Participatory Islamic Finance

"While an option to create resilient financial and economic systems is to adopt risk-sharing financing, the participatory modes of finance are not well-understood and are challenging to apply. This book, participatory Islamic Finance, provides an in-depth discourse on the Shariah, theoretical and practical perspectives on participatory capital and how these can be applied to provide inclusive finance and promote a stable, fair and equitable economy. Focusing on partnership contracts of mudarabah and musharakah and presenting practices from different countries, this study provides unique insights on how these modes of financing can be applied in reality and helps to reduce the use of debt based instruments that increase fragility of businesses and economies."
—Professor Habib Ahmed, *Durham University Business School, UK*

"The authors of *"Participatory Islamic Finance: The Ideals, Contemporary Practices, and Innovations"* have rendered a great service in building the narrative of participatory modes in Islamic finance based on qualitative research methodology. With the case study-based review of the participatory financing practices in Iran, Pakistan, Sudan, Malaysia, and Türkiye, the book presents an innovative approach to both understanding and practicing Islamic finance in various jurisdictions. Risk and reward participation for valid and ethical return is the unique feature of Islamic finance though al lawful modes and tools could lead to the realization of maqāsid al shariah, if applied in their true spirit. Participatory modes are, however, ideal for realizing the objectives of social justice and social inclusion in any economy."
—Professor Dr. Muhammad Ayub, *Riphah University, Islmabad, Pakistan*

"For me the *"Participatory Islamic Finance"* is an exceptional book, which weaves participatory finance, Maqasid al Shariah and higher ethical objectives of Islam in an entirely new foresight. It walks through the developments in participatory finance, historically and through various countries of the world. It has adopted a concrete system approach in addressing the lacunas in participatory finance. It makes the readers and practitioners come out of their comfort zones and look at things with the new wave of awareness just created through their synthesis which is both factual, thorough and interesting."
—Dr. Zohra Jabeen, *Ph.D. and specialized in Sukuks, Institute of Management Sciences, Pakistan*

Muhammad Nouman · Karim Ullah

Participatory Islamic Finance

Ideals, Contemporary Practices, and Innovations

Muhammad Nouman 📵
Institute of Business
and Management Sciences
University of Agriculture
Peshawar, Pakistan

Karim Ullah 📵
Institute of Management Sciences
Peshawar, Pakistan

ISBN 978-981-19-9554-5   ISBN 978-981-19-9555-2 (eBook)
https://doi.org/10.1007/978-981-19-9555-2

© The Editor(s) (if applicable) and The Author(s), under exclusive license to Springer Nature Singapore Pte Ltd. 2023
This work is subject to copyright. All rights are solely and exclusively licensed by the Publisher, whether the whole or part of the material is concerned, specifically the rights of translation, reprinting, reuse of illustrations, recitation, broadcasting, reproduction on microfilms or in any other physical way, and transmission or information storage and retrieval, electronic adaptation, computer software, or by similar or dissimilar methodology now known or hereafter developed.
The use of general descriptive names, registered names, trademarks, service marks, etc. in this publication does not imply, even in the absence of a specific statement, that such names are exempt from the relevant protective laws and regulations and therefore free for general use.
The publisher, the authors, and the editors are safe to assume that the advice and information in this book are believed to be true and accurate at the date of publication. Neither the publisher nor the authors or the editors give a warranty, expressed or implied, with respect to the material contained herein or for any errors or omissions that may have been made. The publisher remains neutral with regard to jurisdictional claims in published maps and institutional affiliations.

This Palgrave Macmillan imprint is published by the registered company Springer Nature Singapore Pte Ltd.
The registered company address is: 152 Beach Road, #21-01/04 Gateway East, Singapore 189721, Singapore

We dedicate this book to our beloved

Prophet Muhammad (SAW)

"Who said: When a man dies, his deeds come to an end except for three things: Sadaqah Jariyah (ceaseless charity); a knowledge which is beneficial, or a virtuous descendant who prays for him (for the deceased)."

Sahih Muslim 4223

Preface

Islamic finance has been evolving to cope with the changing market demands and develop its unique faith-centric identity. Recently, Islamic finance has entered into a new phase of evolution whereby it is forming and re-forming its working models so that these are more substantially understood as 'Islamic' rather than the re-engineering of the conventional finance models. This modulation and re-modulation are characterized by a hidden struggle of the system to establish a new identity by posing itself as being a participatory system, instead of a trade-based system. This book reports the contemporary status and debates on various emergent layers of the participation system and how this system does and should work. In addition, it attempts to unveil more deeply the participatory structures within the Islamic banking and finance, their contemporary practices, and the adaptation and innovations within the participatory system.

Most of the existing books on Islamic finance present general discussion on the origin, concepts, and the importance of participatory finance. However, there is a little published work on the key challenges in implementing participatory finance and how the contemporary practices adapt to these, which is the focus of this book. Therefore, it not only presents a holistic view on the ideals of Islamic finance and the key challenges in practice, but also covers the contemporary practices of participatory finance and the adaptation process within the contemporary participation-based financing products. This struggle is to ensure the overall viability and relevance of the participatory finance.

Since, the contents of the book draw upon the Islamic finance literature and insights from practice, so it is relevant for a wider audience and readership from not only the countries with majority Muslim population but also the leading world financial hubs where Islamic banking finance is growing with a rapid pace. This book, in particular, addresses the need of understanding how organizations can design and develop new participatory financing products. Such a need is globally emerging in a dynamic trend because many Islamic countries and the global financial centers such as the Middle East, Asia, Europe, United States, and other finance centers are in dire need. It is because the financial institutions in these regions are struggling to develop new and flexible Islamic financial products to be able to employ their excess liquidity problems and develop a flexible structure compared to their prevailing sales-based financing system which is characterized by less flexibility and high documentation requirements.

The book starts with the background in Chapter 1, where we explained various modes of Islamic finance, classified as participatory and non-participatory in terms of sharing of resources, contributions, and resultant risks. The participatory modes involve direct participation in the business and its outcomes be it profit or loss, and are claimed to be *Shari'ah*-based modes because these are derived directly from Quran and *Sunnah* of Prophet (Peace and blessings of Allah be upon him). Moreover, these are advocated as the ideal modes for achieving the socio-economic objectives of *Shari'ah*, commonly termed as *Maqasid al Shari'ah*. On the other hand, we claim that the sale-based modes are not sufficiently participatory as the financial institutions do not substantially get involved in the economic activity or the sharing of its profits and losses. One, however, cannot deny the participation involved in it compared to the plain loans as some risk is assumed by the financial institutions too, but these modes usually involve a fixed payment which has to be paid regardless of the business outcomes.

We originated this debated from a brief introduction to Islamic banking and finance and their modus operandi. Next, the participatory and non-participatory paradigms of Islamic finance are elaborated with the major focus on the participatory finance and its legality and origin. The chapter concludes with the detailed discussion of the *Musharakah* and *Mudarabah* modes of participatory finance and their basic principles, particularly the rules related to the contribution of capital, the management of business affairs, treatment of profit and losses, and the termination or maturity of the business arrangement.

In Chapter 2, we moved to the discussion on how *Shari'ah* permeates the financial transactions within the Islamic economic system and provides basic tenets for a unique Islamic financial system to ensure wellbeing of the overall society. For this purpose, it explores the higher ethical objective of *Shari'ah*, commonly known as the *Maqasid al Shari'ah*, to conceptualize the basic philosophy of *Shari'ah*. Moreover, this chapter develops an integrated framework of *Maqasid al Shari'ah* by synthesizing the viewpoints of the leading Islamic philosophers and proponents including imam Ghazali, Abu Zahrah, and Ibn Ahsur. This framework serves a base to build upon the nexus between *Maqasid al Shari'ah* and participatory finance as we further elaborated on in Chapter 3. In addition, Chapter 2 also explores the linkage between *Maqasid Al Shari'ah* and the economic and financial concerns of human life to understand why and how *Shari'ah* permeates the matters related to economic and financial aspects of human life.

Chapter 3 extends the debate presented in Chapter 2 by exploring the philosophical underpinnings of participatory financing models in the wake of conceptualizing the social welfare role of these arrangements. Moreover, the basic philosophy and the axioms of Islamic finance are linked with the participatory financing to highlight its idealization in the Islamic finance literature. Furthermore, building upon the *Maqasid al Shari'ah* framework presented in Chapter 2, and the axioms of Islamic finance, this chapter creates the nexus between participatory financing and the higher ethical objectives of Islam. This nexus is important for the operationalization of *Maqasid al Shari'ah*.

Next in Chapter 4, we present the dilemma of idealization of participatory finance in the theory of Islamic banking and finance, and its marginalization in the practices of Islamic banks from around world. This chapter begins with the detailed discussion on the glorification of participatory finance in the Islamic banking and finance literature and its role in the development of modern banking system. Moreover, the advantages of participatory finance are discussed in detail to conceptualize the reasons for the idealization of participatory finance in the Islamic banking and finance literature. This discussion is followed by the detailed overview of the consistent tendency of Islamic banks to avoid participatory financing arrangements on the assets side. Subsequently, different explanations for the lower preference for participatory financing by banks are also presented.

After establishing the originality of participatory systems, we next identified and explored constraints to the applications of participatory systems and synthesized a coherent constraints framework, in Chapter 5, which was developed by synthesizing the insights from the extant literature using the systematic review approach. The holistic framework of constraints is important because the extant literature provides many explanations for the tendency of Islamic banks to avoid participatory financing. However, literature is divergent and there is no unified understanding of the constraints to participatory financing. Therefore, the proposed framework helps in the unified understanding of the constraints to participatory financing to conceptualize the consistent inclination of Islamic banks toward non-participatory financing throughout the world.

In Chapter 6, we covered the contemporary practices of participatory financing in the major Islamic banking industries of the world. This chapter elaborates how Islamic banks apply participatory financing within the embedded contractual variants of *Musharakah* namely diminishing *Musharakah*, and running *Musharakah*. This chapter covers several applications of participatory financing in Islamic banking, including working capital financing, consumer financing, commodity operations financing, local trade financing, import financing, and *Mudarabah*-based financing.

Chapter 6 suggests that Islamic banks adapt the participatory financing to make it fit for SME financing, corporate financing, consumer financing, and government financing. However, it is not known how Islamic banks assess and mitigate the underlying risks to ensure the viability of *these* participatory arrangements. Therefore, Chapter 7 provides insights into the procedures adopted by Islamic banks for assessing and mitigating the underlying risks associated to the participatory financing, particularly the risk induced by asymmetric information, including adverse selection and moral hazards.

In Chapter 8, we present several case studies of participation system in various regions to show the applications of and experiments with participatory finance. The first case study presents the experience of the Iran in dealing with participatory finance and the steps undertaken to increase the viability and application of participatory finance instruments. This case study also provides thought-provoking evidence of the prevalence of moral commitments and ethical values which resulted in the successful completion of participatory financing arrangements despite the fact that the arrangements were characterized by the asymmetrical information.

The second case study presents the Sudanese experience, where a local bank took the initiative of financing, in innovative ways, the needs of the handicapped rural agriculture sector of Sudan. In this experiment, loopholes were identified in the financing models and an array of innovative products was introduced, most of which were participatory in nature. Interestingly, though these products were offered to the poorest and the most deprived sector of the country, nearly 100 percent recovery rate was witnessed besides a substantial income and relief to the customers.

Next we present the experience of Pakistan, where a state-owned Islamic bank undertook two pure *Musharakah*-based projects. These projects were jointly initiated by the bank and a local entrepreneur for the construction of apartments on *Musharakah* basis. The first project was so successful that it gave the highest return the bank had ever earned from any kind of financing. Consequently, the bank initiated another project with the same partner. However, due to sudden changes in the market conditions, the second project didn't go according to the plan. This case study conceptualizes the constraints and challenges faced by the bank during the course of these projects and how bank dealt with these.

The chapter further presents the story of an innovative participatory finance product in Malaysia using a stand-alone platform. This platform, termed as the Investment Account Platform (IAP), was initiated by the central bank of Malaysia through a consortium of several local banks to channel investors' funds to the business sector. This case study reveals how banks can facilitate and promote participatory financing with minimum involvement in its underlying risks and uncertainties. Finally, the case of Turkiye is presented, where the notion of participation politically used to represent all types of Islamic finance contracts, irrespective of the levels of participation from the financial institution and customers. This case is unique, in a sense of showing how Islamic finance can collectively be presented as participation compared to conventional loan-based financing model.

In the last chapter, we present the curious case of the Islamic banking industry of Pakistan that has revealed a sudden and a significant increase in *Musharakah*-based financing after 2013. The chapter begins with the description of this paradigm shift in the financing portfolio of the overall Islamic banking industry that is characterized by an unexpected surge in the *Musharakah*-based financing and a shift away from *Murabahah*-based financing. This discussion is followed by a brief discussion on the evolution of Islamic baking in Pakistan, and how the evolutionary banking model provides grounds for this paradigm shift. Next, to conceptualize this sudden in participatory finance we attempt to theorize the obscured adaptation in the Islamic participatory financing products to the prevailing constraints and the key outcomes of this adaptation. For this purpose this chapter explores the adaptations and innovations in *Musharakah*-based working capital financing, consumer financing, and commodity operations financing in the Islamic banking industry of Pakistan, and presents the Constraints, Adaptation, and Outcomes (CAO) framework of participatory finance. By developing a pragmatic CAO framework, this chapter not only highlights the typology of adaptation through which Pakistani Islamic banks have achieved innovative output and problem-solving capabilities within participatory financing products; but it also develops a theoretical basis, the researchers, and financial service designers can use to device novel adaptation strategies to meet specific problem-solving and innovation goals.

In summary, we attempted to provide an integrated and a detailed resource on participation finance and innovations in it. This work has benefited from the valuable work of many theologians, practitioners, and academia of Islamic banking and finance. We have duly acknowledged and referenced all such sources throughout this book.

Peshawar, Pakistan   Muhammad Nouman
                                                                  Karim Ullah

A Note on Research Methodology

This research-based book has applied a qualitative narrative strategy in multiple phases, to develop an overall participatory Islamic banking perspective for it being more adaptive and thus innovative approach to theorize and practice Islamic finance. We call it a narrative because we made the participation aspect of Islamic finance a more salient thesis over the non-participatory finance. We tried to establish this story in four phases. Firstly, a comprehensive systematic literature review method is used to carefully select papers on participation finance and the same have then been analyzed qualitatively. We added the systematic literature method in the annexure to this book. Secondly, the initial models, which are conceptualizing the participatory finances, its maqasid, and the constraints to the applications, are more based on a synthesis that has been achieved through qualitative analysis of literature and some observations of the Islamic finance markets. Thirdly, the new market observations, such as the notion of participatory finance spur in Pakistan and the participatory finance experiments in Iran, Pakistan, Sudan, Malaysia, and Turkiye, are added by using qualitative observations, discussions, and mixing the same with the reviewed cases from selected countries. Finally, the concluding framework of constraints, adaptation, and outcomes has been based upon more than forty qualitative interviews and ethnographic experiences of the authors. The book, therefore, presents a balanced account of both theories and empirics, to establish the desired narrative of participatory Islamic finance as a more contemporary and innovative approach to both understanding and practicing of the Islamic finance in various jurisdictions.

CONTENTS

Part I The Ideals of Participatory Finance

1 Introduction to Participatory Finance   3
   1.1 Islamic Banking and Finance   4
   1.2 Participatory vs. Non-Participatory Modes of Islamic
        Finance   8
   1.3 Definition and Forms of Participation in Islam   11
        Shirkat-Ul-Milk *(Participation in Ownership)*   11
        Shirkat-Ul-'Aqd *(Participation by Contract)*   12
   1.4 Legality and Origin of Participation   13
   1.5 Musharakah *and Its Terms and Conditions*   16
        Conditions with Respect to Partners   16
        Conditions with Respect to Capital Contribution   17
        Conditions with Respect to Management   18
        Conditions with Respect to Profit and Loss Sharing   19
        Conditions with Respect to Maturity or Termination
        of Musharakah   20
   1.6 Mudarabah and Its Terms and Conditions   21
        Capital of Mudarabah   21
        Mixing of Capital   22
        Management of the Business Affairs   24
        Distribution of Profit and Losses   25
        Termination/Maturity of Mudarabah   26

xv

1.7	Chapter Summary	27
References		28

2 Maqasid Al Shari'ah and Financial Concern of Human Life — 29

2.1	Shari'ah *and Its Higher Ethical Objectives* (Maqasid al Shari'ah)	30
	The Integrated Framework of Maqasid Al Shariah *(Higher Ethical Objectives)*	30
	Maqasid Al Shari'ah *and the Economic-Financial Concerns of Human Life*	36
2.2	Conclusion	45
References		46

3 Linkage Between Maqasid Al Shari'ah and Participatory Finance — 47

3.1	Aspiration-Oriented Vs Reality-Oriented Schools of Thoughts and the Social Welfare Role of Participatory Finance	48
3.2	The Philosophical Underpinning of Participatory Finance in the Light of the Axioms of Islamic Finance	50
3.3	*The Nexus Between* Maqasid Al Shari'ah *and Participatory Finance*	57
3.4	Conclusion and Implications	58
3.5	Chapter Summary	59
References		60

4 The Paradox of Idealization in Theory and Marginalization in the Practice — 63

4.1	Idealization of Participatory Finance in the Islamic Baking Literature	64
4.2	Role of Participatory Financing in the Development of Islamic Banking System	65
4.3	The Inherent Benefits of Participatory Modes of Finance	68
	Reduced Constraints to SMEs Financing	68
	Promoting Stability of the Financial Sector	69
	Improved Allocative Efficiency	70
	Promotes Innovation	71
	Stability of the Banking System	71
	Effective Distribution of Risks	72

  Closer Coordination Between the Real and Financial
   Sectors of Economy   73
  Higher Return on Investment   73
  Establishing Long-Term Relationships   75
 4.4 *The Marginalization of Participatory Finance*
   in the Practice of Islamic Financial Institutions   76
 4.5 *Chapter Summary*   78
 References   78

Part II The Contemporary Practices of Participatory Finance

5 Constraints to Participatory Finance   85
 5.1 *Overview of the Extant Literature*   86
 5.2 *The Coherent Constraints Framework*   88
   Uncertainty   90
   Lower Demand   94
   Regulatory Constraints   96
 5.3 *Implications of the Constraints Framework*   98
 5.4 *Chapter Summary*   98
 References   99

6 The Applications of Participatory Finance   103
 6.1 *Variants of Participatory Financing in the Major*
   Islamic Banking Industries   104
   Diminishing Musharakah   104
   Running Musharakah   105
 6.2 *Domains of Participatory Finance*   108
   Working Capital Financing   109
   Consumer Financing   110
   Commodity Operations Financing   116
   Domestic Trade Financing   117
   Import Financing   117
   Mudarabah *Based Financing*   119
 6.3 *Chapter Summary*   119
 References   120

7	**Assessment and Mitigation of Risks in the Participatory Financing Arrangements**	121
	7.1 Procedures for Assessment and Mitigation of Risks in Running Musharakah	122
	Mechanism for the Assessment and Selection of Applicants	122
	Strategies for Risk Mitigation in Running Musharakah	124
	7.2 Procedures for Assessment and Mitigation of Risks in Diminishing Musharakah	126
	Procedures for Assessment of Risks in Diminishing Musharakah	127
	Strategies for Mitigation of Risks in Diminishing Musharakah	132
	7.3 Chapter Summary	134
	References	134

Part III The Adaptations and Innovations in Participatory Finance

8	**Experiments with Participatory Financing**	137
	8.1 Iranian Experiments with Participatory Finance	138
	8.2 Sudanese Experiments with Participatory Financing	144
	8.3 Pakistani Experiments with Participatory Financing	147
	8.4 Malaysian Experiments with Participatory Financing	151
	8.5 Turkiye's Experiments with Participatory Financing	152
	8.6 Chapter Summary	153
	References	155
9	**Adaptation in Participatory Islamic Finance to Constraints and Its Outcomes**	157
	9.1 The Curious Case of Musharakah Spur in Pakistan	158
	9.2 Detour: Adaptability of the Islamic Banking in Pakistan	159
	9.3 Constraints, Adaptation, and Outcomes (CAO) Framework of Participatory Islamic Finance	160
	Constraints to Musharakah Financing	164
	Adaptation in Musharakah	165
	Outcomes of Adaptation	173
	9.4 Chapter Summary	180
	References	182

| Annexures | 183 |
| Index | 213 |

About the Authors

Dr. Muhammad Nouman has been serving as Senior Lecturer at the Institute of Business and Management Sciences, the University of Agriculture Peshawar, Pakistan, since 2011. He has also served at a Software house as Project Manager and HR Trainer. Moreover, he also has exposure of working at the GPI Fund (pension fund management department) of Khyber Pakhtunkhwa (a northern province of Pakistan), and a Securities brokerage firm. He has been a part of editorial boards a number of journals related to Islamic banking and finance, investment management, and corporate finance. Moreover, he is member of apex academic and research committees of several universities.

Dr. Karim Ullah is currently working as Tenured Associate Professor at Institute of Management Sciences, Peshawar, Pakistan. He has been awarded twice by the Government of Pakistan Higher Education Commission, for being the author of two books on Islamic Finance, which have been declared as the best books of the country for years 2015 and 2017, respectively. He also led a team to won multiple grants included the financial innovation challenge fund of UK Department for International Development and Central Bank of Pakistan, to lead the establishment of Centre for Excellence in Islamic Finance. He has nearly 15 years of teaching, research, and consulting experience. He is part of multiple editorial boards of impactful journals related to Islamic finance, do consulting and trainings to financiers, and remain part of apex committees related to the policy and standard developments for Islamic finance in multiple countries.

List of Figures

Fig. 1.1	Share of Islamic Finance sectors in the global Islamic Finance Assets	6
Fig. 1.2	Different modes of Islamic finance	10
Fig. 2.1	Maqasid Al Shari'ah integrated framework (*Source* Nouman et al. [2021])	36
Fig. 3.1	The nexus between *Maqasid al Shari'ah* and participatory finance (*Source* Nouman et al. [2021])	58
Fig. 4.1	Mechanism of two-tier *Murabahah* (*Source* Based on Shinsuke [2012])	67
Fig. 4.2	The relative equity risk premium in different markets (*Source* Based on data from Thompson Reuters DataStream)	74
Fig. 5.1	Coherent constraints framework (*Source* Nouman [2019] and Nouman et al. [2018])	90
Fig. 6.1	Mechanism of diminishing *Musharakah*	106
Fig. 6.2	Mechanism of Running *Musharakah*	107
Fig. 6.3	Bank's share in the profit and loss in a RM-based arrangement	107
Fig. 7.1	The business assessment and mode selection process for the eligible firms (*Source* Nouman et al. [2019])	125
Fig. 7.2	The assessment and selection process for house and car financing (*Source* Nouman et al. [2019])	133
Fig. 8.1	Saving in number of steps	140
Fig. 8.2	Saving in time required (in minutes) to complete a transaction	141
Fig. 8.3	Growth of participatory financing in ABI	143

Fig. 8.4	Growth of participatory financing in Iran: ABI versus other banks	143
Fig. 8.5	The functioning of IAP	152
Fig. 9.1	Shift in the share of *Musharakah* and *Murabahah*-based financing	159
Fig. 9.2	Constraints, Adaptation, and Outcomes (CAO) framework of participatory finance (*Source* Nouman, 2019)	163

List of Tables

Table 1.1	Structure of the Islamic finance industry (2019 figures)	5
Table 1.2	The transactions in which each partner is entitled to participate	18
Table 5.1	Factors restraining the application of participatory financing	88
Table 5.2	Factors inducing uncertainty in participatory financing arrangements	91
Table 5.3	Factors leading to lower demand for participatory financing	95
Table 5.4	Regulatory factors restraining the application of participatory financing	97
Table 7.1	Documents required for working capital financing	123
Table 7.2	Terms and conditions of the house financing scheme in Pakistan	128
Table 7.3	Terms and conditions of the car financing scheme	129
Table 7.4	Documents required for house and car financing	130
Table 8.1	Average number of steps and time consumed to conduct a transaction	140
Table 8.2	Percentage share of different modes in the financing portfolio of the Agriculture Bank of Iran (ABI)	142
Table 8.3	Details of the project	149
Table 8.4	Investments and returns of the project	150
Table 9.1	Financing mix of Islamic banking industry of Pakistan (percentage share)	158
Table 9.2	Details of the selected *Musharakah*-based products	162

Table A.1	Overview of the number and the type of selected publications in the refining steps 4 and 5	187
Table A.2	Overview of the Final Sample of selected publications (Step 5)	187
Table A.3	Factors restraining the application of participatory financing	189

PART I

The Ideals of Participatory Finance

CHAPTER 1

Introduction to Participatory Finance

Islam is a complete code of life. Unlike other religions, it is not limited to merely religious rituals, modes of worship, and moral teachings. Rather, it provides a complete set of rules, called *Shari'ah*, which govern every aspect of human life. It constitutes divine guidelines and prohibitions, which when combined together have a cumulative effect of maintaining balance, justice, well-being, and equal opportunities. Moreover, it provides a unique set of legal, political, economic, and social systems to ensure the welfare of individuals and society as a whole in every sphere of life.

Shari'ah also governs financial transactions within the Islamic economic system and provides basic tenets for a unique Islamic financial system. The Islamic financial system outlines a broader set of transactional, financial, and intermediation contracts with varying financing purposes, degrees of risk, and maturities to meet needs of the diverse groups of economic agents in the economy within the boundaries of *Shari'ah*. This system is characterized by two sets of modes of finance called participatory and non-participatory modes. The participatory modes establish partnership between two or more parties whereby each party has to participate directly in the profit and losses.

This chapter intends to introduce the readers to the participatory Islamic finance. It begins with the introduction to Islamic finance followed by an overview of Islamic banking and its modus operandi.

© The Author(s), under exclusive license to Springer Nature Singapore Pte Ltd. 2023
M. Nouman and K. Ullah, *Participatory Islamic Finance*,
https://doi.org/10.1007/978-981-19-9555-2_1

Subsequently, the participatory and non-participatory modes of Islamic finance are briefly discussed. This discussion is followed by detailed overview of participation in Islam, its different forms and origin. The chapter concludes with a detailed discussion on *Musharakah* and *Mudarabah* modes and their terms and conditions.

1.1 Islamic Banking and Finance

Islamic finance constitute the means through which different financial institutions such as banks and other lending institutions invest and raise funds within the boundaries of Islamic law called *Shariah*. Similar to the conventional financial system, Islamic finance features capital markets, money markets, insurance companies, banks, mutual funds, and investment firms. These entities have twofold governance system, i.e., these are not only governed by the rules and regulations of the regulatory authorities that apply to their conventional counterparts but also by the Islamic law.

A financial institution that is governed by the principles laid down by Islamic law and is in consonance with the spirit, philosophy, and the value system of Islam is called an Islamic financial Institution (IFI). IFIs act as intermediaries between the deficit and surplus saving units of the economy just like their conventional counterparts. However, unlike the conventional financial institutions, they use *Shari'ah* compliant instruments instead of charging and paying interest. Their core objective is just price, just wage, reasonable profit, and the welfare of society.

Islamic banking and finance is a rapidly growing phenomenon in the Muslim countries and all over the world. From an obscure financial experiment, Islamic finance clearly has transformed into a major factor in global finance. The worldwide Islamic finance assets grew from US$ 200 billion in 2000 to around US$ 2.88 trillion by 2019, with this figure expected to reach US$ 3.69 trillion in 2024. The services offered by Islamic financial institutions (IFIs) can broadly be categorized into five major services, including Islamic banking, *sukuk*, Islamic funds, *takaful*, and other financial services. Among these Islamic banking has the largest contribution in the global Islamic finance assets. Table 1.1 presents the structure of the Islamic finance industry.

Table 1.1 Structure of the Islamic finance industry (2019 figures)

Islamic finance sector	Industry size	Share in the global islamic finance assets (%)	No. of institutions
Islamic Banking	USD 1993 billion	69	526 in 74 countries
Takaful	USD 51 billion	2	336 in 47 countries
Sukuk	538 USD billion	19	3420 in 25 countries
Other Islamic Financial Institution (OIFI'S)	USD 153 billion	5	645 in 54 countries
Islamic Funds	140 USD billion	5	1749 in 28 countries

Source Islamic Finance Market (2021–2026) report by Mordor Intelligence Analysis

Islamic banking is the most developed among all IFIs. The Islamic banking sector witnessed a 14% growth in 2019, equating to US$ 1.99 trillion constituting 6% share in global banking assets. The size of worldwide assets of Islamic banking sector is expected to reach US$ 2.44 trillion by 2024. Figure 1.1 depicts the share of various Islamic services in the worldwide Islamic finance assets.

Today more than 500 banks including around 200 Islamic banking windows comply with Islamic principles in 74 countries. Interestingly, their customers include not only Muslims but also non-Muslims. Islamic banks are operating and expanding most dominantly in Islamic nations and also in many non-Muslim countries where Muslims are a minority, such as United States, Japan, and UK. The growth of Islamic banking is a result of structural and macro-economic reforms in the financial systems worldwide, global integration of financial markets, privatization, the liberalization of capital movements, and the introduction of new and innovative Islamic products.

Islamic banking is defined as a "banking system which is in consonance with the spirit, ethos and value system of Islam and governed by the principles laid down by Islamic *Shari'ah*." While the prevailing goal of conventional banks is to maximize their profit by charging an optimal rate of interest, whereas that of Islamic banks are to be partners in development and prosperity of society along with the goal of maximization of shareholders' wealth. Therefore, the Islamic banking system makes deposits on the basis of risk of earning profits or facing loss in investment

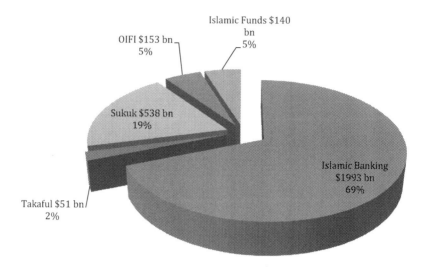

Fig. 1.1 Share of Islamic Finance sectors in the global Islamic Finance Assets

or on *Wakalah* basis against the pre-determined agency fees or service charges.

The main difference between conventional banking and Islamic banking is that in conventional banking system investors do not bear the risk of loss. On the contrary, in Islamic banking, risk remains with the investors in shape of earning profit or facing loss in trading activities. Thus, the Islamic banks play role as intermediaries by channeling savings to the different sectors of the economy, including agriculture, business, and industry; however, their modus operandi are different. The real business activities and goods are their subject matter. On the assets side, the Islamic banks are liable for loss in case of participatory financing (i.e., *Mudarabah* or *Musharakah*). Similarly, risk is taken by them in the trading activities so long as they own the assets to be traded. In transactions based on leasing, the Islamic banks buy assets and then give their assets on rent. They are not risk free in leasing activities as well as they take the ownership risks of those assets and expenses.

An Islamic bank performs all activities of a commercial bank except receiving and giving loans on interest basis. On the liabilities side, Islamic banks accept funds on *Wakalah* (agency) or *Mudarabah* basis. They treat demand deposits of clients as interest-free loans to the bank with guarantee. Islamic commercial banks may use the deposits in investment accounts for investments in suitable projects on partnership basis. In case of investments on partnership basis, the banks may engage in management of enterprise or become a sleeping partner. These funds may also be used for investments in portfolios of (Islamic compliant) financial securities including investment certificates and stocks, etc. They may also engage in leasing of buildings, ships, and industrial goods, etc. On assets side, Islamic banks issue funds to their clients on the basis of profit and loss sharing agreement or debt-creating arrangements in line with the *Shari'ah* principles. Bank acts as a manager of the investment deposit (i.e., time deposits). Moreover, commodity and asset trading and equity holding are also an important part of their operations. They share their net profits with their depositors depending on their deposit nature.

The Islamic banks face criticism on the grounds that their operations resemble that of the conventional banks. It is difficult for Islamic banks to escape this criticism since they cannot engage directly in leasing, trading, or construction activities under their present organizational structure. Therefore, they have to restrict to the financial activities only. Islamic banks may adopt three different models of organizational structures which rely on the nature of activities carried on in the banks. These models include (i) universal banking model whereby different activities including insurance, investment banking, and commercial banking are practiced within the same organization, (ii) bona fide subsidiary model whereby bank establishes different bona fide subsidiaries where each subsidiary has its own operations and separate capital, and (iii) Bank Holding Company Model whereby a banking system was bank owns and controls different organizations for different sort of activities including commercial banking, trading/*Murabahah* activities and investment banking, etc.

Islamic banks do not find the first two models suitable for their operations due to large difference in the nature of activities an Islamic bank will have to carry and the regulatory hurdles. However, the Bank Holding Company Model is more suitable for the Islamic banks and can help in distinguishing their financial operations from the conventional banks. The Bank Holding Company Model will enable them to own separate entity for different sort of activities, including insurance, infrastructure operations, leasing, investment banking, and trade-based operations, etc. Moreover, it will be more convenient for regulatory authorities to regulate and monitor the activities of separate organizations.

Currently, Islamic banking is practiced through three channels including Islamic windows, Islamic banking branches as subsidiary of conventional banks, and specialized Islamic banks. *Islamic window* is an outlet offered by a conventional bank within its existing branch for customers interested in conducting business through *Shari'ah* compatible instruments. Islamic windows are initially offered by commercial banks interested in probing the potential of the Islamic banking market. Such banks take advantage of their existing branch network for opening Islamic windows. The products typically offered at an Islamic window include safekeeping deposits and Islamic trade-finance products (for small and medium enterprises). In the case of an Islamic window, the parent bank's treasury department manages the liquidity requirements of the whole bank, which creates a threat of commingling of the conventional and Islamic funds. The banks, therefore, must establish proper safeguards to avoid the mixing of conventional and Islamic funds.

On the other hand, an *Islamic subsidiary* allows a conventional bank to offer a wider range of *Shari'ah* compliant products under one roof. For example, an Islamic subsidiary is in a better position to fully involve in money market operations, Islamic investment banking, and to manage its separate treasury. However, few Islamic scholars have questioned the legitimacy of Islamic subsidiaries because it is not certain that the initial capital provided by the parent bank has originated from Islamically acceptable sources. On the contrary, a *specialized Islamic bank* is a full-fledged commercial and investment bank that offers only Islamic products and is structured fully on Islamic principles. Such Islamic banks have higher credibility than the Islamic windows and Islamic subsidiaries because it signals that the bank has strong commitment for operating under the principles of *Shari'ah*.

1.2 Participatory vs. Non-Participatory Modes of Islamic Finance

Islamic finance offers a range of distinctive *Shari'ah* compliant modes of finance. The modes of Islamic finance can be broadly classified into participatory and non-participatory modes. Participation, commonly known as the Profit and Loss Sharing (PLS), is the essence of the design of Islamic financial products. This feature allows a financial institution to earn profit on invested capital if the financial institution is willing to tolerate loss in case of the project failure. In a participatory financing arrangement, the allocation of risk and reward to each partner, and the distribution of responsibilities among them are defined in the contract, which is enforced by the social values and the ethical standards set in the *Shari'ah*.

Modes of participatory financing include *Mudarabah* and *Musharakah*. A *Mudarabah* contract is a type of partnership between investor(s) (*Rab-ul-Mal*) and entrepreneur(s) (*Mudarib*). Where an investor contributes capital while the entrepreneur employs effort and exercises complete control over the business. Profits are divided according to a pre-agreed ratio, while in the event of a loss the losses are exclusively borne by the investor. On the contrary, the entrepreneur loses compensation for his efforts. A *Mudarabah* contract is more akin to a limited liability partnership and is further classified into restricted and unrestricted *Mudarabah*. In case of the unrestricted *Mudarabah*, the agreement does not specify the place of business, its period, service, or industry, the specific line of business, and customers or suppliers to be dealt with. On the other hand, the restricted *Mudarabah* has restriction on any of the above-mentioned terms.

On the other hand, a *Musharakah* contract is a type of partnership where all partners jointly contribute capital and manage the business venture. Profits are shared based on a pre-negotiated ratio, while losses are borne in proportion to the capital contributions by the partners. *Musharakah* contracts are considered optimal in the development of Islamic private equity and venture capital markets, which require capital provision with some control and influence over their management.

The non-participatory modes, on the other hand, do not involve profit and loss sharing and usually entail a rather predetermined return. The major modes of non-participatory financing include *Ijarah, Murabahah, Salam,* and *Istisna*. Figure 1.2 presents the classification of different modes of Islamic finance.

Ijarah is the most flexible and efficient way to finance excessive cost and technology-related assets. The bank (lessor) purchases the desired asset and rents it to the customer (lessee). The bank transfers the right to use the asset to the customer while the corpus of the property rests in the bank's ownership. The bank also gives an option to the lessee to purchase the asset during or after the completion of the period of rent.

Similarly, *Murabahah* is a sale contract where buyer, who knows the cost of the commodity being sold, agrees to pay a certain amount above the cost as a profit to the seller. The payment may be made on the spot (lump sum) or on an agreed future date(s) (lump sum or in installments).

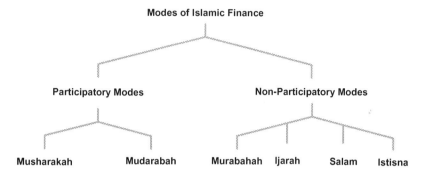

Fig. 1.2 Different modes of Islamic finance

Islamic banks practice *Murabahah* by purchasing the desired asset from a third party instead of lending money to the borrower. The bank then sells it to the borrower at a predetermined higher price. By charging this higher price over installments, the bank has effectively provided credit without charging interest.

On the other hand, *Salam* is an important mode of financing for industrial and agriculture sector. It is a sale contract where the buyer pays full price of some specific goods in advance at the point of contract while the seller agrees to supply the goods to the buyer at an agreed future date. The bank may ask the seller to furnish a security to ensure the delivery of the promised goods on the agreed date. The agreed price in *Salam* is normally lower than the spot price; the bank may sell the delivered goods at a higher price to earn profit. The bank may also sell the promised commodities via parallel *Salam* contracts for the same delivery date.

On the contrary, *Istisna* is a sale agreement where a manufacturer undertakes to construct or manufacture an object for the purchaser, using materials provided by the manufacturer. The time of delivery may or may not be fixed and payment may be made in advance or at any other agreed time. The payment may also be made in installments. It is not necessary for the financier to manufacture/construct the promised object himself. Rather, he [sic] can hire the services of a manufacturer/constructor or may enter into a parallel *Istisna* contract with a third party. The financier estimates the cost and fixes such a price of *Istisna* that may earn him [sic] a reasonable profit. *Istisna* is more suitable for construction projects.

1.3 Definition and Forms of Participation in Islam

Participation, also called profit and loss sharing (PLS) and partnership, is predominantly grounded on the principle of *Shirkah*. In the early books of Islamic Jurisprudence (*Fiqh*), all sort of participatory ventures are covered under the caption of *Shirkah*.[1] It is a set of broad principles that accommodates nearly all forms of joint businesses. The literal meaning of '*Shirkah*' is 'sharing' (Usmani, 2002b). The legality of *Shirkah* stems from the Holy Quran (verse 4:12 and 38: 24), *Sunnah*, and the consensus of the Islamic Jurists. Particularly, the two forms of participatory arrangements including general partnership (*Shirkat al Inan*) and *Mudarabah* are accepted by all jurists without any disagreement.

Few jurists consider *Shirkah* synonymous to *Musharakah*. However, majority of the classical jurists also consider *Mudarabah* as a type of *Shirkah* when used as a broad term. Keeping in view the classical jurists' perspective and the nature of contemporary businesses, *Shirkah* may be defined as the business arrangement whereby two or more parties, sharing similar rights and liabilities, contribute their capital, creditworthiness, or labor together to share the resulting profit, appreciation in the value, or a yield and to share the loss (if any) in the ratio of their respective share in ownership. The profit may be earned through any legitimate (*halal*) way within the parameters of *Shariah*, e.g., through wages, hire, sale, purchase, etc. Following are the different forms of *Shirkah*:

Shirkat-Ul-Milk *(Participation in Ownership)*

Shirkat-Ul-Milk refers to the joint ownership of two or more persons in a property. The purpose of this form of participation may not be profit earning. However, if it involves revenue in any form, it must be distributed among the partners in the ratio of their relative ownership. Moreover, the underlying asset may be used by the partners individually or jointly. If the asset is used by one partner or more than one partners, the non-benefiting partner(s) may charge rental of his (their) share of the asset from the benefiting partner(s).

The *Shirkat-Ul-Milk* may be optional or compulsory. In the optional (*Ikhtiari*) *Shirkat-ul-Milk*, the joint ownership comes into existence at

---

[1] Ayub (2007)—page 307.

the option of the partners since they elect to jointly acquire the asset. On the contrary, the compulsory (*Ghair Ikhtiari*) *Shirkat-ul-Milk* forms automatically without any effort or actions of the co-owners. For example, in case of the death of a person, his property is inherited to his heirs. Thus the co-ownership is formed, without any effort of the partners, as natural consequence of the demise of the actual owner.

Shirkat-Ul-'Aqd *(Participation by Contract)*

Shirkat-Ul-'Aqd refers to the joint ownership in a business enterprise that is formed as a result of mutual contract. Therefore, it can also be termed as a joint commercial enterprise. The AAFOI standards define it as "an agreement between two or more parties to combine their assets, labor or liabilities for the purpose of making profits" (AAOIFI, 2017a, p. 326 Clause 2/1—SS 12). *Shirkah* grants similar, but not necessarily equal, rights and liabilities to all partners. It is governed by the principle of participation in both risk and reward, i.e., a partner who gets share in the profit must also bear the losses. There are four types of *Shirkat-ul-'Aqd*:

a. *Shirkat-ul-Amwal* (Participation in capital)—whereby all partners jointly contribute capital to form co-ownership in a business enterprise. The contribution of partners needs not to be equal. Consequently, partners may have different degree of control over the assets. The profit may be shared among the partners in a pre-agreed ratio, but the losses must be shared in the ratio of capital contribution. This form of *Shirkat-Ul-'Aqd* is also referred to as *Shirkat al 'Inan* or General Partnership.
b. *Shirkat-ul-A'amal* (Participation in services)—whereby all partners join hands to jointly offer services to their customers. The fee or wages earned is shared among them in a pre-agreed ratio. This form of participation is also called *Shirkat Al-Abdan*, *Shirkat Al-Sana'i'*, or *Shirkat-Ut-Taqabbul*.
c. *Shirkat-ul-Wujooh* (Participation in credit worthiness or goodwill)—whereby the partners do not invest capital. Rather, they jointly purchase some commodities on a deferred price which are sold at spot rate. The resulting profit is shared among the partners in a pre-agreed ratio.
d. *Shirkat-ul-Mufawada* *(Universal or Unlimited participation)*—whereby all partners have to share everything on an equal basis

including capital, profit, risk, and management. Thus, each partner acts as an agent, guarantor, and trustee on the behalf of other partners. Moreover, all partners are required to be equal in terms of wealth and privileges to justify unlimited liability and equal rights. However, these conditions are difficult to satisfy because determination of the net worth of another party is not easy. Therefore, this form of participation does not factually exist.

1.4 LEGALITY AND ORIGIN OF PARTICIPATION

The history of participation dates back to pre-Islamic era. It was practiced by people from all religions including, Christians, Jews, and pagans. Prophet Muhammad (peace and blessings of Allah be upon him) witnessed the practice of Shirkah prevailing in the commercial activities in Arabia. He (peace and blessings of Allah be upon him) not only ratified it, but also did business himself on the basis of Shirkah. After migration to Medina, the holy Prophet (peace and blessings of Allah be upon him) created *Mawakhat* (brotherhood) among the *Ansar* (the local Muslims of Medina) and *Muhajireen* (Migrants from Makah). Subsequently, the *Ansar* and *Muhajireen* joined as partners in agriculture, trade, and commerce using different form of participatory arrangements including *Muzara* (partnership in agriculture), *Musaqat* (partnership in gardening), and *Shirkah* (partnership in trade).

The legitimacy of *Musharakah* is derived based on Qur'an, the *Sunnah* of Prophet Muhammad (peace and blessings of Allah be upon him) and the *Ijma* (Consensus of Muslim Jurists). The following verse of Qur'an indicates the validity of *Musharakah*:

> .... *and indeed, many partners oppress one another, except for those who believe and do righteous deeds - and few are they....* (Al-Sad: 24)

Similarly, although the following two verses underlay the rules of inheritance, these also ratify legitimacy of partnership in property. The jurists, however, regard this permissibility as a basis for the permissibility of partnership in any form.

> *Allah instructs you concerning your children: for the male, what is equal to the share of two females. But if there are [only] daughters, two or more, for them is two thirds of one's estate. And if there is only one, for her is half. And*

for one's parents, to each one of them is a sixth of his estate if he left children. But if he had no children and the parents [alone] inherit from him, then for his mother is one third. And if he had brothers [or sisters], for his mother is a sixth, after any bequest he [may have] made or debt. Your parents or your children - you know not which of them are nearest to you in benefit. [These shares are] an obligation [imposed] by Allah . Indeed, Allah is ever Knowing and Wise. (Al-Nisa: 11)

And for you is half of what your wives leave if they have no child. But if they have a child, for you is one fourth of what they leave, after any bequest they [may have] made or debt. And for the wives is one fourth if you leave no child. But if you leave a child, then for them is an eighth of what you leave, after any bequest you [may have] made or debt. And if a man or woman leaves neither ascendants nor descendants but has a brother or a sister, then for each one of them is a sixth. But if they are more than two, they share a third, after any bequest which was made or debt, as long as there is no detriment [caused]. [This is] an ordinance from Allah, and Allah is Knowing and Forbearing. (Al-Nisa: 12)

In addition, several sayings of Prophet (peace and blessings of Allah be upon him) and reports by his Companions (may Allah be pleased with them) also validate participation.

Narrated Abu Hurairah: The Messenger of Allah (peace and blessings of Allah be upon him)having said: Allah, Most High, says: I make a third with two partners as long as one of them does not cheat the other, but when he cheats him, I depart from them. (Sunnan e Abu Dawood, Hadith # 3383)

Ibn Umar narrated that: The Messenger of Allah (peace and blessings of Allah be upon him) said: .... Each partner (who has a share in the flock) should pay [zakat] in proportion to his shares.... (Sunnan e Ibn e Maja, Hadith #1807)

Imam Muhammad Al-Bukhari establishes a separate chapter for *Hadith* on participation (Chapter 48: The book of partnership) in Sahih Bukhari which reports 25 *Sahih Hadith* on *Shirkah* in different forms. Similarly, Imam Ahmad Bin Hanbal and Imam Muslim establish chapter on *Musaqat* (partnership in gardening) and *Muzara* (partnership in agriculture) in Musnad Ahmad (Chapter 97: Discussion on *Musaqat, Muzara,* and giving land on *Ijarah*) and Sahih Muslim (Chapter 23: The book of *Musaqat*), respectively. Some of the *Hadith* that validate participation in commercial activities, property, agriculture, and gardening are as follows:

Narrated Sulaiman bin Abu Muslim: I asked Abu Minhal about money exchange from hand to hand. He said, I and a partner of mine bought something partly in cash and partly on credit. Al-Bara' bin 'Azib passed by us and we asked about it. He replied, I and my partner Zaid bin Al-Arqam did the same and then went to the Prophet [peace and blessings of Allah be upon him] and asked him about it. He said, 'Take what was from hand to hand and leave what was on credit.' (Sahih Bukhari Hadith # 2497)

Narrated Jabir bin 'Abdullah: The Prophet [peace and blessings of Allah be upon him] said, The right of pre-emption [Shufa'a] is valid in every joint property, but when the land is divided and the way is demarcated, then there is no right of pre-emption. (Sahih Bukhari, Hadith # 2496)

Ibn Umar (Allah be pleased with them) reported that Allah's Messenger [peace and blessings of Allah be upon him] contracted with the people of Khaibar the (trees and agriculture lands) on the condition that they would pay half the produce in fruits and harvest. (Sahih Muslim, Hadith # 3962)

Narrated 'Abdullah bin Hisham: that his mother Zainab bint Humaid took him to the Prophet and said, O Allah's Apostle! Take the pledge of allegiance from him. But he said, He is still too young for the pledge, and passed his hand on his (i.e. 'Abdullah's) head and invoked for Allah's blessing for him. Zuhra bin Ma'bad stated that he used to go with his grandfather, 'Abdullah bin Hisham, to the market to buy foodstuff. Ibn 'Umar and Ibn Az-Zubair would meet him and say to him, be our partner, as the Prophet invoked Allah to bless you. So, he would be their partner, and very often he would win a camel's load and send it home. (Sahih Bukhari Hadith # 2501)

Narrated Anas: that Abu Bakr As-Siddiq wrote to him the law of Zakat which was made obligatory by Allah's Apostle. He wrote: 'Partners possessing joint property have to pay its Zakat equally'. (Sahih Bukhari, Hadith # 2487)

Based on Quran the large number of *Hadith* and reports by the companions on partnerships, the jurists are unanimous on the permissibility of Shirkah in all forms. Due to their direct derivation from Quran and *Sunnah*, the participatory modes are termed as '*Shariah* based' while the non-participatory modes are called the '*Shariah* compliant' modes of Islamic finance.

1.5 Musharakah and Its Terms and Conditions

The term *Musharakah* has Arabic origin, and its literal meaning is 'sharing.' Thus both *Shirkah* and *Musharakah* share the same meaning. However, the term *Musharakah* is not used in the books of Islamic Jurisprudence (*Fiqah*). According to Usmani (2002b), the term *Musharakah* is a relatively new terminology which has been recently introduced in the contemporary writings on Islamic banking and finance. Moreover, it has a narrow scope than *Shirkah* since it is restricted only to two particular types of *Shirkat-ul-'Aqad*, namely *Shirkat-ul-Amwal* (participation in capital) and *Shirkat-ul-A'amal* (Participation in services). Thus, it refers to the agreement between two or more partners to invest and engage in a joint business with the aim of sharing profits. This definition infers the following points about *Musharakah*:

a. Musharakah involves joint investment by multiple partners.
b. Partners mutually decide how to share and manage the investment.
c. The investment may be utilized in a business enterprise, whether new or existing, or to own real assets.
d. The investment may be for short-term or long-term.
e. Partners have to share the profit as well the losses.
f. All partners have unlimited liability. Consequently, in the financial matters, each partner is liable for the commitment and actions of the other partners.

The *Musharakah* contract has to fulfill all the conditions that are requisite for the validity of a contract such as *Shariah* permissibility of the subject matter, and free consent of the parties, etc. Apart from these certain other conditions are also mandatory for the validity of Musharakah. These conditions are outlined below:

Conditions with Respect to Partners

Partners can be both individuals and legal persons, e.g., corporate bodies. With respect to individual partners, it is mandatory that they must have sound mind and free consent. Thus, insane and minors cannot become partners. However, a minor can become a partner with the consent of his guardians. *Musharakah* can also be done with non-Muslims or conventional interest-based banks for conducting business[2] within the boundaries of Shariah unless it is evident that funds or assets to be contributed by these entities are from non-permissible sources. Moreover, in case of *Musharakah* with non-Muslims or conventional interest-based banks, necessary guarantees and assurances must be obtained in advance that the *Shariah* rules and guidelines will be followed in the normal course of business and determining the matters of *Musharakah*.[3]

Conditions with Respect to Capital Contribution

Capital of all partners has to be specified and quantified, which can be contributed in lump-sum or multiple payments over time (i.e., when there is need for additional investment to increase the capital). Partners should preferably contribute capital in the form of cash or other monetary assets. However, they can also contribute tangible assets[4] as capital after determining and expressing their value in certain currency so that the capital contribution of each partner is clearly determinable. Moreover, the capital of all partners should be commingled and merged, either in actual or constructive form, so that individual ownership is replaced by the joint ownership.

The constructive commingling is done when the capital contribution in the form of distinguishable commodities. This can be done through valuation using any agreed standard. For example, it can be done by determining the current market value of the asset at the time of contract and considering it as the share of the contributing partner. Consequently, any appreciation in the value of assets reflects the right of all partners in the ratio of their respective capital contribution. Similarly, if the capital contribution by partners is in different currencies, these must be converted in the currency of *Musharakah* at the current exchange rate so that there is no ambiguity in determining liabilities and shares of partners.

---

[2] Excluding all businesses that are not permissible in Islam.

[3] AAOIFI (2017a)—page 327–328, Clause 3/1/1/2.

[4] The contribution in kind must qualify as a commodity having some economic value, i.e., it should not be a free good which is accessible to all.

Conditions with Respect to Management

In a Musharakah arrangement, every partner has the right to participate in the management of the business. However, the partners may agree to assign the task of management to one or more than one selected partners. Thus, *Musharakah*-based ventures may be managed in one of the three possible ways including: management by all partners, management by a single or some identified partners, and management by a third party. If the venture is managed by all partners, each of them serves as the agent of the others in all business matters. Moreover, the actions of one partner, in the normal course of business, are supposed to be authorized by all partners. Table 1.2 summaries the transactions in which each partner is entitled to participate in best interest of the joint venture as per the AAOFI standards:

However, if partners agree to delegate the responsibility of management to one or some selected partners, the sleeping partners cannot participate in the management affairs. The managing partners may charge a predetermined remuneration for their services over and above their share in profit as a partner. According to the AAOFI rules, the services of a partner, to perform a particular job required by the *Musharakah*, may be hired on the basis of an independent employment contract (AAOIFI, 2017a, p. 331 Clause 3/1/3/5). Consequently, this contract may be canceled by the partners without the need of amending the Musharakah

Table 1.2 The transactions in which each partner is entitled to participate

a.	The spot or deferred sales
b.	Making deposits or payments
c.	Requesting credit facilities for the venture
d.	Processing transfers of debts and rights
e.	Renting the venture's assets
f.	Rejection of the defective goods
g.	Taking custody or possession of the receivables
h.	Taking up legal actions
i.	Admission of liabilities
j.	Asking for payment of debts
k.	Receiving or providing mortgage on behalf of the venture
l.	Cancelation of contracts
m.	Doing what is customary in the interest of trading

Source AAOIFI (2017a, p. 329)—SS (12): Clause 3/1/3/1

contract. On the other hand, the sleeping partners are entitled to the profit only to the extent of their investment, i.e., the ratio of their profit should not exceed their ratio of capital contribution. In case of management by third party, the management may be carried out on the bases of different contracts, such as *Mudarabah* (profit sharing), *Ujrah* (Service fee), and *Wakalah* (agency).

Conditions with Respect to Profit and Loss Sharing

The profit and loss sharing ratio should be clearly defined which must relate to the actual profit accrued by the business and not to the invested capital. Similarly, the profit sharing ratio is mutually decided by the partners that may vary from partner to partner. However, a fixed lump-sum amount cannot be agreed upon for any partner. Moreover, the ratio of profit may be different from the ratio of investment for the participating partners, i.e., non-sleeping partners may receive a higher share in profit than their ratio of investment. Thus, a partner with 20% share in the investment may get 30% share in the profit, provided he/she has not put an explicit condition in the partnership agreement to remain a sleeping partner. The share of a partner in the profit cannot exceed share in the capital if he/she is explicitly declared in the partnership agreement as the sleeping partner. However, if the agreement does not stipulate any such condition, a partner will be entitled to additional share over his investment ratio even if he did not work for the venture.[5]

The profit sharing ratio must be determined in advance. However, the partners may agree to alter the profit sharing ratio later on. Moreover, a partner may surrender a part of his/her profit to another partner on the date of distribution. Furthermore, different profit sharing ratios may be agreed upon for different periods or the magnitudes of the realized profit. In the nutshell, the partners may agree on any profit sharing ratio. However, loss must be distributed exactly in the ratio of capital contribution. Any condition to the contrary (in terms of loss sharing) leads to the invalidity of the contract.

---

[5] AAOIFI (2017a)—page 332–333, SS12, Clause 5/1/5/3.

Conditions with Respect to Maturity or Termination of Musharakah

Each partner has the right to terminate or withdraw from the *Musharakah* after informing his partner(s) to this effect though prior notice. In such case, the partner is entitled to his share in the joint venture. However, in case of more than two partners, his withdrawal does not necessitate the termination of the partnership of the remaining partners. Rather the remaining partners can agree to continue the business for a stipulated period of time. In such a case, the price of the share of the leaving partner must be determined through the mutual consent of the partners. However, if the partners fail to arrive on an agreed price, the leaving partners may compel the liquidation or distribution of the assets.

The *Musharakah* stands terminated automatically in the following conditions:

a. if any one of partners dies during the currency of *Musharakah*. His heirs may, however, decide to continue with the *Musharakah* contract. In such case, the deceased partner is replaced by his heir(s);
b. if a partner becomes insane or incapable of affecting commercial transactions;
c. if the purpose of initiating the *Musharakah* is achieved (in case of specific purpose *Musharakah*);
d. on the date of expiry (in case of temporary *Musharakah*).

If assets are liquidated upon the termination of *Musharakah*, the proceeds have to be distributed, on the pro-rata basis, among the partners. Similarly, the partners may also agree to distribute the assets as they are. However, if the partners do not agree on whether to liquidate or distribute the non-liquid assets, the distribution of the non-liquid assets will be preferred. This is because after the *Musharakah* is terminated, the assets become joint property of the partners and a partner has the right to initiate separation or partition and he cannot be compelled on liquidation. However, if the assets are non-distributable such as a vehicle, they shall be liquidated and the proceeds from the sale shall be distributed.

1.6 Mudarabah and Its Terms and Conditions

The *Mudarabah* agreement is also called "*Muqaradah*" and "*Qirad*." Mudarabah is a special form of *Shirkat-ul-'Aqd* in which an investor or a group of investors, called *Rab-ul-Mal*, handover capital to agent(s), called *Mudarib*, to invest in certain business activity. Thus, the investor contributes capital while the entrepreneur employs effort and exercises complete control over the business. The resulting profit is shared in a pre-agreed ratio, while the loss (if any) is borne exclusively by the *Rab-ul-Mal*. Thus, in the event of loss, the *Rab-ul-Mal* incurs financial loss while *Mudarib* losses compensation for his labor and effort. However, if the Mudarabah contract becomes valid due to any reason, the *Mudarib* will continue to manage the business on *Ujrat* (service fee) basis instead of share in the profit.[6] There is no restriction on the number of *Rab-ul-Mal* or number of *Mudarib* in a *Mudarabah* arrangement.

There are two types of Mudarabah contracts namely the restricted and unrestricted Mudarabah: In the restricted Mudarabah (*Mudarabah Al Muqayyadah*), the financier imposes certain restrictions on *Mudarib* in terms of location, time, type of investment, or the products to deal in. However, these restrictions must not be imposed in a manner that would unduly restrain the *Mudarib* in the operations of business. On the contrary, in the unrestricted *Mudarabah* (*Mudarabah Al Mutlaqah*), the financier allows the *Mudarib* to invest the capital without any restrictions. Consequently, the *Mudarib* has a wide range of trade choices and business freedom. However, the *Mudarib* has to assure that the capital of financier is in safe hands. Moreover, he has to try his best to achieve the objectives of the Mudarabah contract and to find best ways for investing the capital in the permissible manner.

Capital of Mudarabah

The capital of *Mudarabah* has to be invested by the *Rab-ul-Mal* which should be in control of the *Mudarib*. For this purpose the capital should be, partially or wholly, at the disposal of *Mudarib*, or the *Mudarib* must have free access to it. In principle, the invested capital should be in the

---

[6] Ayub (2007)—page 321.

form of cash. However, tangible assets may also be contributed to the *Mudarabah*. But the value of non-liquid assets must be determined in the prevailing currency at the time of initiating the *Mudarabah* contract. The valuation of such assets may be performed by experts or as agreed upon by the contracting parties. The capital of *Mudarabah* has to be clearly defined in terms of quantity and quality in such a way that there remains no possibility of ambiguity or uncertainty among the contracting parties.

Mixing of Capital

With the prior consent of the *Rab-ul-Mal*, *Mudarib* can invest his own capital in the *Mudarabah* business. In such case, the business will become a combination of *Musharakah* and *Mudarabah* encompassing the features of both contracts. Thus, *Mudarib* will have dual claim on the profit: first his share as a co-owner and second as a *Mudarib*. For example, a *Rab-ul-Mal* gives USD 200,000 to a Mudarib for investment purpose. The Mudarib also adds USD 100,000 as his own investment with the consent of Rab-ul-Mal. Assume that the partners agree to share the *Musharakah* profit in the ratio of capital contribution. Thus, Mudarib will first get one-third share in the actual profit as a *Sharik*, followed by equal share in the remainder (two-third) profit as a *Mudarib*. The partners may agree on any profit sharing ratio. However, the only condition that has to be fulfilled is that the sleeping partner cannot get a percentage higher than his proportion in investment. For example, in the above example, the *Rab-ul-Mal* cannot claim more than two-thirds of the total profit because his investment is equal to two-thirds of the total capital. See illustration 1.1 for estimation of the partners' share in profit in a *Musharakah* cum *Mudarabah* arrangement.

Illustration 1.1: Estimation of partners' share in profit and loss in a Musharakah cum Mudarabah arrangement

Assume Mr. A and B enters into a *Mudarabah* arrangement whereby A is *Rab-ul-Mal* while B is *Mudarib*. A contributes 3 Million dollars as a *Mudarabah* capital while B agrees to manage the business activities. They agree on a profit sharing ratio of 30:70 where B will get 30% in the net profit as a *Mudarib* while A will get 70% of the net profit as Rab-ul-Mal. However, to initiate this business a total capital of 4 million is required. B agrees to invest the remainder one million dollars as equity. Moreover, they mutually decide to share the profit in the ratio of their respective share in investment. Consequently, B becomes joint owner of the business as well as *Mudarib*. The profit and loss will be shared in the following manner:

Total investment	USD 4 million	
Share of partners in the capital	A's contribution	USD 3 million
	B's contribution	USD 1 million
Capital sharing ratio	75: 25	
	A's share	75%
	B's share	25%
Net Profit	USD 1 million	
Profit sharing ratio Under Musharakah agreement (As per capital contribution ratio)	75:25	
	A's share	75%
	B's share	25%
Share of partners in the profit	A's share @ 75%	1*0.75 = USD 0.75 million
	B's share @ 25%	1*0.25 = USD 0.25 million

Case 1: Distribution of profit

Assume the business earns 1 Million dollars as a net profit in the first year. The profit will be first estimated for the *Musharakah* agreement in the following manner:

The A's share will be further divided between A and B in the ratio of 70 and 30%, respectively, under the *Mudarabah* agreement.

Profit sharing ratio Under Mudarabah agreement	70:30	
	A's share as Rab-ul-Mal	70%
	B's share as Mudarib	30%
Remaining profit to be distributed between A and B	USD 0.75 million	
Share of partners in the profit	A's share @ 70%	0.75*0.70 = USD 0.525 million
	B's share @ 30%	0.75*0.30 = USD 0.225 million

Thus, net share of A and B in profit will be as follows:

Share of A	Share of A as a Co-owner	USD 0.525 million
Share of B	Share of B as a Co-owner	USD 0.25 million
	+ Share of B as a Mudarib	USD 0.225 million
	Total Share of B	USD 0.457 million

Case 2: Distribution of loss

Assume they incur a loss of 0.65 Million dollars in the first year. The loss will be distributed in the following manner:

Total investment	USD 4 million	
Share of partners in the capital	A's contribution	USD 3 million
	B's contribution	USD 1 million
Capital sharing ratio	75: 25	
	A's share	75%
	B's share	25%
Net loss	USD 0.65 million	
Loss sharing ratio Under Musharakah agreement (In the ratio of capital contribution)	75:25	
	A's share	75%
	B's share	25%
Share of partners in the loss	A's share @ 75%	0.65*0.75 = USD 0.4875 million
	B's share @ 25%	0.65*0.25 = USD 0.1625 million

Management of the Business Affairs

Management of the business affairs is the sole responsibility of *Mudarib* while *Rab-ul-Mal* is not allowed to participate in the business activities. Thus, he cannot stipulate to have right to work with the Mudarib and to involve in the routine activities of the business such as sale and purchase, or ordering and supplying of merchandise, etc. However, he has the right to oversee and monitor the business activities to make sure that the *Mudarib* is performing his responsibilities efficiently and honestly. In addition, the *Rab-ul-Mal* can also impose certain restrictions on the *Mudarib* in terms of object, method, place, and timing of trading. For example, he may restrict the *Mudarib* to operate within a specific marketplace. However, restricting the operations to certain commodities is circumscribed with the condition that such commodities must be freely available and should not be scarce, out of season, or in limited supply to make sure that the operations of business are not restrained.

The *Mudarib*, on the other hand, is liable to perform all the tasks that a similar fund or asset manager would be responsible, by custom, to perform. Moreover, he is not entitled to a fee for the work that is part of his responsibilities. Similarly, if he appoints someone else to carry out any such work, the wage of the worker has to be paid from his personal funds. However, he can appoint another party, against the *Mudarabah* funds, to perform the tasks that are not by custom the responsibility of the *Mudarib*.

Distribution of Profit and Losses

The mechanism for profit distribution must be determined in advance. It must be explicit and clear so that the possibility of any dispute and uncertainty is ruled out. Moreover, the partners can agree on any profit sharing ratio. However, if no such ratio is determined, the customary practice shall be followed to determine the partners' share in profit. In case, if no customary practice is found in this regard, the *Mudarabah* contract stands void ab-initio, and the *Mudarib* becomes entitled to a common market service charges for the amount and kind of services being rendered by him.[7] Moreover, the distribution of profit must be based on the agreed percentage of the actual profit and not on the lump-sum payment or a percentage of investment. Similarly, it is not allowed to assign the profit from one period or a particular transaction to *Mudarib* and profit from another period or transaction to the *Rab-ul-Mal*.

However, it is permissible to assign different profit sharing ratios in different conditions.[8] For example, if *Mudarib* trades in rice, he will receive 40% share in profit but if he trades in wheat he will receive 30% share. Similarly, a two-tier profit sharing ratio is also permissible.

---

[7] AAOIFI (2017b)—page 373–374, SS 13, Clause 8/4.

[8] Usmani (2002a)—page 104, Usmani (2002b)—page 33, Ayub (2007)—page 325.

In the two-tier profit sharing a ceiling rate is determined on the mutual consent. If the profit exceeds the ceiling rate, the partners may agree on the distribution of the profit above ceiling in an agreed ratio which may be different from the original profit sharing ratio. For example, partners may mutually decide that the profit that is less than or equal to 2 million dollars will be distributed in the 30:70 ratio (i.e., tier 1). While the profit above 2 million will be distributed equally (i.e., tier 2). Thus, if 3 million dollars profit is incurred, 2 million will be shared in the 30:70 ratio while 1 million will be shared equally (50:50 ratio).

In addition, *Mudarib* is not entitled to any periodical fee or salary for his services to the *Mudarabah* business over and above his pre-determined share in the profit. However, the partners can sign a separate independent contract for assigning any task to Mudarib, which is by custom not part of the *Mudarabah* business, against a fee over and above his share in the profit. This contract must be independent of the original *Mudarabah* contract so that the original *Mudarabah* contract remains intact if *Mudarib* is terminated from the additional service. Similarly, the *Mudarib* is not allowed to withdraw daily expenses from the *Mudarabah* account. However, Imam Ahmad Ibn Hanbal allows withdrawal of daily expenses of food only, while Imam Abu Hanifa allows charging only the expenses incurred during the journeys undertaken for the business purpose.

Similarly, *Mudarabah* is a trust-based contract whereby the relationship between *Rab-ul-Mal* and *Mudarib* is based on trust. Therefore, *Mudarib* is not liable for the losses except in the case of breach of trust such as negligence, misconduct, or breach of the terms of *Mudarabah* contract. In any of such case, the *Mudarib* become liable for the loss. Similarly, partners can create reserve from the profit, with the mutual consent, to compensate the future losses. Thus, loss can be compensated by the reserves maintained in the past or by the expected profit of future operations. If losses exceed the profits at the time of liquidation, the net loss shall be deducted from the capital.

Termination/Maturity of Mudarabah

A restricted *Mudarabah* will terminate automatically after the intended objective is achieved. While in case of general Mudarabah, the termination is contingent on the mutual consent of the partners. In case of disagreement among partners on whether to terminate or continue the joint venture, reconciliation may be sought through court or any other arbitration. However, the unlimited power of a partner to terminate the *Mudarabah* agreement creates complexities in the context of contemporary business environment, because businesses usually demand time and continuous efforts to establish. Moreover, it is usually unlikely for the business to earn a significant return in the early phases after inception. Thus, if the *Rab-ul-Mal* losses hope in the early phase of the business, the early termination will cause a severe set-back to the *Mudarib* who will end up earning nothing despite his sincere efforts. To cope with this problem, the partners can mutually decide, at the time of inception, that no party shall terminate the contract during a specified period except in specified circumstances.[9]

Put differently, the terms of a *Mudarabah* contact are not binding and the contract can be terminated unilaterally by any partner except in the following cases[10]:

a. When the *Mudarabah* business has already been commenced, in such case, the contract becomes binding upon all partners till the date of actual or constructive liquidation.
b. When the duration of *Mudarabah*, for which the business will remain in operation, has been agreed upon by the partners, in such a case, the *Mudarabah* cannot be terminated before the designated period, except by the mutual consensus of the partners.

1.7 Chapter Summary

The modes of Islamic finance can be broadly classified into participatory and non-participatory modes. The participatory modes, as their name suggests, involve direct participation in the business and its outcomes be it profit or loss. The participatory modes are called the *Shari'ah*-based modes because these are derived directly from Quran and *Sunnah* of Prophet (Peace and blessings of Allah be upon him). Moreover, these are advocated as the ideal modes for achieving the socio-economic objectives of *Shari'ah*. On the other hand, the non-participatory modes are called the sales-based modes which do not involve profit and loss sharing. These

---

[9] Usmani (2002b)—page 35.
[10] AAOIFI (2017b)—page 371, SS 13 Clause 4/3.

modes usually involve a fixed payment which has to be paid regardless of the business outcomes.

This chapter introduces participatory finance, its origin and modes to build an overall context for the book. The thesis argument is built by introducing Islamic banking and finance and their modus operandi. Next, the participatory and non-participatory paradigms of Islamic finance are elaborated with the major focus on the participatory finance and its legality and origin. The chapter concludes with the detailed discussion of the *Musharakah* and *Mudarabah* modes of participatory finance. The basic rules of *Musharakah* and *Mudarabah* are discussed particularly the rules related to the contribution of capital, the management of business affairs, treatment of profit and losses, and the termination/maturity of the business arrangement.

References

AAOIFI. (2017a). Shari'ah Standards. In AAOIFI (Ed.), *Shari'ah Standard No. (12): Sharikah (Musharakah), and Modern Corporations* (Vol. 2). Accounting and Auditing Organization for Islamic Financial Institutions.

AAOIFI. (2017b). Shari'ah Standards. In AAOIFI (Ed.), *Shari'ah Standard No. (13): Mudarabah*. Accounting and Auditing Organization for Islamic Financial Institutions.

Ayub, M. (2007). *Understanding Islamic Finance*. John Wiley & Sons Ltd.

Usmani, M. I. A. (2002a). *Meezan Bank's guide to Islamic banking* (1st ed.). Darul-Ishaat.

Usmani, M. T. (2002b). *An introduction to Islamic finance*. Kluwer Law International.

CHAPTER 2

Maqasid Al Shari'ah and Financial Concern of Human Life

The religion Islam is more broadly comprehended as a complete code of life. As a consequence, the Islamic society and its framework are developed through the divine law called *Shari'ah* and rigorous Islamic jurisprudence called *Fiqh*. Its foremost message is that every follower must struggle, at the individual as well as social level, to attain the potential for good. Besides other aspects of human life, it also governs the behavior in the economic monarchy. This chapter explores the higher ethical objective of *Shari'ah* to conceptualize the basic philosophy of *Shari'ah*. For this purpose this chapter develops an integrated framework of *Maqasid al Shari'ah* by synthesizing the viewpoints of the leading Islamic philosophers and proponents including imam Ghazali, Abu Zahrah, and Ibn Ahsur. This framework serves a base to build upon the nexus between *Maqasid al Shari'ah* and participatory finance as we further elaborated on in Chapter 5. In addition, this chapter also explores the linkage between *Maqasid Al Shari'ah* and the economic and financial concerns of human life to understand how and why *Shari'ah* permeates the matters related to economic and financial aspects of human life.

2.1 SHARI'AH AND ITS HIGHER ETHICAL OBJECTIVES (MAQASID AL SHARI'AH)

Islamic rules and laws, known as *Shari'ah*, i.e., Islamic jurisprudence, govern all aspects of Islamic matters including faith, worship, social, cultural, political, legal, and economic concerns of Islamic societies. The literal meaning of *Shari'ah* is the "way" or "path to the water source." Technically, *Shari'ah* refers to the laws derived from or contained in The Holy Qur'an and *Sunnah* of the Prophet Muhammad (Peace Be Upon Him) and represents all facets of Islamic faith including the belief system and practices.

Shari'ah defines a system of values and ethics governing intellectual, moral, personal, economic, political, and social behaviors. The utmost objective of *Shari'ah* rests within the concepts of guidance and compassion, which seek to alleviate hardships, eliminate, prejudice, and establish justice by promoting mutual support and cooperation within the society. These two concepts can be manifested through the realization public wellbeing which the *Shari'ah* scholars generally consider as the all-pervasive objective and value of *Shari'ah* and synonymous with compassion.

Numerous Islamic scholars have attempted to comprehend the objectives of *Shari'ah*, called the *Maqasid al Shari'ah*. *Maqasid al Shari'ah*, refers to the underlying logic or rationale for *Shari'ah* principals and rulings. In other words, it highlights the importance and benefits of using the Islamic lens in every aspect of life. It comprises of the underlying advantages, benefits, and welfare for which Allah has revealed His *Shari'ah*. Ibn Qayyim al-Jawziyyah (d.1356) states that *Shari'ah* aims to safeguard the interest of people in both the worlds, including this world and hereafter. Similarly, Sheikh Mohammad Abu Zahrah viewed it as the 'mercy to humanity.'

The Integrated Framework of Maqasid Al Shariah *(Higher Ethical Objectives)*

Different authors have outlined different dimensions of *maqasid al Shari'ah*. For example, Sheikh Mohammad Abu Zahrah has classified *Maqasid al Shari'ah* into three subgroups namely educating the individual (*Tahdhib al-Fard*), establishing justice (*Iqamah al-ʿAdl*) and public Interest (*al-Maslahah*). On the other hand, few scholars, including Ibn ʿAshur, have divided the *Maqasid al Shari'ah* into three main categories including (i) *maqasid ammah* (general objectives), (ii) *maqasid khassah* (specific objectives), and (iii) *Maqasid juz'iyyah* (partial objectives). General objectives include the objectives and goals that are reflected in all or most facets of religious legislations. The specific objectives, on the other hand, are concerned with specific discipline such as private conduct, family law, and financial transactions, while partial objectives relate to a particular issue or question, or to a particular proof that acts a base for the deduction of the larger purpose of *Shari'ah*.

This chapter seeks to develop an integrated framework to conceptualize different dimensions of *Maqasid al Shari'ah* and their typology to build upon the nexus between *Maqasid al Shari'ah* and participatory finance.[1] For this purpose the present study adopts the imam Ghazali's classification coupled with the Abu Zahrah and Ibn Ahsur classification. Figure 2.1 presents the integrate model of *Maqasid al Shari'ah*.

Sheikh Mohammad Abu Zahrah has classified *Maqasid al Shari'ah* into three subgroups, namely educating the individual (*Tahdhib al-Fard*), establishing justice (*Iqamah al-'Adl*), and public interest (*al-Maslahah*). *Tahdhib al-Fard* (educating the individual) refers to the human's development that focuses not only on knowledge and skills but also their spiritual values. Therefore, it can be viewed in the broader spectrum of *Falah* (success) in this world and hereafter. Educating the individuals to perform a dual function. Firstly, it enlightens them about the moral values and worldview of Islam and their mission in this world as *Khalifahs* (vicegerents) of Allah Almighty. Secondly, it not only improves the individual's efficiency to perform their jobs, but also expands the society's technological base and knowledge. The moral uplift and expansion of the technological base and knowledge would untimely lead toward development.

Similarly, *Iqamah al-'Adl* (Establishing justice) encompasses equal treatment among individuals, and avoidance of discrimination to ensure peace and moral and social uplift of the society. Qur'an has emphatically commanded people to stand firmly to justice (Qur'an, 16:90 and 4:135). Establishment of justice has been the primary mission of all Messengers of Allah (Qur'an, 57:25). The absence of justice cannot but lead ultimately to misery and destruction (Qur'an, 20:111). Hence, the goals

---

[1] See Nouman et al. (2021) for detailed discussion on how this framework was developed.

of social well-being, equality, brotherhood, and human dignity remain hollow concepts unless not accompanied by socio-economic justice.

Al Maslahah, on the other hand, refers to interest or benefit, advantage or welfare. Its literal meaning is to secure benefits or repel harm. *Maslahah* is synonymous to public interest and is employed in Islamic legal theory as a juristic device for promoting public well-being and repelling corruption or social evils. Al-Ghazali reinforces the fundamental meaning of *Maslahah* as the preservation of the *Shari'ah's* objectives. He defines *Maslahah* as:

> *Maslahah is essentially an expression for the acquisition of benefit or the repulsion of injury or harm, but that is not what we mean by it, because acquisition of benefits and the repulsion of harm represent human goals, that is, the welfare of humans through the attainment of these goals. What we mean by Maslahah, however, is the preservation of the Shari'ah's objectives.* (Al-Raisuni, 1992, p. 41)

Kamali (2008) expands the *Maslahah's* meaning to the realm of justice. He asserts that the aim of *Maslahah* is to ensure justice that refers, not merely in its retributive sense to repelling harm but, to establish the equilibrium of advantages and benefits, and distributive justice in the society. He further adds that the failure of *Shari'ah* to preserve public well-being would imply the failure of Islam to serve its followers. Thus, the meaning of *Maslahah* is in lined with the *Maqasid al Shari'ah* in terms of promoting social well-being, utility, and benefits.

Maslahah is further classified into three main components by several *Shari'ah* scholars, including Imam Al-Ghazali, Al-Shatibi, and Abu Zahrah namely: (i) *Daruriyyat* (necessities or essentials), (ii) *Hajiyyat* (complement), and (iii) *Tahsiniyyat* (embellishments). *Daruriyyat* (essentials) encompasses primary or basic necessities for well-being of mankind. These necessities include fundamental needs for the survival of humanity including right to religion, right to live peaceful life, and right to have food for survival. Accomplishment of theses necessities guarantees the progressive life for individuals in particular and for the society in general. Imam Ghazali specifically highlighted five main areas for *daruriyyat* or the essentials as protection of religion (*Al-Din*), protection of life (*Al-hayah*), protection of mind (*Al'Aql*), protection of wealth (*Al mal*), and protection of family/linage (*Nasal*). According to Imam Al-Ghazali:

The objective of the Shari'ah is to promote the well-being of all mankind, which lies in safeguarding their faith (din), their human self (nafs), their intellect ('aql), their posterity (nasl) and their wealth (mal). Whatever ensures the safeguard of these five serves public interest and is desirable.

When *Daruriyyat* are fulfilled, individuals look for the fulfillment of *Hajiyyat* (complements) to attain the higher level of economic and social growth. *Hajiyyat* (complements) are categorized as secondary needs or requirements of well-being of mankind. Individuals and society can survive without realization of these; however, these are important for the normal functionality of the various activities and functions of the society in the normal course of life. For example, in the dominion of economic affairs, *Shari'ah* allows hire and lease (*Ijarah*) and forward buying (*Salam*) keeping in view needs of the society, though both of these entail certain anomaly.

Tahsiniyyat (embellishments), on the contrary, addresses the prestigious type of needs of individuals and society and refers to those needs that, when fulfilled, would consequently result in the perfection and refinement in the conduct and customs of society. Thus, embellishment helps to achieve the ultimate level of development and advancement, for individual and social well-being. Some examples of *Tahsiniyyat* (embellishments) for *ibada* (worship) are, *sadaqah (charity)*, ethical value, and moral values.

While achieving the above levels of *maqasid*, wealth is considered one of the fundamental means for it in the society and hence requires protection. Ibn Ashur has further deliberated five subcategories of the protection of wealth *(hifz al-mal)* under *Maqasid al Shariah* including rawaj (circulation), wuduh (clarity), thubat (stability and proof), and 'adl (justice) and *tanmiyah* (growth and development).

i. *Rawaj* (circulation)

Rawaj refers to the fair circulation of wealth in the hands of as many people as possible. It governs all facets of wealth circulation including investments, exchange, benevolence, and inheritance. *Shariah* promotes the circulation of wealth and discourages its wasteful concentration to provide equal opportunities to all. For this purpose *Shariah* obligates the wealthy people to share their fortunes with the poor and forbids the accumulation of gold and silver for their own sake, profiteering, monopoly, and hording. The main channels for circulation in Islamic include *Sadaqat* (voluntary charity), *Zakat* (obligatory alms), *Kaffarat* (expiations), *Waqf* (charitable endowments), and *Hibah* (gifts). These are in addition to other permissible means of investments through which the wealth circulation is enhanced.

ii. *Wuduh* (Clarity)
Wuduh as a higher ethical objective refers to clarity and transparency in the ownership of wealth and its transactions. Shariah seeks to prevent the disputes caused by ambiguities and confusions in the ownership, contracts, and transactions due to the lack of clarity. Thus, clarity ensures the protection of wealth by preventing destruction of property and thereby helps in warding off evil in the society. Ownership is protected by clarity in its modes of transfer and acquisition, inheritance, *Iltizam* (unilateral commitment), and contracts of exchange. Moreover, the ownership rights are protected against unfounded claims through witnessing, documentation, reconciliation, judicial order, and others.

iii. *Thubat* (Stability and Proof)
Thubat in the contemporary context refers to stability and proof. According to Ibn Ashur, the application of *thubat* is imperative to avoid conflicts and establish the legal claim or right for assets and business transactions. Thus, stability and proof is imperative for preservation of wealth since ownership claim and any contract can only be verified to be true if it has some legal proof (*thubat*). Moreover, it also serves as a means (*Wasilah*) toward ascertaining clarity (*Wuduh*) because legal proof is required for determining the ownership of an asset. Thus, clarity can only be maintained if the stability and proof exists. Stability and proof are ascertained through transactions, contracts, and regime of law that establish an environment conducive to the stable exchange, transfer, and ownership of goods and services.

iv. *'Adl* (**Justice**)
   According to Ibn Ashur, in the economic and business realm, 'Adl (Justice) refers to the equality before the law in terms of ownership rights and economic activities. Justice induces the protection of wealth and its growth by ensuring a secure environment which is characterized by protection of ownership rights and equitable distribution of opportunities and wealth. Shariah ascertains justice in economic and business realm by laying down the principles of economic and distributive justice that ensure the fair production and distribution of wealth in the society. Moreover, Shariah bounds the state authority through divine injunctions to regulate the economy in a way that is conducive to the justice and economic security of people.

v. *Tanmiyah* (**Growth and Development**)
   Islam necessitates not only the circulation and preservation of existing wealth, but also its growth and development *(tanmiyah)*. It can be achieved through generation of more through investment, profitable trade and work. Thus, all legal and legitimate mechanisms and means to the development and growth of trade and property fall within the purview of *tanmiyah*. Moreover, it also includes development of agriculture and health sector, cleanliness and environmental safety, import and export activities, deepening and diversification of market, savings, food security, and development of employment opportunities.

Figure 2.1 presents the integrated model of *Maqasid al Shari'ah* based on the models of Imam Ghazali, Imam Abu Zaharah, and Ibn Ashur.

Based upon the above discussion and the proposed integrated framework, it can be concluded that *Maqasid al Shari'ah* proposes a value system for the proper functioning of the society, and a strong framework for alleviating troubles and hardships of humans and establishing justice. Its foremost message is that we must struggle, at the individual as well as social level, to attain the potential for good. Thus, all aspects of human life including intellectual, moral, personal, economic, political, and social should strictly be in lined with *Maqasid al Shari'ah* to ensure social well-being in all spheres of life.

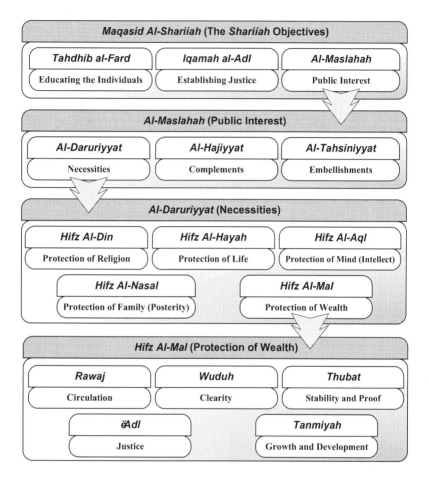

Fig. 2.1 *Maqasid Al Shari'ah* integrated framework (*Source* Nouman et al. [2021])

Maqasid Al Shari'ah *and the Economic-Financial Concerns of Human Life*

Shari'ah considers the issues of social justice, equity, and fairness in all spheres of human life including the economic concerns. In fact, *Shari'ah* provides the basic framework for an Islamic economic system, where the economic motives are integrated fully with the ethical behavioral norms (discussed as *maqasid* in the preceding section). This framework emphasizes a social welfare system based on care and dignity for the poor, mutual help, behavioral reforms, character building, and the system of *Zakat* to uplift the economically suppressed class of the society.

Islamic economic system is characterized by socio-economic and distributive justice, and entails a comprehensive system of moral values and ethics. It does not allow hoarding, destruction of output, fictitiously forcing, or maintaining high prices. Similar to a free-market system, Islamic economic system entails private property and enterprise, market mechanisms, fare competition, and self-interest. Within this overall frame work, government has to ensure, through effective supervision, that markets function freely under a competitive price mechanism, disclosures and transparency, without being distorted by the stronger and influential segments of the society. Moreover, individuals have the right of free enterprise and private property, and are allowed to earn profit through value creation and profit and loss sharing. State has to assume the role of overseeing to ensure that the linkage between real economy and finance contributes to growth and fare distribution of income.

In the economic realm, Islamic law regulates both the methods, i.e., method of earning money and the method of spending it. Acquirement of wealth is permitted and encouraged through those conducts which are justified to all concerned parties. Individual profit, exploitation and subjective taxation, which lead to social harms, are not permitted in Islamic law. Such laws put various limitations on business practices employed to make profits. For example, selling products that lead to moral exploitation or polluting the environment are not permitted in Islamic law.

According to Islamic point of view, the acquired wealth becomes personal property, which is both a test and a trust. According to the test aspect, those who have wealth over and above their needs must take care of needy ones. According to the trust aspect, property should be used in such a way that it benefits both the individual and society. Islamic law also focuses the ways of utilizing or spending acquired wealth. Therefore, Islamic law encourages the struggling to acquire wealth and to spend it for personal as well as family needs. Thus, people are not allowed to ask from others and are expected to struggle for self-reliance and independence. Moreover, Islam encourages a relaxed and happy living standard and does not encourage strictness. Similarly, Islam strongly dejects spending on idle wishes, luxuries, and flashiness. Instead, spending on social welfare is strongly encouraged. These vital principles for wealth acquisition and its proper utilization and spending influence all the dominions of economic activity. Ensuring the delivery of fairness and justice is the key objective of an Islamic state. The Islamic public finance aims at with outlining the firm implication for this purpose.

Economic affair is among one of the most important issue discussed in teachings of Islam. *According to Qur'an* "Allah hath bought from the believers their lives and their wealth in return for Paradise" (Qur'an, 9: 111). According to Islamic view, one of the five questions that Muslims will have to answer on the Day of Judgment is that how they earned their wealth and how did they spend it. According to Islamic law, all of our incomes must come from *Halal* means, and we should spend these incomes to fulfill our *Halal* needs of expenditure. To properly govern an expanding and growing territory (empire), the early Muslim writers were led to discuss *Halal* means of generating incomes for the state and its obligations to spend this income on their public. Therefore, public finance is a classy and well-developed area within the Islamic doctrine. These early Islamic teachings permeate modern Islamic economics which has also been robustly molded by the colonization of Islamic countries, attempts for their independence, and the requisite to act in response to the proclamations of the Western knowledge supremacy.

The transition from Biblical "love of money is the root of all evil" to the George Bernard Shaw's "lack of money is the root of all evil" (Shaw, 1903) fittingly summarizes the growing materialism, varying approach toward poor people, and other repercussions of the expansion of capitalism. On the contrary, Islam doesn't priorities economics. However, as economic system (i.e., socialism, communism, and capitalism) is a major characteristic of Western identity, Muslims need to respond in this regard. According to Mufti Muhammad Shafi:

> No doubt, Islam is opposed to monasticism, and views the economic activities of man as quite lawful, meritorious, and some-times even obligatory and necessary. It approves of the economic progress of man, and considers "Lawful or righteous livelihood" as "an obligation next to the obligation" that is to say, an obligation of the secondary order. Notwithstanding all this, it is no less a truth that it does not consider "economic activity" to be the basic problem of man, nor does it view economic progress as the be-all and end-all of human life. (Shafi, 1978)

Islamic economic system is largely based on some certain encouragements and prohibitions. In Islamic economic system, *Riba* (Interest) is prohibited whereas trade is permitted. "Allah has allowed (profit from) trade and prohibited *Riba*" (verse 2: 275 of the Holy Qur'an). Such teachings of *Qur'an* imply that financial activities involved in an Islamic economic system should be asset-backed transactions and businesses. This suggests that all the financial transactions ought to illustrate real transactions or sale of goods, benefits, or services. Along with this, Islam also suggests a behavioral/moral standard which is almost similar in all the civilized culture of the world.

Along with the prohibition of interest, taking excessive risk or involvement in the games of chance is also prohibited in Islamic finance because these involve exploitations and cause loss to at least one or both parties involved in the contract. The Islamic finance philosophy stems the following rules and principles:

a. **Avoiding Interest**

Islamic financial structure revolves around prohibition of *Riba* or interest and the permissibility of the profit. Interest or *Riba* is basically an increase or extra amount that is paid by the lender as a premium. It signifies the return on such transactions which involves the exchange of money for money and the payment of certain or agreed amount of money in case of any delay in payment of loan.

As per *Shari'ah* doctrine and the Islamic Finance philosophy, lender will lend money without expecting any return.

> From Anas ibn Malik (Gbpwh): "The Prophet said: 'When one of you grants a loan and the borrower offers him a dish, he should not accept it; and if the borrower offers a ride on an animal, he should not ride, unless the two of them have been previously accustomed to exchanging such favours mutually'."[2]

Therefore, Islamic banks are not allowed to lend or borrow in a way that would ensure excess receipt or payment over the principal amount. On the other hand, selling or purchasing of goods, both on the basis of cash payment and credit, for profit earning purpose is permitted. Along with

---

[2] Baihaqi, 1344 H, Kitab al-Buyu,' Bab kulli qardin jarra manfa'atan fa huwa riban.

this, the pricing of goods with taking into consideration the time given for price payment in transactions of credit is also permissible but with the condition that there must not be any involvement of any kind of increase or enhancement to the principal amount of loan resulting from of the transaction of sale. This concept suggests seller has no right to charge or demand over and above the specified credit price, after the creation of debt.

However, barter exchange of certain commodities, e.g., foodstuff or currencies involving excess, or delay, is prohibited. The following *Hadith* suggests the rules for *Riba* in sales called the *Riba al Fadl*:

> The holy Prophet (Pbuh) said, "Gold for gold, silver for silver, wheat for wheat, barley for barley, dates for dates and salt for salt – like for like, equal for equal, and hand to hand; if the commodities differ, then you may sell as you wish, provided that the exchange is hand to hand."[3]

This *Hadith* prohibits the exchange of six commodities involving delay or excess. However, jurists have extended the scope of this type of prohibition (Riba al Fadl) to other commodities on the basis of the *'Illah* (effective cause) and *Qiyas* (analogical reasoning) (see for details Ayub, 2007; Vogel & Hayes, 1998).

The *Shari'ah* has forbidden *Riba* because it is harmful and vicious, as it generates economic imbalances and exploitations. An interest based is contract involves injustice to one of the parties, sometimes to the borrower and sometime to the lender. It is unjust on lender's part to ask for a predetermined rate of return if borrower incurs loss. On the other hand, if the borrower earns huge profits, it is injustice on the part of borrower to give a meager portion of profit to the lender.

Charging interest is among those facets of immoral behavior that promotes injustice and corrupts the whole society. *Riba* involves injustice in two ways: firstly, in loans involving *Riba*, a positive return is guaranteed to the lender (who does not assume a share of risk with the entrepreneur) regardless of the outcomes of the project. Instead, all types of risks are assumed by the entrepreneur along with the contribution of his labor and skills.

---

[3] Muslim, 1981, Kitab al Musaqat, chapter on Riba.

Secondly, Islam strictly forbids appropriation of other's property through unfair means (see, e.g., *Qur'an*, 2:188, 4:29, 4:161, and 9:34). Two types of property rights are recognized in Islam:

1. the property rights resulting from combining natural resources and labor of a person; and
2. the claims or right to the property gained through inheritance, exchange, and outright grants.

Money denotes the owner's monetized claim to the property rights that were gained through either or both of these ways. Borrowing money, in effect, transfers these property rights of lender to the borrower, and lender can in return claim no more but its equivalent. Charging interest on the money lent represents unjustified instantaneous claim to the property rights. It is considered unjustifiable since it does not fall within the legitimate property rights framework recognized by Islam. Moreover, this claim is considered instantaneous since as soon as the contract is finalized, lender obtains right to the property of borrower.

Moreover, it hampers the sense of brotherhood and cooperation and promotes *fasad* in the society. If a person needs loan for acquiring stuff necessary for survival, charging interest is demeaning, violating the nature of social life which demands help, care, and cooperation for the needy people from the rich. Imam Razi in his *Tafsir* discusses the following wisdoms of the Qur'anic prohibition of *Riba*:

- It leads to appropriation of the property of another person without giving him anything in return.
- It diminishes the value of work and thus refrains people from working to earn money. The rich people will not be interested in risking his capital in business or trade. As a result, it paralyzes industry, trade, and commerce.
- It also hampers the borrower's sense of friendliness and goodwill toward the lender. Moreover, it reduces benevolent acts which are key to brotherhood.
- It allows the rich to exploit the poor. Moreover, it widens the gap between rich and poor.

Since all the interest bearing transactions are strictly prohibited in Islam thus the contracts are not allowed to be sold at discount or premium. Along with this all such transactions that involve exchange of money or near to money goods like silver or gold are required to be "equal for equal" and must be "hand to hand." The term "equal for equal" is clear which means that any increase on the one side would be *Riba*. The term "hand to hand" means that the exchange of money ought to be on spot, because in the adverse case a party may use the money for their benefit but in return has delivered no counter value to the second party to take benefit from.

In Islamic finance context, lending and investments are two different things. Lending is a benevolent act and loan is a financial or monetary transaction where money exchange hands with the assurance for the full reimbursement without any compensation for the lender. On the other hand, from Islamic viewpoint, investment is not just a monetary or financial transaction which just involves transfer of funds. Investment actually represents a real activity or becomes part of a real economic activity. Therefore, buying a bond issued by corporation or government or depositing an amount in any conventional bank as a loan will not be considered as an investment due to the fact it is only a financial transaction involving no real activity. The real investment is the one that involves the use of funds for purchasing of real goods or services and selling of such goods or services at profit. However, using funds being acquired through interest-based loans for building or purchasing or physical assets is not allowed. In the same way, selling or purchasing of financial securities/documents is not an investment either because the holder does not involve in any real activity at all. Thus any income generated on loans in the form of interest is forbidden while any income generated from investment activities is allowed.

b. *Avoiding Gharar*

Another main prohibition in Islamic finance is *Gharar*. The term *Gharar* refers to the hazard or uncertainty due to non-clarity in the price or subject matter in an exchange or contract. In other words, *Gharar* means engaging in a contract whose final outcome, delivery date, or subject matter of the assets or goods under contract has absolute uncertainty.

Concealing the following elements of a contract leads to uncertainty, ambiguity, or doubt thus induces *Gharar* in the contract:

a. the types of entity and its attributes;
b. the object's quality; and
c. payment time in case of deferred sale.

Moreover, the following factors may also induce *Gharar* in the contract:

a. inability [probable or explicit] to deliver the object;
b. contracting for an object that does not exist; and
c. signing a contract without seeing the object.

Gharar leaves one or more vital elements of contracts, concealed, doubtful or uncertain, ambiguous or unclear. Therefore, *Gharar* also entails a contract which lacks sufficient value-relevant information or if the available information is inaccurate because it results into uncertainty, and may open ways for exploiting any of the party involved in the contract. Thus, fraud, deception, or deliberate withholding of vital information is equivalent to *Gharar*.

Any business transaction that involves the element of *Gharar* is strictly prohibited in Islamic finance. Islamic banks are not permitted to involve in any contract where the results are concealed, as in case they are not certain about the delivery of the product since it is compulsory for the accomplishment of the transaction. Thus, the contemporary practices of the insurance companies and financial institutions in the options and futures market are not permissible as per *Shari'ah* rules due to the fact that they involve gambling, interest, and *Gharar*, etc. However, if such elements are removed from transactions of the contemporary stock markets, it would then become Islamic.

In order to avoid *Gharar*, Islamic banks are required to avoid speculative trade in stocks, short-selling, trading in unidentified items and discounting of securities and bills. In the same way, Islamic investment banks should also take great care to avoid *Gharar* while involving in the Initial Public Offerings (IPOs) of the joint stock companies due to the reason that asymmetry of information between promoters and investors during early phases of the inception of companies may also involve

Gharar. Similarly, *Gharar* is also involved while trading in derivatives; therefore, it is also a gray area for the Islamic banks.

Though *Shari'ah* prohibits excessive *Gharar* in exchanges, however *Gharar* is inevitable in some contracts. Moreover, it is usually not possible to eliminate it completely from such contracts. For example, if someone is buying a house, there is uncertainty about the quality of material used in its foundations. However, such *Gharar* does not make this contract void. Some extent of *Gharar* in the form of uncertainty is allowed in Islamic finance. Therefore, a question arises how much *Gharar* is tolerable in a contract. Jurists have provided the following guidelines for deciding whether a *Gharar* in a contract may be considered ignorable or excessive because exorbitant or excessive *Gharar* make a contract void:

a. A contract should not be dominated by *Gharar*, in a way that the contract is characterized by *Gharar* to the extent that it becomes the hallmark of the contract.
b. The notion of *Gharar* applies only to the contracts involving exchange. Therefore, *Gharar* in the contracts that involve the sharing of profit or output is not prohibited.
c. A useful exchange or trade [which is need of the society] involving *Gharar* should not be prohibited.

The useful trade is the one which is a need, having no alternative, and the society or individual may face difficulty or hardship if it is not allowed. It is important to note that Islam makes distinction between *Gharar* and risk. Islam prohibits *Gharar* not commercial risk. Indeed, Islam encourages commercial risk if is shared equitably.

c. *Avoiding Qimar* (or *Maysir*)

Qimar (or *Maysir*), which refers to games of chance or gambling, is also a major prohibition in Islamic finance. This prohibition is based on the *Qur'an*'s injunction (see, e.g., *Qur'an* 5:90, 5:91, and 2:219). All such instruments like lotteries or prize bonds in which tabs or coupons are provided and incentives are given by unknown and an uncertain event that depend on the chance, or uneven rewards are distributed through lotteries, or where the parties taking part are intended to get benefited from the chance at prizes are inacceptable in *Shari'ah*. Similarly, gambling is involved in several schemes or products of the conventional banks and their financial transactions which are not permitted to Islamic banks. Since, conventional insurance involves both *Maysir* and *Riba*; therefore, it cannot be deemed as *Shari'ah* compliant.

Private and public sector corporations mobilize their resources through draws and lotteries which directly involve gambling; therefore, it is prohibited according to injunctions in Islam. Along with this, contracts like futures and options contracts that are based on generating benefit through the differences or gaps in price only also come under gambling. The most important of all are prize-carrying bonds/schemes or lotteries which the conventional institutions launch in order to mobilize their resources from time to time are also considered as gambling. Because only a very few of the participants receive reward at the other bondholders cost in these schemes, without performing any activity or taking any kind of liability.

2.2 Conclusion

It is evident from the above discussion that *Shari'ah* permeates financial transactions within the Islamic economic system and provides basic tenets for a unique Islamic financial system to ensure well-being of the overall society. The prohibition of *Riba* (lit. addition), i.e., interest in general, lies at the core of Islamic finance. However, simply describing an Islamic financial system as interest-free does not show a true representation of the system. Prohibition of interest is no doubt the essence of the Islamic financial system. However, in addition it is also characterized by other principles including protection of property rights, individuals' duties and rights, risk sharing and promotion of entrepreneurship, prohibition of speculative behavior, and the sanctity of contractual obligations. In the nutshell, charging interest, taking excessive risk or involvement in the games of chance, is prohibited in Islamic finance because these involve exploitations and cause loss to at least one or both parties involved in the contract. Therefore, a commercial or financial transaction is permissible in *Shari'ah* if it is free from excessive *Gharar* (uncertainty), *Riba* (interest), *Haram* (prohibited) activities, and *maysir* (gambling).

REFERENCES

Al-Raisuni, A. (1992). *Nazariah al-Maqasid 'inda al-Imam al-Shatibi*. Riyadh: Dar al-'Alamiyah Kitab al-Islami.
Ayub, M. (2007). *Understanding Islamic finance*. John Wiley & Sons Ltd.
Kamali, M. H. (2008). *Maqasid Al-Shariah made simple*. The Islamic Institute of IslamicThought.
Nouman, M., Siddiqi, M. F., Ullah, K., & Jan, S. (2021). Nexus between higher ethical objectives (Maqasid Al Shari'ah) and participatory finance. *Qualitative Research in Financial Markets, 13*(2), 226–251. https://doi.org/10.1108/QRFM-06-2020-0092
Shafi, M. (1978). *Distribution of wealth in Islam* (M. H. Askari & K. Husain, Trans.). Aisha Bawani Waqf and Ashraf Publications.
Shaw, G. B. (1903). *Man and superman: A comedy and a philosophy*. Cambridge University Press.
Vogel, F. E., & Hayes, S. L. (1998). *Islamic law and finance: Religion, risk and return*. Kluwer Law International.

CHAPTER 3

Linkage Between *Maqasid Al Shari'ah* and Participatory Finance

Islam is a system of beliefs based on the Holy *Qur'an*, *Hadith* (the sayings of the Prophet Muhammad peace be upon him), *Sunnah* (the tradition and practices of the Prophet Muhammad peace be upon him), and *Ijma* (lit. consensus), of the religious authorities. Islamic rules and laws, known as *Shari'ah*, govern all aspects of human life, whether related to faith, worship, social, cultural, political, legal, or economic concerns. The major goal of *Shari'ah* is the promotion of fairness, justice, and general welfare of people in the society.

Shari'ah also permeates financial transactions within the Islamic economic system and provides basic tenets for a unique Islamic financial system. The objective of Islamic financial system is to provide the financial solutions to the modern world that should be aligned with the *Shari'ah*. Within this system, *Shari'ah* rulings determine the operational nature of financial institutions, while the normative nature of their operations is defined by the precepts of Islamic Moral Economy (IME) which implies that their operations should comply with the ethical norms and account for the social impact consequences. Consequently, the Islamic financial institutions are supposed to fulfill the IME's normative expectations as articulated by the objectives of *Shari'ah*, referred to as the *Maqasid al Shari'ah*. This chapter, therefore, explores the philosophical underpinnings of participatory financing arrangements to conceptualize the social welfare role of these arrangements. Moreover, the basic philosophy and the axioms of Islamic finance are linked with the participatory financing to highlight its idealization in the Islamic finance literature. For this purpose it strives to create nexus between participatory financing and *Maqasid al Shari'ah*.

3.1 ASPIRATION-ORIENTED Vs REALITY-ORIENTED SCHOOLS OF THOUGHTS AND THE SOCIAL WELFARE ROLE OF PARTICIPATORY FINANCE

The Islamic financial system is characterized by an array of *Shari'ah* compliant participatory and non-participatory modes. The participative modes of finance, including *Musharakah* and *Mudarabah*, are widely accepted as the ideal modes of Islamic finance, because these are acclaimed to be inconsonance with the true spirit of *Shari'ah* and the IME. However, over the years, there seems to be widening gap between the theory and practice of Islamic finance that has led to the dissection of the advocates into two schools of thoughts including the aspiration-oriented and the reality-oriented schools.

The aspiration-oriented school adheres to the ideal of Islamic economics and finance and advocates a financial system based upon participation.[1] This group, mainly comprising of the Islamic economists, considers participation encompassing *Mudarabah*, *Musharakah*, and their variants as the main tool for replacing interest-based system. It is usually argued that the non-participatory modes though meet the requirements for *Shari'ah* compliance, but these do not have the ability to achieve the *Maqasid al Shari'ah* and the specific goals of Islamic economics and finance. Therefore, this group unanimously believe that the Islamic financial institutions must rely on partnership contracts to achieve the objectives of the economic system stability, efficiency, and socio-economic justice. However, their priorities and approach vary slightly.

For example, S.M. Hasanuz Zaman prefers *Musharakah* over *Mudarabah* for financing the non-trade operations.[2] On the other hand, Nejatullah Siddiqi and many other scholars are in the favor of

---

[1] See, e.g., Uzair (1978), Ahmad (1947), Qureshi (1946), Maududi (1969), Siddiqi (1969), Ghanameh (1973).

[2] See Zaman (1966).

the extensive utilization of *Mudarabah*.[3] Similarly, some scholars favor both *Musharakah* and *Mudarabah* equally. For example, according to Umar Chapra, the unanimously agreed upon financing of the Islamic financial institutions, particularly Islamic banks, should be based upon participatory modes or acquisition of shares of joint stock companies.[4]

The reality-oriented school, on the other hand, is indifferent toward participatory and non-participatory modes.[5] They rather emphasize the economic feasibility of Islamic finance in the contemporary business environment. This group, mainly comprising of the practitioners and academicians, believe that the non-participatory modes are equally legitimate as per the injunctions of Qur'an. Moreover, these modes are more viable and relevant to IFIs. Thus giving preference to participatory modes, as per the popular Islamic finance theory, is incorrectly devised. Moreover, they accuse the theory of preferring participation of not being derived from Holy Qur'an.

A stream of divergent literature has stemmed from the dissenting views of two schools of Islamic finance. An array of modern Islamic economists, who support the aspiration-oriented school, advocates a financial system based upon participation and risk sharing.[6] Some of them have strived to highlight the theoretical advantage of participatory finance using different economic models.[7] Moreover, others have pursued the potential of participatory modes to boost rural development and reduce poverty in the context of social role of participatory finance.[8]

On the other hand, the literature that adheres to the reality-oriented school advocates that the social welfare is the responsibility of government, while the core responsibility of financial institutions is toward their depositors and shareholders.[9] Therefore, it is not justified to overburden them with other responsibilities. For example, Asutay (2007) regards the

---

[3] See Siddiqi (1991), Sadique (2010).

[4] See Chapra 1985.

[5] E.g., Ismail (2002), Yaquby (2005), Kahf (1999), Lewis and Algaoud (2001), Ismail (1989), Humud (1976), Al-Amine (2015).

[6] E.g., Sadr (1982), Siddiqi (1983a), Siddiqi (1985), Ahmad (2000), Naqvi (2003).

[7] See, e.g., Khan (1986), Mansour et al. (2015), Bacha (1997), Yousfi (2013), Jaffar (2010), Presley and Sessions (1994), Elhiraika (1996), Iqbal and Llewellyn (2002).

[8] See, e.g., Sadr (1999), Abdalla (1999), Nouman and Ullah (2014), Osman (1999), Said and Elangkovan (2014).

[9] E.g., Ismail (2002), Yaquby (2005), Kahf (1999), Lewis and Algaoud (2001).

economic development and social justice to be the exogenously developed objectives of Islamic finance because *Maqasid Al Shari'ah* does not entail the social welfare dimension. He asserts that, according to the Ghazali's framework, the key objective of *Shari'ah* is to ensure the well-being of all human beings which can be achieved through *protection of their: (i) religion (Al-Din), (ii) life (Al-hayah), (iii) intellect(Al'Aql), (iv) wealth (Al mal), and (v) family/linage (Nasal)*. This indicates that all of these objectives are individual oriented with none having explicit social connotation. Thus, referring to *Maqasid al Shari'ah* as the source of social dimensions in Islamic economics and enforcing these on Islamic finance is unrealistic. Therefore, social welfare does not have epistemological source and merely represents the aspirational expectations.

On the other hand, few authors have even gone beyond denying the social welfare role of Islamic finance and have questioned the ability of participatory modes of financing to achieve social well-being. For example, Choudhury (2001) criticizes participatory modes as not being able to internalize the value of work and the socio-economic justice. While Nagaoka (2010) claims that if participatory modes indeed have superiority in the light of *Shari'ah*, they must entail a substantial economic and social wisdom, particularly behind their risk-sharing features. Moreover, he advocates the need for reconsidering the wisdom of participatory finance.

Against this backdrop, it is imperative to consider the underlying philosophy of *Shari'ah* and how participatory finance fits in its ethos and value system. The chapter, therefore, investigates the role of social well-being in basic philosophy of the *Maqasid Al Shari'ah* and participatory finance. Moreover, it strives to integrate insights from the both the classical and the contemporary Islamic economics and finance literature to conceptualize the missing link between the philosophy of *Maqasid Al Shari'ah* and participatory finance by developing their nexus.

3.2 The Philosophical Underpinning of Participatory Finance in the Light of the Axioms of Islamic Finance

Islamic envisions a financial system where the economic and social ends of financial transactions are prioritized over the contract mechanics for achieving the financial ends. The core difference between Islamic financial institutes and their conventional counterparts lies not only in their way of doing business but the value system which guides the overall operations and outlook of Islamic financial institutes. These values should not only be expressed in the minutiae of their transaction, but in their overall role in the society. This demands the internalization of the underlying philosophy of Islamic finance in its true spirit, form, and substance, particularly in their financing patterns.

The major goal of *Shari'ah* is the promotion of fairness, justice, and general welfare of people in the society. In banning *Riba*, Islam seeks to establish a society based upon fairness and justice (Holy Qur'an 2:239). Since, an interest-based loan promises a fixed return to the lender irrespective of the outcomes of the venture. On the other hand, sharing the outcomes of the venture (whether profit or loss) is fairer instead. Therefore, participatory financing encompassing *Mudarabah*, *Musharakah*, and their variants is the main tool near the majority of Islamic economists for replacing interest-based system and achieving social well-being.

Participatory financing is governed by the following underlying axioms of Islamic finance:

a. ***Brotherhood and Cooperation***

Islam endeavors to establish a society where all individuals are unified by the bonds of affection and brotherhood like members of a single family. Brotherhood entails a relationship of universal welfare and mutual care where all Muslims are considered as one *Ummah* (nation, or community), and recognizes the collective responsibility of guarantying the welfare of each individual in the society. It obliges humankind to uphold trust among the *Ummah* and to renounce *fasad* (corruption, animosity, and mischief) (Qur'an 2: 205). However, the sense of brotherhood could be hampered through lie, oppression, unjust dealings, and other means of appropriation of other's property. The sense of brotherhood is further promoted by Allah's directive to cooperate with one another in righteousness and piety and not on sinful acts and enmity (Qur'an 5: 2).

Islamic finance is based on the principle of brotherhood and cooperation, which appeal for a system of risk sharing, equity sharing, and stake-taking between the financier and entrepreneur. Islam bans *Riba* because it hampers the sense of brotherhood and cooperation and promotes *fasad* in the society. To replace *Riba*, Islam advocates the principle of participation (profit and loss sharing) which fosters the spirit of cooperation, unity, and brotherhood among the concerned parties. Participatory finance works on the principle of shared responsibility and cooperation. Unlike *Riba*-based and non-participatory financing, if business incurs losses, the burden of losses is distributed among the partners, thus promoting solidarity and cooperation among the partners.

b. *Social justice and fairness*

Justice is a basic theme in social life which permeates all facets of social interaction. It provides legitimacy to religious, social, political, and legal practices and institutions. Philosophers and social thinkers have shown immense concern in the issue of justice. Justice means morally treating people in a proper way. According to Chryssides and Kaler (1995):

> justice is about ensuring that what is done to people is what ought to be done to them and assessing action affecting people in terms of the treatment those affected people are morally required to receive, and dealing with these moral requirements as both constraints on action and also as imperative to action. In everyday language, justice is about giving people what is fair what they have a right to and whatever it is that, to their advantage or disadvantage, they deserve. (pp. 167–168)

Shari'ah lays emphasis on moral, ethical, religious, and social factors to promote equality and fairness for the welfare of the whole society. Moreover, it strictly prohibits all forms of exploitations and stands for fair play and justice. Qur'an categorically forbids Muslims to wrongfully acquire the property of each other (Qur'ān 2: 188 and 4: 29; see also 4: 161 and 9: 34).

Justice is a broad term in Islam which has to be ensured in every aspect of human interaction be it legal, social, political, or economic. A Muslim has to be just with not only human beings but also with, insects, animals, and the environment. Jabir ibn 'Abdullah reported that Prophet Muhammad (Peace Be Upon Him) said, "Fear injustice. Injustice will appear as darkness on the Day of Rising. Fear avarice. Avarice destroyed people before you and led them to shed one another's blood and to make lawful what was unlawful for them" (*Al-Adab Al-Mufrad*, 28, 483).

The essence of Islamic finance is to endorse justice and fairness in the society. Islam has banned *Riba* in order to establish a society based upon justice and fairness. Islam strictly forbids appropriation of other's property and wealth through unfair means (see, e.g., Qur'an 2:188, 4:29, 4:161, and 9:34). Charging interest is among those facets of immoral behavior that promote injustice and corrupts the whole society. Two types of property rights are recognized in Islam:

a. The property rights resulting from combining natural resources and labor of a person; and
b. The claims or right to the property gained through inheritance, exchange, and outright grants.

Money denotes the owner's monetized claim to the property rights that were gained through either or both of these ways. Borrowing money, in effect, transfers these property rights of lender to the borrower, and lender can in return claim no more but its equivalent. Charging interest on the money lent represents unjustified instantaneous claim to the property rights. It is considered unjustifiable since it does not fall within the legitimate property rights framework recognized by Islam. Moreover, this claim is considered instantaneous since as soon as the contract is finalized, lender obtains right to the property of borrower.

The permission of profit and loss sharing in Islam, on the other hand, is based on the arguments of social justice, fairness, property rights, and equality. Islam promotes the profit and loss sharing but bans *Riba* because profit being decided ex-post, signifies the creation of additional wealth and successful entrepreneurship. On the other hand, interest, being decided ex ante, is a cost that has to be paid irrespective of the result of business operations and may not signify wealth creation if business incurs losses. Social justice requires that the profits as well as the losses are shared by the lender and borrower in a fair manner to ensure the protection of wealth. Moreover, it demands that the process of wealth creation and its distribution in the society should be just and representative of true productivity.

Furthermore, participatory modes of finance are more consistent with the *Maqasid al Shari'ah* under the protection of wealth. This is because the participatory modes of finance are more conducive to the circulation of wealth *(rawaj)*, clarity and transparency *(wudu)*, stability and proof *(thubat)*, and its growth and development *(tanmiyah)* compared to the other modes in several ways. For example, *Mudarabah* contracts channel the idle funds toward the production of goods and services. Thus, it provides an opportunity to the entrepreneurs with different risk appetites to grow their wealth which consequently creates a balance between savings and investments. This also calls for the establishment of a sophisticated investment infrastructure that would employ hedging mechanisms, financial engineering, and sound business strategies. Consequently, a stable financial environment is created that is conducive to the protection and growth of wealth.

Musharakah, on the other hand, has much sophisticated and wider application. It can be effectively applied for venture financing, but its real potentials can be witnessed when applied in the Islamic capital markets where idle funds are channelized. Thus, it can prove as an efficient tool to ensure circulation and generation of wealth. That is why many Muslim economists[10] favor participatory financing and put upon Islamic financial institutes the greater social welfare responsibility and religious obligation to achieve the *Maqasid al Shari'ah* with respect to financial and economic transactions, including social justice, fair allocation of income and wealth, and endorsing economic growth and development. Although these Muslim economists do not fully reject the utilization of the *Shari'ah* compliant debt-based contracts together with the participatory financing, they claim that the socio-economic objectives of Islamic finance including social justice, and the economic stability, economic growth, and efficiency induced by the protection of wealth of all parties can better be achieved if Islamic banks resort to primarily participatory financing.

c. *Distributive justice*

Islam endeavors to establish a social order where all individuals are unified by the bonds of affection and brotherhood like members of a single family. The notion of equal treatment and brotherhood in the society is hollow unless accompanied by economic justice in a way that there is no exploitation in the society and each individual acquires due return for his contribution to the social product or to the society.

---

[10] E.g., Sadr (1982), Siddiqi (1983b, 1985), Chapra (2000a, 2000b), Usmani (2002), and Naqvi (2003), and many others.

Economics justice involves the utilization of resources in an equitable way so that the generally accepted humanitarian goals are realized including the general need-fulfillment, equitable distribution of wealth and income, full employment, optimum growth, and economic stability. It is a broad term and has many aspects. One of the important aspects of economic justice is the distributive justice. According to Ahmad and Hassan (2000) "distributive justice is concerned with the norms of resource allocation and perception of fairness by the recipients. The norms may be merit, need or equality" (p. 159).

Though concerns with the allocation of resources to the individuals in a society has a long history (e.g., Aristotle, J. S. Mill, Hobbes, and Marx), social scientists started paying attention to this basic facet of human behavior after George C. Homans propounded the concept of distributive justice in 1961. The Homans theory of distributive justice inspires from the work of Aristotle which associates justice with the appropriate proportion of contributions to compensations. In this view justice demands that a person should receive returns that match with his investments. This principle was developed as a four-term theory, by Homans, which claims that if the contributions of two persons are equal; their reward should also be equal.

Homans theory of distributive justice is extensively accepted. The equity theory considers social interactions of human beings as a series of exchanges with just and fair distribution being the core of these exchanges. The social scientists generally believe that every culture needs to institutionalize a proper system for the just distribution of resources among all members of society.

Islam has provided guidance in the personal distribution of income. The Islamic view of "distributive justice" consists of the following three elements:

1. Guaranteeing that the basic needs of every individual in the society are fulfilled;
2. Equity in the personal incomes of members of society, not equality; and
3. Eliminating the severe disparity in the personal wealth and income of individuals.

The Islamic prohibition of interest is largely based on the notion of negative distributive justice and equity effects. An interest based is contract involves injustice to one of the parties, sometimes to the borrower and sometime to the lender. It is unjust on lender's part to ask for a predetermined rate of return if borrowers incur loss. On the other hand, if the borrower earns huge profits, it is injustice on the part of borrower to give a meager portion of profit to the lender.

Moreover, interest widens the gap between rich and poor in the society. The rich entrepreneurs borrow depositors' money from the banks for utilizing it in their lucrative ventures. After earning huge profits they share only its negligible portion in the form of interest. This amount is also taken back by the entrepreneurs by adding it (the interest paid to the lenders) to the cost of the products they produce. Thus, in reality depositors get nothing. Thus interest leads to imbalance and inequity in the distribution of income and wealth.

Participatory financing is contrary to this because the outcome of the venture is shared equitably by both parties. Entrepreneurs have to share actual profits with the depositors which may in normal cases be much larger than the rate of interest. Moreover, since profits are unknown unless the products get sold, the share of profit paid to the financier cannot be added to the product's cost. Therefore, contrary to the interest-based system, entrepreneurs cannot take back the profit paid to the lenders.

Thus interest creates unequal and unjust distribution of resources and opportunities. On the other hand, participatory financing ensures that profit or loss resulting from investment is distributed among the contracting parties in a fair way. Thus participatory financing creates fair and just distribution of resources and risk. These contracts may be high risk, but it focuses more on resource mobilization, social justice, and fair distribution of profit and resources.

It is evident from the above discussion that the participatory modes of finance are grounded on the moral and ethical framework of *Shari'ah* and entail well-being of overall society. Moreover, these represent the true spirit of the Islamic financial system. This is because the participatory modes of finance do not involve *Riba*, coercion, exploitation, fraud, and *Qimar*. That is why advocates of the Islamic finance are almost unanimous on the fact that the Islamic financial institutions must rely on participatory modes to achieve the objectives of the economic system stability, efficiency, and socio-economic justice.

3.3 The Nexus Between *Maqasid Al Shari'ah* and Participatory Finance

In view of above discussion, it is evident that Islam bestows an economic vision that entails a social and economic order capable of ensuring social well-being along with economic prosperity. This vision is deeply inscribed in the *Maqasid al Shari'ah*. Complying with the *Maqasid* imply that businesses and individuals should not be solely profit oriented. Rather they must strive to protect the society's needs and promote social well-being. Thus, in the light of *Maqasid Al Shari'ah* integrated framework, it is worthy to conclude that social well being is the core of *Maqasid Al Shari'ah* (Nouman et al., 2021).

Similarly, keeping in view the axioms of Islamic finance, it is evident that the participatory modes of finance, being characterized by social commitments and ethical norms, are grounded on the moral and ethical framework of *Shari'ah* and entail well-being of overall society. Therefore, participatory finance fits well in the ethos and value system of Islam. Moreover, it represents the true spirit of the Islamic financial system.

Thus, keeping in view the *Maqasid Al Shari'ah* integrated framework and the axioms of Islamic finance it is evident that social well-being provides the nexus between *Maqasid al Shari'ah* and participatory finance.[11] Figure 3.1 shows the nexus between *Maqasid al Shari'ah* and participatory finance, based on the dimensions of *Maqasid al Shari'ah* and the axioms of participatory finance.

The *Shari'ah* permissibility of all basic Islamic modes of finance, either based upon direct participation or non-participation. However, participatory modes, being more consistent with the axioms of Islamic finance including brotherhood and cooperation, fairness and social justice, and distributed justice, have a greater capability of ensuring the social well-being. Therefore, these can serve as a mean to achieve the *Maqasid al Shari'ah*.

Therefore, Islamic financial institutes, being *Shari'ah*-based firms, should apply and promote participatory finance to fulfill the social obligations that go far beyond the traditional capitalist worldview of mere profit maximization. A move toward policy and goals rather than the

---

[11] See Nouman et al. (2021) for detailed discussion on how the nexus between *Maqasid al Shari'ah* and participatory finance was developed.

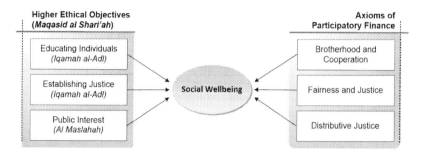

Fig. 3.1 The nexus between *Maqasid al Shari'ah* and participatory finance (*Source* Nouman et al. [2021])

legal and mechanistic structure of Islamic finance would ultimately lead to the materialization of the economic and social well-being objectives of *Shari'ah*.

3.4 Conclusion and Implications

This chapter explores the extent literature for the possible existence of philosophical linkage between the axioms and propositions of *Maqasid al Shari'ah* and participatory finance. It is evident from the extant literature that social well-being lays at the core of *Shari'ah*. *Maqasid al Shari'ah* represents the realistic and holistic view of Islam as a complete code of life, encompassing the well-being of both individuals and society. Hence, compliance to the *Maqasid al Shari'ah*, in true sense, requires the commitment of each organization and individual to realize welfare, brotherhood, cooperation, and justice to ensure social well-being.

Moreover, participatory modes of finance, being characterized by social commitments and ethical norms, are grounded on the moral and ethical framework of *Shari'ah*. Therefore, these can be used as effective means toward creating a just society and fulfillment of the socio-economic objectives within the broader framework of *Maqasid al Shari'ah*. Thus, participatory finance has an enormous potential of creating a financial system consistent with the true spirit of Islam in which morality is not limited only to the prohibition of interest.

The non-participatory modes, on the other hand, are acclaimed to lack the capacity to avoid the evils and injustices of interest-based system because they by far mimic the conventional debt-based arrangements.

Thus, a financial system based on non-participatory modes does not have superiority over the conventional interest-based system in terms of growth, stability, efficiency, and equity. Moreover, it neither represents the philosophy and aspirations of Islamic economic system, nor it meets the expectations of the less developed Muslim societies for whom it was anticipated as a way out. Therefore, it is necessary to change the prevalent approach of *Shari'ah* compliance merely in terms of the legal form of the contract. Rather the 'substance' of *Shari'ah*, that has the greater implications for realization of the core objective of *Shari'ah*, should be equally considered particularly in designing the financial products.

In this regard, the derived framework provides important policy implications for substantiation of Islamic financial practices, in terms of providing two levels of principles to make up regulatory and functional frameworks at institutions and markets. First, the proposed framework provides interpretations for how educating people, establishing justice, and promoting justice be made as key bases for not only to establish benchmarks for *Maqasid al Shari'ah*-based policy guidelines for economy but also to demonstrate such substance-in-economy as, when and where, the people in systems and organizations experience social well-being as evidence of being *Shariah* based. Second, the framework also informs policy at the second level of abstraction in practice, by interpreting how finance as a sub-system of economy be managed, as it being leading to well-being, through relatively concrete principles of enhancing participatory finance as a construct of cooperation, fairness, and distributive justice. These two levels of policy practice, namely economy and finance, can thus be converged toward a unified outcome of well-being as evidence of the systems being *Shariah* based.

3.5 CHAPTER SUMMARY

Islamic finance not only provides guidelines for investment, but also a set of unique contracts. The Islamic financial system outlines a broader set of transactional, financial, and intermediation contracts with varying financing purposes, degrees of risk, and maturities to meet needs of the diverse groups of economic agents in the economy in accordance with the rules of *Shari'ah*.

Participation, commonly known as the Profit and Loss Sharing, is the essence of the design of Islamic financial products. This feature allows a financier to earn profit on invested capital if the financier is willing to tolerate loss in case of the project failure. In a participatory financing arrangement the allocation of risk and reward to each partner, and the distribution of responsibilities among them are defined in the contract, which are enforced by the social values and the ethical standards set in the *Shari'ah*. This chapter, therefore, explores the philosophical underpinnings of participatory financing arrangements to conceptualize the social welfare role of these arrangements and create the nexus between participatory financing and *Maqasid al Shari'ah*.

Building upon the *Maqasid Al Shari'ah* integrated framework and the axioms of Islamic finance, this chapter implies that social well-being is the core of *Maqasid al Shari'ah* and the essence of participatory finance. Therefore, participatory arrangements have an immense potential for creating a just society and fulfillment of the socio-economic objectives within the broader framework of *Maqasid al Shari'ah*. Thus, it is necessary to change the prevalent approach of *Shari'ah* compliance merely in terms of the legal form of the contract. Rather Islamic financial institutions ought to apply and promote participatory financing so that the 'substance' of *Shari'ah* could also be achieved.

REFERENCES

Abdalla, M. G.-E. (1999). Partnership (Musharakah): A new option for financing small enterprises? *Arab Law Quarterly, 14*(3), 257–267.
Ahmad, K. (2000). Islamic finance and banking: The challenge and prospects. *Review of Islamic Economics, 9*, 57–82.
Ahmad, K., & Hassan, A. (2000). Distributive justice: The Islamic perspective. *Intellectual Discourse, 8*(2), 159–172.
Ahmad, M. (1947). *Economics of Islam: A comparative study*. Muhammad Ashraf.
Al-Amine, M. A.-B. (2015). Product development and Maqāṣid in Islamic finance: Towards a balanced methodology. *Islamic Economic Studies, 23*(1), 33–71.
Asutay, M. (2007). Conceptualisation of the second best solution in overcoming the social failure of Islamic finance: Examining the overpowering of homoislamicus by homoeconomicus. *IIUM Journal in Economics and Management, 15*(2), 167–195.
Bacha, O. I. (1997). Adapting mudarabah financing to contemporary realities: A proposed financing structure. *The Journal of Accounting, Commerce & Finance, 1*(1), 26–54.
Chapra, M. U. (1985). *Towards a just monetary system*. The Islamic Foundation.

Chapra, M. U. (2000a). *The future of economics: An Islamic persepective*: Islamic Foundation.
Chapra, M. U. (2000b). Why has Islam prohibited interest: Rationale behind the prohibition of interest. *Review of Islamic Economics, 9*, 5–20.
Choudhury, M. A. (2001). Islamic venture capital: A critical examination. *Journal of Economic Studies, 28*(1), 14–33.
Chryssides, G. D., & Kaler, J. H. (1995). *An introduction to business ethics*. Chapman and Hall.
Elhiraika, A. B. (1996). Risk-sharing and the supply of agricultural credit: A case study of Islamic finance in Sudan. *Journal of Agricultural Economics, 47*(3), 390–402.
Ghanameh, A. H. (1973). *The interest less economy in contemporary aspects of economic and social thinking in Islam*. Muslim Students Association of U.S. and Canada.
Humud, S. (1976). *Tatwir Al-A'mal Al-Masrifiyya bima Yattafiqu wa Al-Shari'ah Al-Islamiyya (Arabic)*. Dar Al-Ittihad Al-'Arabi lil-Tiba'a.
Iqbal, M., & Llewellyn, D. T. (Eds.). (2002). *Islamic banking and finance: New perspectives on profit-sharing and risk*. Edward Elgar.
Ismail, A. H. (1989). *Al Qur'an on deferred contracts of exchange*. Prime Minister's Secretariat (Mimeograph).
Ismail, A. H. (2002). *The deferred contracts of exchange: Al Qur'an in contrast with islamic economists: Theory of banking and finance*. Institute of Islamic Understanding.
Jaffar, M. M. (2010, December 5–7). *Mudharabah and musyarakah models of joint venture investments between two parties*. Paper presented at the International Conference on Science and Social Research (CSSR 2010), Kuala Lumpur, Malaysia.
Kahf, M. (1999). Islamic banks at the threshold of the third millennium. *Thunderbird International Business Review of Financial Economics, 41*(4–5), 445–460.
Khan, M. S. (1986). Islamic interest-free banking: A theoretical analysis. *IMF Staff Papers, 33*(1), 1–27.
Lewis, M. K., & Algaoud, L. M. (2001). *Islamic banking*. Edward Elgar.
Mansour, W., Abdelhamid, M. B., & Heshmati, A. (2015). Recursive profit-and-loss sharing. *Journal of Risk, 17*(6), 21–50.
Maududi, S. A. A. (1969). *Ma'ashiyat e Islam (Urdu)*. Islamic Publications.
Nagaoka, S. (2010). Reconsidering mudarabah contracts in Islamic finance: What is the economic wisdom (hikmah) of partnership-based instruments? *Review of Islamic Economics, 13*(2), 65–79.
Naqvi, S. N. H. (2003). *Perspectives on morality and human well-being: A contribution to Islamic economics*. Islamic Foundation.

Nouman, M., & Ullah, K. (2014). Constraints in the application of partnerships in Islamic banks: The present contributions and future directions. *Business & Economic Reivew, 6*(2), 47–62.
Nouman, M., Siddiqi, M. F., Ullah, K., & Jan, S. (2021). Nexus between higher ethical objectives (Maqasid Al Shari'ah) and participatory finance. *Qualitative Research in Financial Markets, 13*(2), 226–251. https://doi.org/10.1108/QRFM-06-2020-0092
Osman, B. B. (1999). The experience of the Sudanese Islamic bank in partnership (Musharakah) financing as a tool for rural development among small farmers in Sudan. *Arab Law Quarterly, 14*(3), 221–230.
Presley, J. R., & Sessions, J. G. (1994). Islamic economics: The emergence of a new paradigm. *The Economic Journal, 104*(424), 584–596.
Qureshi, A. I. (1946). *Islam and the theory of interest* (1st ed.). Muhammad Ashraf Publishers.
Sadique, M. A. (2010). Islamic banks' dilemma between ideals and practice: Debt or equity. *Global Journal of Management and Business Research, 10*(2), 147–150.
Sadr, A. S. M. B. (1982). *An introduction to principles of Islamic banking.* Bunyad Be'thet.
Sadr, K. (1999). The role of Musharakah financing in the agricultural bank of Iran. *Arab Law Quarterly, 14*(3), 245–256.
Said, M. M., & Elangkovan, K. (2014). Prosperity and social justice consequences of applying ethical norms of islamic finance: Literature review. *Journal of Economics and Sustainable Development, 5*(2), 99–107.
Siddiqi, M. N. (1969). *Ghair Soodi Bank kari (Urdu).* Islamic Publications.
Siddiqi, M. N. (1983a). *Banking without interest.* Islamic Foundation (originally published in Urdu).
Siddiqi, M. N. (1983b). *Issues in Islamic banking.* The Islamic Foundation.
Siddiqi, M. N. (1985). *Partnership and profit-sharing in Islamic law.* The Islamic Foundation.
Siddiqi, M. N. (1991). Some economic aspects of mudarabah: Review of Islamic economics. *Journal of the International Association for Islamic Economics, 1*(2), 21–34.
Usmani, M. T. (2002). *An introduction to Islamic finance.* Kluwer Law International.
Uzair, M. (1978). *Interest-free banking.* Royal Books.
Yaquby, S. N. (2005). Shariah requirements for conventional banks. *Journal of Islamic Banking and Finance, 22*(3), 45–50.
Yousfi, O. (2013). Does PLS solve moral hazard problems? *Journal of Islamic Economics, Banking and Finance, 9*(3), 1–14.
Zaman, S. M. H. (1966). Islam vis-à-vis Interest. *Islamic Culture, 40*(1), 1–12.

CHAPTER 4

The Paradox of Idealization in Theory and Marginalization in the Practice

Participatory financing dominates Islamic banking literature. The participation model calls for a banking system which is akin to equity-based model whereby depositor in essence has equity position in the banks. The banks, in turn, purchase equity position in the ventures being financed. This system is acclaimed to have several advantages over the non-participatory Islamic banking models and the conventional interest-based banking system. These advantages include the risk sharing and avoidance of any conflict of interest, as all partners have common interest in the ultimate success of the projects. Moreover, the viewpoint, that profit sharing has *Shariah* legitimacy, provides basis for the development and implementation of the contemporary Islamic banking in various legal contexts. Therefore, advocates of Islamic banking argue that participatory financing is the essence of Islamic banking and the true spirit of the Islamic banking system.[1] Moreover, the basic philosophy of Islamic finance cannot be translated into reality unless Islamic banks expand the use of participatory financing.

This chapter presents the dilemma of idealization of participatory finance in the theory of Islamic banking and finance and its marginalization in the practices of Islamic banks throughout the world. This chapter

[1] E.g., Chapra (1985), Iqbal and Mirakhor (2011), Sadique (2012), Siddiqi (1983b, 1985), Usmani (2002), and Warde (2000).

begins with the detailed discussion on the idealization of participatory finance in the Islamic banking and finance literature and its role in the development of modern banking system. Moreover, the advantages of participatory finance are discussed in detail to conceptualize the reasons for the idealization of participatory finance in the Islamic banking and finance literature. This discussion is followed by the detailed overview of the consistent tendency of Islamic banks to avoid participatory financing arrangements on the assets side. Moreover, different explanations for the lower preference for participatory financing by banks are also presented.

4.1 Idealization of Participatory Finance in the Islamic Baking Literature

Participatory finance is believed to be enhancing Justice, brotherhood, and character, which are the important pillars of an ideal Islamic economic system. Therefore, a substantial Islamic economy cannot be conceived without (i) the social and individual character being emphasized by Islam, (ii) the mutual support system, and solidarity induced by the Islamic brotherhood, and (iii) the eradication of every type of injustice that Islam absconds. That is why Islam bans *Riba* and proposes an alternative system based on participation and risk sharing to establish a society based upon fairness and justice.

As discussed in Chapter 3, participatory finance fits well in the ethos and value system of Islam. This is because the participatory modes of finance are grounded on the moral and ethical framework of *Shari'ah* and entail well-being of overall society. Moreover, participatory finance represents and attempts to reduce injustice, coercion, and exploitation, which may otherwise exist in more binding contracts. That is why participatory financing, encompassing *Mudarabah*, *Musharakah*, and their variants, is the main tool near the majority of Islamic economists for replacing interest-based system.

However, in practice the financing portfolios of the Islamic banks around the world are predominantly characterized by non-participatory agreements, particularly *Murabahah*, whereby banks merely get the sheer mercantilist business return in the form of mark-up on the merchandise being financed. These returns (mark-ups) have nothing in common with the real economic return resulting from the participatory financing, where the financial institutions have long-term commitment to create value. Consequently, the mobilization of resources using non-participatory financing alone has neither helped in boosting the inter-communal trade financing in Muslim world, nor did it improve returns to the depositors/investors. This problem has stemmed mainly from the Islamic banks' tendency to mimic the conventional banking model which calls for financial competition, rent-seeking economic behavior, and risk-averse attitude rather than promoting justice, cooperation, and risk sharing among various stakeholders of the Bank.

Building upon these notions, advocates of the Islamic banking and finance are unanimous on the fact that the Islamic financial institutions must rely on partnership contracts to achieve the objectives of the economic system stability, efficiency, and socio-economic justice. On the other hand, the non-participatory modes, also called trade-based financing modes, are acceptable only for those situations where participatory financing arrangements are clearly not suitable, e.g., in the case of consumer financing or exceedingly small loans.

The non-participatory modes (particularly *Murabahah* and *Ijarah*) are criticized on the basis outcomes, which are claimed to be materially the same as that of the interest-based borrowing, when these are used within the framework of the conventional benchmarks like LIBOR and others. Therefore, the *Shari'ah* supervisory boards have accepted that these are not the ideal models of financing and therefore should only be used in case of absolute need, with full and vigilant observation of the *Shari'ah* prescribed conditions. Moreover, this allowance should not be taken as a permanent rule for all sorts of transactions and the entire operations of Islamic banks should not revolve around it (Usmani, 2002).

4.2 Role of Participatory Financing in the Development of Islamic Banking System

The participatory financing has provided the foundation for Islamic banking. The idea of using profit and loss sharing instead of interest in the depositor vs. bank and bank vs. business (borrower) relationships was first introduced during the time period 1940s to 1960s. However, this idea gained significant acceptance in the 1980s and 1990s. The earliest references to the reorganization of banking system on the basis of participation instead of interest can be found in the pioneering work by Anwar Iqab Qureshi, Mahmud Ahmad, and Naiem Siddiqi in late forties, followed by Abul A'ala Mawdudi in 1950.

Two pioneering works by Islamic economists Anwar Iqbal Qureshi and Mahmud Ahmad proposed a banking system based on participatory financing. Anwar Iqbal Qureshi in his book "Islam and the Theory of Interest" stated that interest is prohibited in Islam, but partnership is not. In Islamic system there is no objection against a bank if it becomes partner with business ventures, sharing profit and loss, instead of giving them loans (Qureshi, 1946). His statement implies that the participatory financing arrangements i.e., *Musharakah* and *Mudarabah*, are more appropriate for the Islamic financial system. Around the same time, Mahmud Ahmad mentioned his preference for participation-based systems in his book (Ahmad, 1947). He stated that "The *Shirakat* banks would lend money to industry and commerce on the basis of *Shirakat*, that is, they would share the profit with their debtors rather than burden industry and commerce with a fixed rate of interest" (Ahmad, 1947, p. 170).

Nejatullah Siddiqi called the work of Anwar Iqbal Qureshi and Mahmud Ahmad pioneering in the literature of Islamic economics, because most Islamic economists of the next generation followed their lead and encouraged participatory financing (see Siddiqi, 1981). Muhammad Uzair and Muhammad Nejatullah Siddiqi, among the next generation scholars, made important contributions in developing the theory to make the proposed Islamic banking feasible in practice. In 1951, Uzair proposed the practical idea of *Mudarabah*, which was later on known as "two-tier *Mudarabah*" where both sides of the balance sheet of a bank were established through participatory modes.

The idea of "two-tier *Mudarabah*" was to use two *Mudarabah* transactions in one scheme, where depositors (*Rab-ul-Mal*) would invest money with the bank (*Mudarib*) on *Mudarabah* basis, while bank (*Rab-ul-Mal*) would invest this money with the borrower (*Mudarib*) on *Mudarabah* basis. Thus, the depositors (*Rab-ul-Mal*) and the bank (*Mudarib*) would conduct the first *Mudarabah*, while the bank (*Rab-ul-Mal*) and the borrower (*Mudarib*) would conduct the second *Mudarabah* (see Fig. 4.1). Parties of the first *Mudarabah* would share the bank's profit while those of the second *Mudarabah* would share the borrower's profit. In 1969, Siddiqi contributed by developing a comprehensive picture of a *Mudarabah*-based Islamic financial system (Siddiqi, 1983a). He not only elaborated the theory of two-tier *Mudarabah*, but also expanded its application to the relationship between central bank and commercial banks.

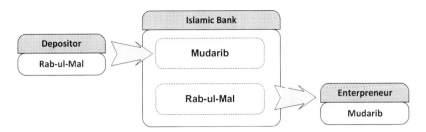

Fig. 4.1 Mechanism of two-tier *Murabahah* (*Source* Based on Shinsuke [2012])

The Siddiqi's model was followed by the work of Mohsin Khan who has proposed two window participatory banking model in 1986. Under this model, banks are supposed to adopt a two-window model on the liabilities side namely demand deposit window and equity or profit and loss window (Khan, 1986). In the first window the deposits of the risk-averse depositors, who are interested merely in safe keeping of their deposits, would be treated as demand deposits. This window would entail a 100% reserve requirement placed on the demand deposits to ensure that these funds are not utilized for iterative credit creation. On the other hand, the equity window would treat depositors as shareholders in the bank, with no guarantee of return on their deposits or nominal value of their share. Moreover, this window would entail no reserve requirement since deposits would be treated as investment. Therefore, banks would accept such deposits on the basis of profit and loss sharing and invest them directly in the business ventures by purchasing their equity shares.[2]

It is evident from the above discussion that the proposed Islamic banking models were supposedly based on the principle of participation and risk sharing. These models placed the religious obligation and greater social welfare responsibility upon Islamic banks to strive for achieving the broader goals of *Shari'ah* that could be realized by synthesizing the operations of Islamic banks on participation basis. Moreover, these models provided foundation for the development and implementation of Islamic banking. However, no attention was paid to developing theoretical arguments or mechanism to assure the capital protection. Similarly, the mechanism for consumer loans and the non-participatory modes of

---

[2] For details see Khan (1986) and Iqbal and Mirakhor (2011).

financing were totally ignored in the proposed participatory banking models. That is why soon after the advent and proliferation of *Murabahah* financing,[3] it conquered the operations of Islamic banks and pushed participatory financing to a corner accounting for less than ten percent in the operations of Islamic banks (Siddiqi, 2006).

Thus building upon these notions, participatory financing is widely accepted as the essence of Islamic banking system. That is why the aspiration oriented advocates of Islamic banking and finance claim that Islamic banks are supposed to act as suppliers of venture capital, financing promising ideas, and worthy ventures in exchange for share in the profits. Moreover, they assert that the basic philosophy of Islamic banking and finance cannot be translated into reality unless Islamic banks expand the use of participatory financing.

4.3 THE INHERENT BENEFITS OF PARTICIPATORY MODES OF FINANCE

Participatory financing is an area that has considerable potential. Participatory financing can play an important role in gearing up economic growth in several ways. Moreover, these can be used as effective means toward creating a just society and fulfillment of the socio-economic objectives within the broader framework of *Maqasid al Shari'ah*. Thus, participatory finance has an enormous potential of creating a financial system consistent with the true spirit of Islam in which morality is not limited only to the prohibition of interest.

The participatory financing arrangements are preferable to the non-participatory arrangements for several reasons. Some of the reasons are briefly discussed in the subsequent sections.

Reduced Constraints to SMEs Financing

Promoting participatory financing in IFIs can reduce the financial constraints faced by SMEs and new firms in connection to their overall financial inclusion. The small and new firms hardly have any access to finances from traditional financial institutions because these firms often do

---

[3] Murabahah was first modified by Humud (1976) as a tool for extending credit without violating the Shari'ah rules.

not have enough acceptable physical collateral or track record to obtain finances from institutional sources. Moreover, the distribution of credit is skewed in favor of the wealthy class of the society. In fact, most of the funds flow to the multinational corporations, and large industries while low and medium class entrepreneurs do not have sufficient access to the finances even for their viable projects. The participatory financing, on the contrary, favors SMEs because in such a system the selection of projects is based on the viability of the venture, not on the sheer size or creditworthiness of the business.

In addition, participatory financing best suit the needs of such businesses because the financier has to share in the success of the enterprise, without penalizing the business unduly for any failure. This inherent characteristic would resolve the financial problems of small enterprises and startups because they often face the problem of predatory lending which involves high interest rate and/or abusive and unfair loan terms which often leads to business failure. Therefore, promoting participatory financing in IFIs will elevate economic growth by promoting Small Medium Enterprises (SMEs) because SMEs have significant role in employment creation and growth of gross domestic products of developing countries.

Promoting Stability of the Financial Sector

Participatory financing makes the financiers participate in the risks of venture, which induces them to assess the risks with utmost care and to monitor the borrowers. The twofold assessment of investment proposals by both the borrower and the lender would help introduce greater health and stability into the financial sector. In addition, interest has to be paid in both good and bad times alike, whereas dividends can be reduced in bad times and can even be skipped in extreme situations. This factor significantly reduces business failures and in turn promotes economic stability.

Similarly, both speculation and inflation-driven instability are initiated through debt-based instruments. With the continuation of financialization of capitalism, the reduced emphasis upon "real" assets heightens this danger. On the other hand, the participatory financing model assures that the supply of money does not overstep the supply of goods and services and therefore restrains inflationary pressure unlike "modern" and sort of fiat finance which allows the money supply to easily exceed the real production of goods and services when various documentary contracts start working as assets in themselves.

In addition, the banking system based on participation would also limit the supply of money because it does not foster credit creation or money creation "ex nihilo" (i.e., money creation out of thin air) predominantly due to the fact that this system entails 100% reserve requirement on demand deposits and the investment of saving deposits in equity shares. That is, in the participatory system banks have to follow a two-window model namely demand deposit window and equity or profit and loss window, whereby the demand deposit window entails a 100% reserve requirement to ensure that demand deposits are not utilized for iterative credit creation.[4]

On the contrary, banks would accept deposits in the equity window on the basis of profit and loss sharing (treating depositors as shareholders in the bank) which would be ultimately directed toward the business ventures as equity (by purchasing their equity shares). Consequently, the banks would perform the function of wealth creation instead of being credit multipliers. The participatory system, therefore, induces a stable growth of financing activities which is determined by the real growth in the economic activities, rather than being the outcome of speculative financial activities or money creation by banks and other financial institutions. Consequently, the Islamic financial system is not expected to face the deep cycles of boom and bust which are inherent in the conventional interestbased system. That is why several eminent economists with predominately Western economic thinking also advocate the participatory banking system (see, e.g., Fernandez, 1984; Simons, 1948).

Improved Allocative Efficiency

The participatory system results in the improved allocative efficiency compared to the interest-based system. This is because interest-based system banks rationally are not sufficiently vigilant about the project itself as their primary interest is in the borrowers collateral and repayment ability. Thus in the conventional system only those projects are financed

---

[4] The 100% reserve requirements have proponents in the mainstream economics as well. Several eminent economists criticize the fractional reserve banking system and call for 100% reserve requirements (see, e.g., Friedman, 1969; Golembe & Mingo, 1985; Kareken, 1985; Karstens, 1982; Simons, 1948).

which are capable of repaying the principal amounts and interest, while other projects, in spite of their potential long-term profitability, might be ruled out. On the contrary, the Islamic bank has more interest in the return and viability of the project itself because their profit is linked to the return of the project. Therefore, Islamic banks have to evaluate and select projects very carefully. Thus, allocating projects solely on the basis of their potential productivity and profitability, instead of their creditworthiness, opens a door for increased and more efficiently utilized employment. Consequently, adopting a participatory system could increase the volume of investments and thus increase worthwhile employment opportunities.

Promotes Innovation

Introduction of a financial intermediation system based on the principle of participation will have a positive impact on the behavior of surplus and the deficit economic units (savers and entrepreneurs respectively) as well as the financial intermediaries (banks). This is because this system converts savers into entrepreneurs instead of lenders, by inducing them to participate directly in business ventures, thereby becoming partners in the risks and return of the business. Similarly, the banks operating on the principle of participation will be more concerned with the efficient channeling of the funds than the traditional banks because, being partner in the profit and losses of the venture, they would tend to allocate their deposits to viable and productive investment avenues. This will in turn favor new entrepreneurs particularly those who are innovative but have not yet established their creditworthiness because participatory modes of financing do not involve collateral requirements. Therefore, participatory system promotes innovation.

Stability of the Banking System

A number of studies have attempted to model the working of an Islamic banking system based on the participation principle which makes the Islamic system akin to an equity-based system. On the liabilities side, these models treat depositors as shareholders whereby bank does not guarantee the rate of return on deposits. Similarly, on the assets side, the bank itself becomes partner with the entrepreneurs to whom funds are extended on profit and loss sharing. Thus, the payment commitments take the form of dividends which have to be paid only if profit is incurred. These models suggest that participatory system has the inherent capability of adjusting to shocks that lead to banking crises compared to the interest-based banking system (Khan, 1986). This is because in this system the shocks to asset positions of the bank are absorbed by the changes in the nominal value of deposits held by depositors in the bank at the liabilities side and essentially the risk is shared.

Due to this risk-sharing system, the actual value of bank's liabilities and assets would be equivalent all the time. This in turn shields the bank from credit risk and interest rate risk to much extent and reduces the probability of insolvency by a greater extent. In the interest-based banking model, on the contrary, an adverse shock to assets can result into divergence between real liabilities and assets which may in turn lead to reduction in the bank's net worth. This is because the bank guarantees the nominal value of the deposits in the conventional baking system. Thus, the correction of the disequilibrium becomes a real challenge for the bank. Moreover, the process of adjustment could be time consuming process.

Thus, in the participatory system the chances of bank's insolvency are very low compared to the conventional interest-based system. In participatory system, a bank can only become insolvent if its commitments and out-of-pocket costs exceed the revenues. However, such situation is not inherent in the participatory system and can rather happen only due to extraneous economic factors or poor management (Iqbal & Mirakhor, 2011).

Effective Distribution of Risks

The participatory system results in better distribution of risk. Unlike the conventional risk-based financing arrangement where only entrepreneur bears the risk, the business risk is distributed among the bank, depositor, and the entrepreneur in a participatory system. In such a system, the entrepreneur risks his labor, bank risks its time, effort and skills, while depositors risk their capital and thus get entitled to the return. That is why greater dependence on equity financing has supporters even in mainstream economics. Rogoff, a Harvard Professor of Economics, argues that "In an ideal world equity lending and direct investment would play a much bigger role." He further claims that: "With a better balance between debt and equity, risk-sharing would be greatly enhanced and financial crises sharply muted" (Rogoff, 1999, p. 40).

Closer Coordination Between the Real and Financial Sectors of Economy

According to Iqbal and Mirakhor (2011), the inherent capability of the participatory arrangements to spread of risk forges a strong and healthy coordination between the real and financial economic sectors. On the contrary, the risk is transferred in interest-based debt arrangements which ultimately weakens this linkage. Consequently, in the highly leveraged economies, the growth of interest-based debts and financial derivatives—that have no or little connections to real assets—may outpace the real sector's growth.

This noxious growth may end up in the liabilities that are several times larger than the real assets needed to support these. This loss of connection between the finance and real assets, termed as "financialization" or "financial decoupling," ultimately leads to financial crises. Therefore, by far risk transfer rests at the core of all historical financial crises in the conventional interest-based economies including the most popular US Subprime Mortgage Crisis of 2008.

This calls for limiting leveraging and credit expansion and the development of an alternative equitable system based on participation and risk sharing that could ensure economic growth and development and equitable distribution of wealth and income. This is because the participatory finance is inherently characterized by a direct link between the activities of the real and financial sectors. Consequently, the credit cannot contract or expand independently of the real sector. Therefore, unlike the conventional system, the decoupling of the real and financial sectors is not possible in the system based on participation.

Higher Return on Investment

Mostly the rate of inflation is high in most of the countries. However, the rate of interest paid on deposits usually does not match the rate of inflation. In addition, the interest rate does not adjust automatically with the rate of inflation. Therefore, the real rate of interest may even become negative in the periods of high inflation. Consequently, the lenders are at disadvantage most of the times. On the contrary, in the participatory system, as the prices increase, the rate of return also increases to adjust with the inflation. Thus, it is possible to maintain a positive real rate of return. Therefore, depositors are not prone to loss in the form of negative real rate of return because entrepreneurs and the depositors share the actual rate of return.

In addition, the participatory system promises higher return than the interest-based system due to the inherent equity premium. The debate on debt and equity by Mehra and Prescott (1985), referred to as the "equity premium puzzle" clearly suggests with evidence that in the long-term the return on equity-based investments significantly outplace real returns on safe debt-based investments such as treasury bills. This is because equity has to be compensated for the risk borne by paying higher return than the debt (risk premium). Figure 4.2 depicts the historical equity risk premium in the emerging markets, United States, and other developed markets (excluding United States) which is measured as the return over and above the risk free rate.

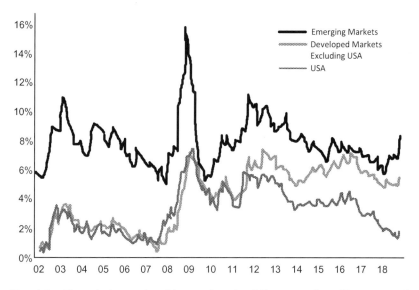

Fig. 4.2 The relative equity risk premium in different markets (*Source* Based on data from Thompson Reuters DataStream)

Establishing Long-Term Relationships

Unlike the conventional and non-participatory financing, the participatory arrangement have greater tendency to form long-term relationship between the entrepreneurs and banks due to its inherent superior risk management properties. On the contrary, in case of interest-based and non-participatory arrangements, the entrepreneur's ability to pay off the liability is contingent on the business condition. Consequently, if entrepreneurs face temporary difficulty in debt servicing, e.g., due to a short-term adverse demand shock, it may have a magnification effect. That is, the credit channel may dry up due to the lenders' overreaction to the temporary inability of the entrepreneur to service the debt (Iqbal & Mirakhor, 2011).

This may happen even if the bank suspects that the entrepreneur's ability to service the debt may be compromised in future due to possible fluctuations in its profitability. Put differently, interest payments are due irrespective of the outcomes of the entrepreneur's investment whether sweet or sour. The bank may experience change in fortune only if entrepreneur is not able to service the bank's debt. Therefore, bank may view a few delayed payments, or a temporary cash flow problem of the entrepreneur as a regime change which could ultimately blow up into a sudden stop in lending.

On the contrary, these temporary shocks are viewed differently in a participatory arrangement because the bank, being a partner in the business, regularly receives information on the ups and downs of the venture to calculate their share in the profits. Moreover, the adverse shocks in the business are automatically absorbed in the form of a low or no periodic return to partners rather than pilling up as outstanding payments to the lenders. Consequently, the short-run loss or temporary cash flow problem does not result in putting an end to the relationship between entrepreneurs and capital providers because investors expect that the low or no return in one period might be compensated by a higher return in future.

4.4 The Marginalization of Participatory Finance in the Practice of Islamic Financial Institutions

Paradoxically, while the pertinent literature continues to emphasize participatory modes as the main modes, in practice Islamic Financial Institutions (IFIs) tend to deliberately and systematically avoided (Chong & Liu, 2009; Khan, 2010). The IFIs, particularly Islamic banks, adopt partnership contracts for the scheme of deposits, especially for term deposit accounts (Nouman & Ullah, 2014, 2016). However, it is usually claimed that they do not adopt participatory financing as the main financing scheme due to their inherent high risks. In practice, Islamic banks mainly rely on the non-participatory modes of financing particularly *Murabahah* in the majority Islamic banking industries. Even specialized IFIs, e.g., Mudarabah Companies in Pakistan, which are supposed to be functioning purely on a PLS basis, have a negligible proportion of their funds invested on a *Mudarabah* or *Musharakah* basis. The strong and consistent tendency of IFIs to rely on debt-like instruments, particularly *Murabahah*, while investing funds is referred to as *Murabahah* syndrome (Yousef, 2004). It is because the trend has been followed by the IFIs across the world, to mimic conventional investing of funds.

Islamic banking face a great deal of criticism due to the overwhelming use of non-participatory financing. It is usually argued that though non-participatory modes of finance are *Shariah* compliant; these are not consistent with the true spirit of Islamic finance. Moreover, these are clearly incapable to achieve the specific objectives of the Islamic banking and finance and the broader goals of *Shariah*. According to Mansoori (2011) the contemporary Islamic banks do not give sufficient consideration to *maqāsid al Shari'ah* in practice. Consequently, their transactions do not involve exchange of benefits and real economic activities in most cases. He further argues that the advocates of Islamic banking defend the current banking model by stressing the *Shari'ah* compliance of the transactions, which in their view refers to adherence to the mechanics of the contracts. However, in order to develop a distinct Islamic identity of Islamic banking, their transactions should predominantly focus the high purposes of Islamic finance and *maqāsid al Shari'ah* instead of the contract mechanics. Consequently, it will transform from merely *Shari'ah*-compliant banking into a truly *Shari'ah*-based banking system.

The extant literature suggests that Islamic banks avoid participatory financing because the viability of *Musharakah* and *Mudarabah*-based financing is restrained by several factors. The extant literature highlights several reasons for marginalization of participatory financing in the practices of IFIs. However, literature remains scattered, with diverse studies focused on different dimensions of the issue. For example, Ascarya (2010) and Sadique (2012) claim that upper management of Islamic financial institutions is not committed and sincere in adopting participatory arrangements. On the other hand, Akacem and Gilliam (2002), Khan (1995), and Samad et al. (2005) argue that projects and clients to be financed through participatory contracts require to be evaluated very carefully for which managerial skills and expertise are required. However, IFIs lack skillful human resource in this regard. Similarly, Ascarya and Yumanita (2006) claim that there is a low demand for financing through participatory financing as they are hesitant to make bank partners in their businesses.

On the contrary, Dar et al. (1999), Dar and Presley (2000), Farooq (2007) argue that Islamic banks avoid participatory contacts because these are less applicable in the current business environment. While according to Adnan and Muhamad (2008), Aggarwal and Yousef (2000), Akacem and Gilliam (2002), Amrani (2012), Bacha (1997), Chong and Liu (2009), Hasan (2002), Kayed (2012), Khan and Ahmed (2001), Mirakhor and Zaidi (2007), Sarker (1999), and Siddiqi (1983b, 2006), the inherent agency problems are the most dominant hurdle in the application of these contracts.

In the nutshell, the literature is not only diverse but also divergent. Therefore, although the seemingly rather abstract elements are actually interconnected, it is difficult to conceptualize the big picture since the typology of constraints is missing. Therefore, it is important to have a unified understanding of the constraints to participatory financing to conceptualize the consistent inclination of Islamic banks toward non-participatory financing throughout the world. To bridge this gap a coherent framework has been proposed in the proceeding chapter that outlines the typology of constraints participatory financing.

4.5 Chapter Summary

Participatory finance has an enormous potential of creating a financial system consistent with the true spirit of Islam in which morality is not limited only to the prohibition of interest. It is usually argued that participatory financing ensures availability of more financial resources to small businesses, make accruing unearned income more difficult, and promote justice and equity in society since it would finance all deserving ventures, not just the ventures with well-established credit history or excellent collateral. Thus, most advocates of IBF hold that a financial system based on risk sharing would lead to greater allocative efficiency, equity, GDP growth, and financial system stability. Moreover, participatory financing is considered as the essence of Islamic banking and finance and the true spirit of the Islamic financial system.

The non-participatory modes, on the other hand, are acclaimed to lack the capacity to avoid the evils and injustices of interest-based system because they by far mimic the conventional debt-based arrangements. Thus, a financial system based on non-participatory modes does not have superiority over the conventional interest-based system in terms of growth, stability, efficiency, and equity. Building upon these notions, advocates of the Islamic banking and finance are unanimous on the fact that the Islamic financial institutions must rely on partnership contracts to achieve the objectives of the economic system stability, efficiency and socio-economic justice.

References

Adnan, M. A., & Muhamad. (2008). Agency problems in mudarabah financing: The case of Sharia (Rural) banks, Indonesia. In M. Obaidullah & H. S. H. A. Latiff (Eds.), *Islamic finance for micro and medium enterprises* (pp. 107–130): Islamic Research & Training Institute, Islamic Development Bank.

Aggarwal, R. K., & Yousef, T. (2000). Islamic banks and investment financing. *Journal of Money, Credit and Banking, 32*(1), 93–120.

Ahmad, M. (1947). *Economics of Islam: A comparative study*. Muhammad Ashraf.

Akacem, M., & Gilliam, L. (2002). Principles of Islamic banking: Debt versus equity financing. *Middle East Policy, 9*(1), 124–138.

Amrani, F. (2012, June 28–29). *Financing cost and risk sharing in Islamic finance: A new endogenous approach*. Paper presented at the 29th International Symposium on Money, Banking and Finance, Nantes-France.

Ascarya. (2010). The lack of profit-and-loss sharing financing in Indonesia's islamic banks revisited. *Review of Indonesian Economic and Business Studies, 1*(1), 57–80.

Ascarya, & Yumanita, D. (2006). *The lack of profit and lost sharing financing in Indonesian Islamic banks: Problems and alternative solutions.* Paper presented at the INCEIF Islamic Banking and Finance Educational Colloquium, KL Convention Center, Kuala Lumpur, Malaysia.

Bacha, O. I. (1997). Adapting mudarabah financing to contemporary realities: A proposed financing structure. *The Journal of Accounting, Commerce & Finance, 1*(1), 26–54.

Chapra, M. U. (1985). *Towards a just monetary system.* The Islamic Foundation.

Chong, B. S., & Liu, M.-H. (2009). Islamic banking: Interest-free or interest-based? *Pacific-Basin Finance Journal, 17,* 125–144.

Dar, H. A., Harvey, D. I., & Presley, J. R. (1999). *Size, profitability, and agency in profit and loss sharing in Islamic banking and finance.* Paper presented at the Second Harvard University Forum on Islamic Finance: Islamic Finance into the 21st Century, Cambridge, Massachusetts.

Dar, H. A., & Presley, J. R. (2000). Lack of profit loss sharing in Islamic banking: Management and control imbalances. *International Journal of Islamic Financial Services, 2*(2), 3–18.

Farooq, M. O. (2007). Partnership, equity-financing and Islamic finance: whither profit-loss sharing? *Review of Islamic Economics, 11*(Special Issue), 67–88.

Fernandez, R. B. (1984). Implicancias dinamicas de la propuesta de Simons para reforma del sistema financiero. *Ensayos Económicos, Banco Central de la Republica Argentina (Buenos Aires), 29* (March 1984), 1–30.

Friedman, M. (1969). The Monetary Theory and Policy of Henry Simons. In M. Friedman (Ed.), *The Optimum Quantity of Money and Other Essays.* Chicago: Aldine.

Golembe, C. H., & Mingo, J. J. (1985). *Can Supervision and Regulation Ensure Financial Stability?* Paper presented at the The Search for Financial Stability: The Past 50 Years, San Francisco (Federal Reserve Bank of San Francisco).

Hasan, Z. (2002). Mudaraba as a mode of finance in Islamic banking: Theory, practice and problems. *The Middle East Business and Economic Review, 14*(2), 41–53.

Humud, S. (1976). *Tatwir Al-A'mal Al-Masrifiyya bima Yattafiqu wa Al-Shari'ah Al-Islamiyya (Arabic).* Cairo: Dar Al-Ittihad Al-'Arabi lil-Tiba'a.

Iqbal, Z., & Mirakhor, A. (2011). *An introduction to Islamic finance: Theory and practice* (2nd ed.). Singapore: John Wiley & Sons (Asia) Pte. Ltd.

Kareken, J. H. (1985). *Ensuring Financial Stability.* Paper presented at the The Search for Financial Stability: The Past 50 Years, San Francisco (Federal Reserve Bank of San Francisco).

Karstens, I. (1982). Islam and financial intermediation. *Staff Papers International Monetary Fund (washington)*, 29, 108–142.
Kayed, R. N. (2012). The entrepreneurial role of profit-and-loss sharing modes of finance: Theory and practice. *International Journal of Islamic and Middle Eastern Finance and Management*, 5(3), 203–228.
Khan, F. (2010). How 'Islamic' is Islamic banking? *Journal of Economic Behavior & Organization*, 76, 805–820.
Khan, M. S. (1986). Islamic interest-free banking: A theoretical analysis. *IMF Staff Papers*, 33(1), 1–27.
Khan, T. (1995). Demand for and supply of PLS and mark-up funds of Islamic banks: Some alternative explanations. *Islamic Economic Studies*, 3(1), 1–46.
Khan, T., & Ahmed, H. (2001). *Risk management: An analysis of issues in Islamic financial industry*. Jeddah: Islamic Research and Training Institute-Islamic Development Bank.
Mansoori, M. T. (2011). Is "Islamic Banking" Islamic? Analysis of current debate on Sharī'ah legitimacy of Islamic banking and finance. *Islamic Studies*, 50(3/4), 383–411.
Mehra, R., & Prescott, E. C. (1985). The equity premium: A puzzle. *Journal of Monetary Economics*, 15(2), 145–161.
Mirakhor, A., & Zaidi, I. (2007). Profit-and-loss sharing contracts in Islamic finance. In K. Hassan & M. Lewis (Eds.), *Handbook of Islamic banking* (pp. 49–63). Edward Elgar Publishing.
Nouman, M., & Ullah, K. (2014). Constraints in the application of partnerships in Islamic banks: The present contributions and future directions. *Business & Economic Reivew*, 6(2), 47–62.
Nouman, M., & Ullah, K. (2016). *New perspectives on partnership contracts in Islamic banks*. Paper presented at the 1st CEIF International Conference on Towards Financial Inclusion: Developments in Islamic Economics, Banking and Finance, Peshawar, Pakistan.
Qureshi, A. I. (1946). *Islam and the theory of interest* (1st ed.). Muhammad Ashraf Publishers.
Rogoff, K. (1999). International institutions for reducing global financial instability. *The Journal of Economic Perspectives*, 13(4), 21–42.
Sadique, M. A. (2012). *Capital and profit sharing in Islamic equity financing : Issues and prospects*. The Other Press.
Samad, A., Gardner, N. D., & Cook, B. J. (2005). Islamic banking and finance in theory and practice: The experience of Malaysia and Bahrain. *The American Journal of Islamic Social Sciences*, 22(2), 69–86.
Sarker, M. A. A. (1999). Islamic business contracts, agency problem and the theory of the Islamic firm. *International Journal of Islamic Financial Services*, 1(2).

Shinsuke, N. (2012). Critical Overview of the history of Islamic economics: Formation, transformation, and new horizons. *Asian and African Area Studies, 11*(2), 114–136.

Siddiqi, M. N. (1981). *Muslim economic thinking.* Islamic Foundation.

Siddiqi, M. N. (1983a). *Banking without interest.* Islamic Foundation (originally published in Urdu).

Siddiqi, M. N. (1983b). *Issues in Islamic banking.* The Islamic Foundation.

Siddiqi, M. N. (1985). *Partnership and profit-sharing in Islamic law.* The Islamic Foundation.

Siddiqi, M. N. (2006). Islamic banking and finance in theory and practice: A survey of state of the art. *Islamic Economic Studies, 13*(2), 1–48.

Simons, H. C. (1948). *Economic policy for a free society.* Univ. of Chicago Press.

Usmani, M. T. (2002). *An introduction to Islamic finance.* Kluwer Law International.

Warde, I. (2000). *Islamic finance in the global economy.* Edinburgh University Press.

Yousef, T. M. (2004). The murabaha syndrome in Islamic finance: Laws, institutions and politics. In C. Henry & R. Wilson (Eds.), *The politics of Islamic finance.* Edinburgh University Press.

PART II

The Contemporary Practices of Participatory Finance

CHAPTER 5

Constraints to Participatory Finance

Participatory modes of financing are the ideal modes of financing and represent the true spirit of Islamic banking and finance, as discussed in the context of *Shari'ah*, Islamic economic principles, and advocacy of the Islamic banking essence and models, covered in previous chapters. It, therefore, seems important that Islamic banks may promote participatory financing. However, in practice Islamic banks tend to avoid participatory financing even though acknowledging its originality. This chapter, therefore, attempts to identify and describe the constraints to participatory finance.

For this purpose, this chapter presents a holistic constraints framework[1] which was developed using the systematic review approach.[2] Whereby, a systematic review[3] of the literature was conducted to identify and describe constraints to participatory financing and develop a holistic constraints framework by synthesizing the insights from the extant literature. The typology of constraints is important because the extant literature provides many explanations for the tendency of Islamic banks to avoid participatory

---

[1] This framework was first published in Nouman, Ullah, and Gul (2018).

[2] See Annexure 1 For detailed discussion on how the coherent constraints framework was developed.

[3] Systematic reviews aim to *"answer a specific question, to reduce bias in the selection and inclusion of studies, to appraise the quality of the included studies, and to summarize them objectively"* (Petticrew, 2001, p. 99).

financing. However, literature is divergent and there is no unified understanding of the constraints to participatory financing (See Sect. 5.1 for details). Therefore, it is important to have a unified understanding of the constraints to participatory financing to conceptualize the consistent inclination of Islamic banks towards non-participatory financing throughout the world.

5.1 Overview of the Extant Literature[4]

The earliest writings on the subject of Islamic finance can be traced back to the forties of the twentieth century (Siddiqi, 1981). Whereas, the contemporary practice of Islamic banking date backs to late fifties which started with the establishment of the first modern banking venture based on the tenets of Islamic laws in a rural area of Pakistan in the late 1950s (Roy, 1991), Tabung Haji (formerly known as Lembaga Urusan dan Tabung Haji) in Malaysia in 1963, and Mit Ghamr Savings Bank in Egypt in 1963 (Siddiqi, 2006). These were having interest free operations based up on profit sharing. Among these only Tabung Haji survived due to its narrow focus, strong roots in the community, clear business-based structure, and official blessings (Siddiqi, 2006). The modern Islamic banking with full fledge operations incepted with the establishment of more than a half dozen Islamic banks in 1970s across many Muslim countries including UAE, Kuwait, Sudan, Egypt, Jordan, and Bahrain (Shinsuke, 2012). The Islamic banks from the inception were not pure profit-and-loss sharing banks; they made use of non-participatory financing to a rather significant extent including leasing of capital goods and mark-up trading (Nienhaus, 1983).

According to Nienhaus (1983) and Siddiqi (2006) the early literature till the end of nineteen-seventies, which can be characterized as the theory of Islamic banking, was largely a supplication for the replacement of interest with profit and loss sharing in banks (See for example, Ahmad, 1972; Ghanameh, 1973; Maududi, 1969; Qureshi, 1946; Siddiqi, 1969). The main emphasis of the early literature was on highlighting the evils of interest and emphasizing the underlying benefits of the participatory financing (Nienhaus, 1983; Siddiqi, 2006). Moreover, it placed the religious obligation and greater social welfare responsibility upon Islamic

---

[4] Based on insights from Nouman, Ullah, and Jan (2022b)

banks to strive for achieving the broader goals of *Shari'ah* that could be realized by synthesizing their operations on partnership basis (Dusuki & Abozaid, 2007). However, no attention was paid to developing theoretical arguments or mechanism to assure the capital protection in the system based on partnership and the non-participatory modes of financing were totally ignored (Hasan, 2005; Ismail, 2002). That is why soon after the advent and proliferation of *Murabahah* financing during the late nineteen-seventies and early eighties,[5] it conquered the operations of Islamic banks and pushed participatory financing to a corner accounting for less than ten percent in the operations of Islamic banks (Siddiqi, 2006).

In the late 1980s, when the prevailing divergence in the theory and practice of the Islamic banks became evident, the researchers and Islamic economists started paying attention to its possible explanations and solutions. The study by Nienhaus (1983) was among the first studies aiming at describing the problems of the newly born Islamic banking including factors hindering the application of the participatory financing. Similarly, Waqar Masood Khan in his Ph.D. dissertation (Khan, 1983) created the moral hazard hypothesis for the very first time as an explanation of the constraints faced by Islamic banks in the application of the participatory financing (Khan, 1995). Similarly, the study by Nadeem Ul Haque and Abbas Mirakhor was the first attempt toward modeling the Islamic participatory financing arrangements and analyzing their implications. Moreover, they used the lens of agency theory for the first time to explain constraints to participatory financing arrangement (Haque & Mirakhor, 1986). Their study aimed at formulating investment behavior in a participatory financing arrangement as a principle-agent problem and analyzed the relevant issues under the moral hazard and uncertainty conditions.

These studies were followed by a stream of the literature, providing divergent explanations for the tendency of Islamic banks to avoid participatory financing. For example, Ascarya (2010) and Sadique (2012) claim that upper management of Islamic financial institutions is not committed and sincere in adopting participatory financing. On the other hand, Akacem and Gilliam (2002), Khan (1995), and Samad et al. (2005) argue that projects and clients to be financed through participatory financing require to be evaluated very carefully for which managerial skills and

---

[5] *Murabahah* was first modified by Humud (1976) as a tool for extending credit without violating the *Shari'ah* rules (El-Gamal, 2006).

Table 5.1 Factors restraining the application of participatory financing

1. Untrustworthiness	2. Reluctance to share profit
3. Lack of skilled HR	4. Severe competition
5. Weak accounting procedures	6. Higher appraisal and monitoring costs
7. Unawareness	8. Cost preference
9. Higher risk	10. Disclosure of business secrets
11. Less applicability	12. External interference
13. Complications	14. Weak properly rights
15. Protection of depositors' interest	16. Shallow secondary market
17. Weak regulatory and legal framework	18. Risk-averse depositors
19. Asymmetric information	20. Adverse selection
21. Moral hazards	22. Non-supportive government
23. Tax shield benefits	24. Inefficient accounting and auditing systems

Source Based on Nouman (2019) and Nouman et al. (2018)

expertise is required; however, IFIs lack skillful human resource. Similarly, Amrani (2012) and Kayed (2012) claimed that there is a low demand for participatory financing. On the contrary, according to Bacha (1997), Chong and Liu (2009) agency problems are the most dominant hurdles in the application of participatory financing.

Due to the divergence in the literature, there was no unified understanding of the constraints to participatory financing. To bridge, this chapter attempts to integrate the divergent literature and develop the holistic framework of the constraints. The analysis of the extant literature suggests that there are 24 different factors that restrain the application of the participatory financing. Table 5.1 summaries the constraints to participatory.

5.2 The Coherent Constraints Framework

The constraints presented in Table 5.1 suggest that the strong and consistent tendency of Islamic financial institutions to rely on non-participatory financing results from necessity, not from preference. *Musharakah* and *Mudarabah* have serious practical problems. In fact, all the distinct factors highlighted in Table 5.1 contribute together toward the less popularity of the participatory financing and put the non-participatory financing at a comparatively advantageous position. Therefore, Islamic financial institutions rely mainly on non-participatory modes of financing to avoid these problems.

Although, the seemingly rather abstract elements are actually interconnected, it becomes difficult to conceptualize the big picture since the typology of constraints is missing. Therefore to bridge this gap, a holistic typology is proposed for better conceptualization of the underlying constraints to participatory financing. This framework is developed in two stages. In the first stage, a systematic review of the literature was conducted to identify all those factors that contribute to the lower preference for *Musharakah* and *Mudarabah*-based financing. In the second stage, the identified constraints were synthesized, using the thematic synthesis method,[6] to develop a coherent constraints framework,. This framework outline the typology of the constraints by categorizing the constraints into three distinct categories namely uncertainty, low demand, and regulatory hurdles. Figure 5.1 presents the coherent constraints framework.

The constraints framework highlights that the seemingly rather distinct and abstract constraints interact together to make the participatory financing a less attractive option for Islamic banks. This framework suggests that there are mainly three facets of lower preference for participatory financing. First, there are several factors in the contemporary business settings, prevailing social setting, and the bank's internal environment that underpin uncertainty in the success of participatory financing arrangements. Second, there is a lower demand for participatory financing in the market, i.e., entrepreneurs prefer to use non-participatory arrangements for financing their ventures due to the inherent restraining characteristics of the participatory financing arrangements. Finally, there are certain factors in the regulatory framework that restraints the extensive

---

[6] The thematic synthesis is a qualitative evidence synthesis method that follows a highly structured approach for the selection, organizing, and tabulation of the primary research data. It mainly entails listing the findings of selected studies and then combining them into similar descriptors or themes to develop a general description of the problem at hand (Hannes & Lockwood, 2012). The thematic synthesis 'uses thematic analysis techniques, as well as adaptations from grounded theory and meta-ethnography, to identify themes across primary research studies. Synthesis component entails an iterative process of inductively grouping themes into overarching categories that capture the similarities, differences, and relationships between the themes' (Paterson, 2012, p. 17).

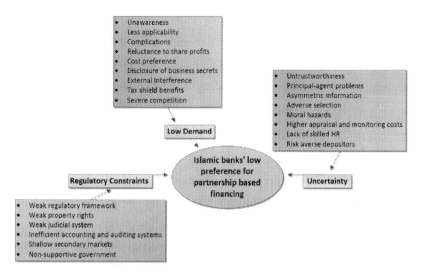

Fig. 5.1 Coherent constraints framework (*Source* Nouman [2019] and Nouman et al. [2018])

utilization of participatory financing arrangements by Islamic banks.[7] The following subsections present a detailed discussion on the three constructs of the constraints framework.

Uncertainty

The practical application of participatory financing has always been restricted by the business ethics constraints and operational difficulties in the Islamic banking industry. The current economic structure is biased, supporting the interest-based (and the non-participatory) system rather than the partnership paradigm. There are several factors in the contemporary business settings that induce uncertainty in participatory financing arrangements and in turn restrain their application in the Islamic banking industry. Table 5.2 summarizes the factors that induce uncertainty in

---

[7] Regulatory hurdles are a set of restraining factors derived from the regulatory structures, courts, laws, and government agencies exerting conformance pressures and shaping the lower preference of Islamic banks for participatory financing.

Table 5.2 Factors inducing uncertainty in participatory financing arrangements

1. Low levels of reliability and trustworthiness in the market
2. Asymmetric information
3. Adverse selection
4. Moral hazards
5. Participatory financing arrangements involve higher project appraisal and monitoring costs which induces Islamic banks to bear additional costs of operation
6. Projects and clients to be financed through participatory financing arrangements require to be evaluated very carefully for which managerial skills and expertise is required. However, there is a lack of skilled human resource in the Islamic banks
7. Depositors of Islamic banks are risk-averse. Thus, investing their funds in risky projects could prompt their depositors to withdraw their funds

the successful commencement and operation of participatory financing in Islamic banking.

Fairness is important to success of partnership arrangements. An experimental study by Zhou and Wu (2011) which employed different economic games suggests that people have increased demand for fairness when they have to share losses with others. People demand justice in wealth allocation in both the loss and gain domains, but this preference in the context of loss sharing might not be the same as in the context of gain sharing. Potential losses have greater impact on fairness preference and choice behavior than the equivalent gains. Therefore, unfairness in division schemes would originate stronger reactions (higher rejection rates) among partners in loss sharing compared to gain sharing.

Similarly, Williamson in the Transaction Cost Theory suggests two other important behavioral premises of human agents: bounded rationality and opportunism.[8] Bounded rationality means that although human beings intend to behave rationally, their rationality is limited by their ability to "formulate and solve complex problems and to process information". Therefore, in (neo-) classical economic sense, their decisions are hardly ever optimal. Opportunism may be defined as "self-interest seeking with guile", which means that parties are willing to provide incomplete or false information to complete a transaction that will provide them with advantage.

[8] See Williamson (1981, 1985, 1993).

Given bounded rationality, opportunism and increased demand for fairness under adversity, participatory financing arrangements are more exposed to compatibility, conflicts, and other contracting problems. Therefore, existence of a supportive and cooperative social environment is conducive to the successful operation of the partnership paradigm. High moral standards in the society are prerequisite for the success of participatory financing arrangements. These contracts are not workable in an environment which lacks honest and fair dealings.

The lack of reliability and trustworthiness in the society leads to agency problems in participatory financing including the asymmetric information, adverse selection, and moral hazards problems. Asymmetric information is a situation that arises when insufficient knowledge of one party involved in the transaction about the other one, makes it impossible to take accurate decisions while conducting a transaction. Since, participatory financing arrangements are formulated in the form of principal-agent arrangements, these are prone to the asymmetric information problem. The agent (an entrepreneur who seeks funds) being the insider (active) party has better knowledge about the project they wish to undertake. While the principal (a bank which provides the funding needed to initiate the project) being the outsider (passive) party usually has less knowledge about the potential returns and the associated risks of the project than the agent does. The asymmetric information in turn creates problems in the partnership arrangements on two fronts: before the project is initiated (adverse selection) and after the initiation of the project (moral hazard).

Adverse selection is the problem faced due to asymmetric information before occurrence of the transaction. Borrowers have better inside information about themselves (including their abilities and intentions) and project (including its potential returns and likelihood of success), but they may not credibly signal it to the bank in the wake of exploiting interest of bank for their own benefits. Since it is difficult for banks to determine the quality of a loan applicant, this creates several adverse selection problems. Given the asymmetric information, the adverse (undesirable) selection is more likely to occur in case of partnership arrangements because the following type of borrowers actively seek funds on partnership basis and are therefore more likely to be selected:

1. The borrowers expecting their projects to provide low profits, but high non-monetary benefits prefer partnership arrangements because they expect to realize high total returns at artificially low cost of capital.
2. The borrowers expecting high profit from a risky project prefer partnership arrangement because their risk will be shared or even completely borne by bank (i.e., in case of *Mudarabah* because if the project fails, losses will be exclusively borne by the bank whereas, the entrepreneur will lose his efforts).
3. When the ratio of profit sharing is decided on the basis of expected profit, potential borrowers inflate their declared profit expectation in the hope of profit sharing ratio being set low by bank.

Due to adverse selection it is more likely that funds might be lent to inappropriate applicants, banks decide not to invest on partnership basis even though there are suitable parties (with promising projects) in the marketplace.

Moral hazard, on the contrary, is the problem faced due to asymmetric information after a project is initiated. Moral hazard in partnership arrangements is the risk (hazard) that the working partner might involve in activities that are undesirable (immoral) from the bank's point of view. These problems are associated with the under reporting or artificial reduction of the actual profit and the difficulty of observing the entrepreneur's actions. Since, participatory financing arrangements are formulated in the form of principal-agent arrangements, the moral hazard problems in such contracts are similar to those found in agency relationships. The principal-agent problem arises when the entrepreneur (agent) involves in activities that maximizes his interest at the cost of bank's (principal) interest. The moral hazard problem arises in such set-ups if an agent is slack about the firm's management, misuses the funds, and is not honest.

Mudarabah contracts are more vulnerable to agency problems and moral hazards, compared to *Musharakah* contacts since financier has no right to interfere in the business although he is required to bear all losses. The prevalence of poor systems of accounting and auditing in most of the Muslim countries, and failure of the judicial systems in helping financial systems in case of default strengthen the probability of moral hazard in participatory financing arrangements. The problem of adverse selection and moral hazards induce the risk of default in the participatory financing arrangements which ultimately harm the interest of depositors.

The Islamic banks would, therefore, need to evaluate the projects and clients to be financed through participatory financing very carefully. Moreover, they need to incur costly monitoring expenses to ensure that the behavior of entrepreneur is consistent with the bank's interests. The additional dead weight costs in pre-contract project appraisal and post-contract monitoring to control the adverse selection and moral hazards make partnership agreements costly compared to the non-participatory arrangements. Furthermore, the pre-contract project appraisal and post-contract monitoring is not only expensive but also non-feasible for Islamic banks because it requires managerial skills and expertise. However, there is a serious lack of qualified credit personnel for the evaluation and monitoring of the projects in the Islamic banks.

In the nutshell, there are several distinct but interdependent operational factors in the contemporary business settings that underpin uncertainty in the participatory financing arrangements, which in turn restrict the commencement and successful operation of the participatory financing arrangements.

Lower Demand

The extant literature grants the contractual choice exclusively to the bank, assuming that the avoidance of the participatory financing comes from the supply side in the market. However, there are many factors on the demand side that hinder the application of participatory financing. Table 5.3 summarizes the factors that hamper the demand for participatory financing.

Participatory financing arrangements have been widely criticized for being "old instruments" that are neither fitting for contemporary financial needs nor comparable with what the state-of-the-art conventional banking can offer. The reluctance of the Islamic banks to adopt participatory financing arrangements have been widely attributed to the construct and the disposition of the participatory financing arrangements themselves which in turn lead to the lower demand for the participatory financing. For example, it is generally claimed that *Musharakah* and *Mudarabah* are less applicable. Moreover, these arrangements are more complicated to structure and deal with.

In addition, customers (borrowers) refuse the participatory financing arrangements for a given quality of their projects, since these arrangements become more expensive to the entrepreneurs if their profitability

Table 5.3 Factors leading to lower demand for participatory financing

1. Participatory financing arrangements are less applicable
2. More complicated to structure and deal with partnership financing
3. Profitable businesses are not willing to share their expected high profits with Islamic banks
4. Businesses are interested in the cost; not in the mode of financing
5. Low demand for participatory financing because it may disclose business operations and its secrets to the financier and other parties
6. Entrepreneurs prefer to maintain independence and avoid external interference
7. Unfair treatment in taxation: Interest is tax deductible, but profits are not
8. Lack of understanding and knowledge in the society regarding the fundamentals of the Islamic finance and banking
9. Due to severe competition from conventional banks and other financial institutions, Islamic banks have to offer comparable products

exceeds a certain level. Therefore, they prefer non-participatory financing and interest bearing financing since they do not have to share their high business profits with the financier. Similarly, unfair treatment in taxation also contributes toward comparatively higher cost of participatory financing arrangements. Profit is taxed while interest is exempted. Thus, the tax shield benefit feature of the interest bearing modes of finance makes participatory financing the least attractive option. Furthermore, the need of rigorous accounting and periodic audits make participatory financing more complicated to deal with. Moreover, entrepreneur loses exclusive control over his business. Thus, many entrepreneurs reject participatory financing because they do not want to disclose their operations and trade secrets to the financiers and tend to protect their business from external interference. Moreover, depositors of Islamic banks are risk-averse. Thus, investing their funds in risky projects could prompt their depositors to withdraw their funds.

Bearing all these factors in mind it can be concluded that customers have lower preference for participation-based financing which ultimately put the non-participatory modes of financing at a comparatively advantageous position. Moreover, it share the tendency of banks to avoid participatory finance on the assets side.

Regulatory Constraints

The economic and legal mechanisms underpin financial systems around the globe. These economic and legal mechanisms depend on the political structures, regulatory institutions, legal tradition, and institutional variables such as bureaucratic quality, corruption, and expropriation risk. The presence of a sound regulatory framework is prerequisite for the effective regulation of Islamic financial institutions and growth of participatory financing. A sound regulatory framework for Islamic banking comprises of various components including the securities law, *Shari'ah* law, insolvency law, property law, business law, tax law, common law, civil law, and employment law. Following are the features of a sound regulatory framework:

1. A supportive financial environment that assists and promotes the development of the industry.
2. A sound legal framework offering a comprehensive and proficient system conducive to the successful operation of the participatory financing arrangements.
3. A reliable and credible forum for clearing the legal disputes of the parties involved in the Islamic financing arrangements.

However, a sound regulatory framework is missing in Muslim countries. For example, in most of the Muslim countries property rights are neither properly defined nor well protected, the judicial system is not capable of enforcing the terms of the contacts, secondary market for Islamic financial instruments is shallow and illiquid, the taxation policies are biased, the auditing and accounting systems are weak and inefficient (Nouman et al., 2022a; Shah et al., 2021). These constraints ultimately leave participatory financing a less attractive option for Islamic banks. Table 5.4 summarizes the regulatory factors that restrain the application of participatory financing.

Prudential regulations imposed by the regulatory authorities also play an important role in restraining the application of participatory financing on a large scale. Sound regulations help in mitigating the problems of asymmetric information. On the other hand, regulations that are over restrictive can prove counterproductive, since it may restrict the number of products being offered by Islamic banks, increase transaction costs, and decrease financial efficiency. In addition, Islamic banks are exposed to the

Table 5.4 Regulatory factors restraining the application of participatory financing

1. Absence of a supportive regulatory framework
2. Banking laws enforce rules and controls on the allocation of bank's funds in direct investment
3. Lack of properly defined or protected property rights in Muslim countries
4. Weak judicial system in Muslim countries
5. Inefficient accounting and auditing systems
6. Lack of sound accounting procedures and standards consistent with the Islamic laws
7. Illiquid and shallow secondary market for Islamic financial instruments
8. The Islamic bank acting as managing partner for depositors is bound to protect the interest of depositors and to invest their money in less risky avenues
9. Lack of commitment and support from government

equity investment risk that arises from investing funds on participation basis. Moreover, the value of their deposits is not guaranteed. The value of deposits may become at stake in the event of severe losses. Consequently, in the wake of securing depositors interests the regulatory bodies impose various controls on the allocation of funds in direct investments involving profit and risk sharing. Therefore, Islamic banks are bound to invest their money in less risky avenues.

In case of participatory financing arrangements bank shares in profits and losses of venture. It is not a matter of concern if the bank is allowed, and is able to keep a close eye on the operations of the firm. However, suitable monitoring mechanisms have not been devised yet for the participatory financing arrangements, especially for *Mudarabah* arrangements where financier does not have the control right. Since, the bank cannot control the entrepreneur who manages the venture being financed through *Mudarabah*. Moreover, the bank cannot reduce the risk in participatory financing by requiring guarantee or collateral. Therefore, supportive prudential regulations are crucial for the successful operation of the participatory financing in the modern world.

In Pakistan various *Mudarabah* laws attempt to outline a basic regulatory framework including the *Mudarabah* companies and *Mudarabahs* Ordinance 1980, the *Mudarabah* Rules 1981, the State Bank of Pakistan's prudential regulations, and the Guidelines for Issuance of *Musharakah* Certificates for *Mudarabah*. However, standardized participatory financing contracts or bylaws need to be constructed keeping in view the legal frameworks of Islamic countries.

5.3 Implications of the Constraints Framework

The constraints framework strengthens the axiom that Islamic finance is a dependent system requiring an economy based on Islamic setting. The viability of Islamic finance especially participatory financing depends on the presence of a "true Islamic state" where its religious, social, political, economic, legal, and educational institutions complement each other and function as a whole toward the accomplishment of common values and the desired goals. Moreover, it highlights the factors in the contemporary social, economic, and regulatory settings that strengthen the non-cooperative and risk-averse attitudes and hinder the viability of the participatory financing.

This framework implies that compared to the participatory financing, the non-participatory financing is more consistent with the conventional banking traditions in the present setting. Banking culture, professional orientation of staff, similarity of products and services being offered, laws and regulations, and premises of competition, all put the non-participatory modes of financing at a comparatively advantageous position. Thus, given the lack of trustworthiness and cooperation in the market, lower demand for the participatory financing and absence of supportive regulatory framework and enabling institutions, the main challenge faced by the Islamic financial service industry is the development of a mechanism that would reveal the fruits of Islamic finance to the global economy. Thus, there is serious need of policy implications, institutional reforms, and introduction of incentive compatible contracts based upon partnership principle. Unless serious steps are taken by Islamic banks, academia, and regulatory and legal bodies, the non-participatory financing will continue to dominate the operations of Islamic banks.

5.4 Chapter Summary

This chapter proposes a coherent constraints framework to conceptualize the constraints to participatory finance. This framework synthesizes the several abstract explanations provided by the extant literature regarding constraints to participatory financing to develop the typology of the constraints to participatory financing. The constraints framework indicates that three major constraints contribute to the lower preference of Islamic banks for participatory financing:

First, there are several factors that induce uncertainty in the participatory financing arrangements. These factors include agency problems (encompassing the asymmetric information, adverse selection and moral hazard problems), risk-averse depositors, high project evaluation and monitoring costs, lack of skilled human resource for project evaluation and selection, and lack of reliability and trustworthiness in the society.

Second, the entrepreneurs have lower demand for participatory financing due to certain inherent characteristics of *Mudarabah* and *Musharakah* and other related factors including: lack of familiarity and understanding among the customers and entrepreneurs, severe competition, unfair treatment in taxation, fear of external interference in the business matters, fear of losing independence and secrecy, high financing cost, complications in structuring and dealing with participatory arrangements, and less applicability of participatory financing.

Third, the current regulatory structure restrains the viability of participatory financing in several ways. The major regulatory constraints include lack of government support, lack of deep and liquid secondary markets, inefficient accounting and auditing systems, weak judicial systems, weak property rights, restrictive prudential regulations, and non-supportive regulatory framework.

This framework implies that the contemporary social, economic, and regulatory settings are not conducive to the participatory financing and put the interest based and non-participatory financing at an advantageous position compared to the participatory financing. Therefore, the non-participatory financing is expected to dominate the Islamic banking operations unless serious steps are taken by the Islamic banks and regulatory bodies.

REFERENCES

Ahmad, S. M. (1972). *Economics of Islam: A comparative study*. Mohammad Ashraf.

Akacem, M., & Gilliam, L. (2002). Principles of Islamic banking: Debt versus equity financing. *Middle East Policy*, 9(1), 124–138.

Amrani, F. (2012, June 28–29). *Financing cost and risk sharing in Islamic finance: A new endogenous approach*. Paper presented at the 29th International Symposium on Money, Banking and Finance, Nantes-France.

Ascarya. (2010). The lack of profit-and-loss sharing financing in Indonesia's Islamic banks revisited. *Review of Indonesian Economic and Business Studies*, *1*(1), 57–80.

Bacha, O. I. (1997). Adapting mudarabah financing to contemporary realities: A proposed financing structure. *The Journal of Accounting, Commerce & Finance*, *1*(1), 26–54.

Chong, B. S., & Liu, M.-H. (2009). Islamic banking: Interest-free or interest-based? *Pacific-Basin Finance Journal*, *17*, 125–144.

Dusuki, A. W., & Abozaid, A. (2007). A critical appraisal on the challenges of realizing Maqasid al-Shariah in Islamic banking and finance. *IIUM Journal of Economics and Management*, *15*(2), 143–165.

El-Gamal, M. A. (2006). *Islamic finance: Law, economics, and practice*. Cambridge University Press.

Ghanameh, A. H. (1973). *The interest less economy in contemporary aspects of economic and social thinking in Islam*. Muslim Students Association of U.S. and Canada.

Hannes, K., & Lockwood, C. (Eds.). (2012). *Synthesizing qualitative research: Choosing the right approach*. John Wiley & Sons Ltd.

Haque, N. U., & Mirakhor, A. (1986). Optimal profit-sharing contracts and investment in an interest-free Islamic economy. *International Monetary Fund Working Paper*, WP/86/12.

Humud, S. (1976). *Tatwir Al-A'mal Al-Masrifiyya bima Yattafiqu wa Al-Shari'ah Al-Islamiyya (Arabic)*. Cairo: Dar Al-Ittihad Al-'Arabi lil-Tiba'a.

Kayed, R. N. (2012). The entrepreneurial role of profit-and-loss sharing modes of finance: Theory and practice. *International Journal of Islamic and Middle Eastern Finance and Management*, *5*(3), 203–228.

Khan, T. (1995). Demand for and supply of PLS and mark-up funds of Islamic banks: Some alternative explanations. *Islamic Economic Studies*, *3*(1), 1–46.

Khan, W. M. (1983). *Towards an interest free Islamic economic system: A theoretical analysis of prohibiting debt financing*. (Ph.D.), Boston University.

Maududi, S. A. A. (1969). *Ma'ashiyat e Islam (Urdu)*. Islamic Publications.

Nienhaus, V. (1983). Profitability of Islamic PLS banks competing with interest banks: Problems and prospects. *Journal of Research in Islamic Economics*, *1*(1), 37–47.

Nouman, M. (2019). *Constraints, adaptation, and outcomes framework of participatory financing in Islamic banking (PhD)*, Institute of Management Sciences, Peshawar Pakistan.

Nouman, M., Ullah, K., & Gul, S. (2018). Why Islamic banks tend to avoid participatory financing? A demand, regulation, and uncertainty framework. *Business & Economic Review*, *10*(1), 1–32.

Nouman, M., Ahmad, I., Siddiqi, M. F., Khan, F. U., Fayaz, M., & Shah, I. A. (2022a). Debt maturity structure and firm investment in the financially constrained environment *International Journal of Emerging Markets.* https://doi.org/10.1108/IJOEM-08-2020-0908

Nouman, M., Ullah, K., & Jan, S. (2022b). Domains and motives of Musharakah spur in the Islamic banking industry of Pakistan. *The Singapore Economic Review, 67*(1), 381–409. https://doi.org/10.1142/S0217590819500620

Paterson, B. L. (2012). It looks great but how do I know if it fits? An introduction to meta-synthesis research. In K. Hannes & C. Lockwood (Eds.), *Synthesizing qualitative research: Choosing the right approach.* John Wiley & Sons, Ltd.

Petticrew, M. (2001). Systematic reviews from astronomy to zoology: Myths and misconceptions. *British Medical Journal, 322*(13), 98–101.

Qureshi, A. I. (1946). *Islam and the theory of interest* (1st ed.). Muhammad Ashraf Publishers.

Roy, D. A. (1991). Islamic banking. *Middle Eastern Studies, 27*(3), 427–456.

Sadique, M. A. (2012). *Capital and profit sharing in Islamic equity financing: Issues and prospects.* The Other Press.

Samad, A., Gardner, N. D., & Cook, B. J. (2005). Islamic banking and finance in theory and practice: The experience of Malaysia and Bahrain. *The American Journal of Islamic Social Sciences, 22*(2), 69–86.

Shah, I. A., Shah, S. Z. A., Nouman, M., Khan, F. U., Badulescu, D., & Cismas, L. M. (2021). Corporate governance and cash holding: New insights from concentrated and competitive industries. *Sustainability, 13*(9), 1–18. https://doi.org/10.3390/su13094816

Shinsuke, N. (2012). Critical overview of the history of Islamic economics: Formation, transformation, and new horizons. *Asian and African Area Studies, 11*(2), 114–136.

Siddiqi, M. N. (1969). *Ghair Soodi Bank kari (Urdu).* Islamic Publications.

Siddiqi, M. N. (1981). *Muslim economic thinking.* Leicester: Islamic Foundation.

Siddiqi, M. N. (2006). Islamic banking and finance in theory and practice: A survey of state of the art. *Islamic Economic Studies, 13*(2), 1–48.

Williamson, O. E. (1981). The economics of organization: The transaction cost approach. *The American Journal of Sociology, 87*(3), 548–577.

Williamson, O. E. (1985). *The economic institutions of capitalism* (3rd ed.). Free Press.

Williamson, O. E. (1993). Opportunism and its critics. *Managerial and Decision Economics, 14*, 97–107.

Zhou, X., & Wu, Y. (2011). Sharing losses and sharing gains: Increased demand for fairness under adversity. *Journal of Experimental Social Psychology, 47*, 582–588.

CHAPTER 6

The Applications of Participatory Finance

The participatory modes of Islamic financing including *Musharakah* and *Mudarabah* are widely accepted as the ideal modes of financing among the jurists of Islamic banking and finance. However, paradoxically, these are not the most popular modes of financing in practice. This is because the practice of the participatory financing in Islamic banking is constrained by several factors. Therefore, Islamic banks apply the adapted variants of *Musharakah* throughout the world. This chapter explores the prevailing variants of participatory financing in the major Islamic banking industries around the globe. The design and structure of two major variants of *Musharakah* are explored in detail including diminishing *Musharakah* and running *Musharakah*. Moreover, it elaborates the domains of participatory financing in the major Islamic banking hubs. Several applications of participatory financing are covered including working capital financing, consumer financing, commodity operations financing, local trade financing, import financing, and *Mudarabah*-based financing.

© The Author(s), under exclusive license to Springer Nature Singapore Pte Ltd. 2023
M. Nouman and K. Ullah, *Participatory Islamic Finance*,
https://doi.org/10.1007/978-981-19-9555-2_6

103

6.1 Variants of Participatory Financing in the Major Islamic Banking Industries

Islamic banks apply participatory modes of financing (*Mudarabah*) on the deposits side. However, these are seldom applied on the assets side in the original form due to several constraints to pure *Musharakah* and *Mudarabah* modes of finance (see Chapter 5 for details). Therefore, the practice of participatory financing is predominantly based on the adapted variants of *Musharakah* in the major Islamic banking industries. Presently, the Islamic banks mainly apply two variants of *Musharakah*, namely diminishing *Musharakah* and running *Musharakah*. These variants have been developed by adapting the design of pure *Musharakah*.[1]

Diminishing Musharakah

Diminishing *Musharakah*, also known as *Musharakah Mutanaqisah*, is a variant of *Musharakah* which enables a partner to gain ownership of the asset gradually overtime. It is based on the principle of *Shirkat ul Milk* and *Ijarah*. The Accounting and Auditing Organization for Islamic Financial Institutions (AAOIFI) defines diminishing *Musharakah* as "a form of partnership in which one of the partners promises to buy the equity share of the other partner gradually until the title to the equity is completely transferred to him" (AAOIFI, 2008: 217). It is tailored to the needs of the customers who are interested in a temporary co-partnership with the bank in a certain project or asset, and eventually want to gain ownership of the asset/project within a stipulated period of time.

In the diminishing, *Musharakah*-based financing arrangement the customer and bank jointly acquire an asset which is leased back to the customer. The customer in return promises to pay rent to the bank for using the asset which is estimated on the basis of bank's outstanding share in the asset. Moreover, the customer gradually redeems the bank's share in the asset, at the price prevailing at the time of sale, until the asset is fully owned by the customer. The diminishing *Musharakah* agreement concludes upon the full redemption of the bank's share in the asset by the customer followed by the transfer of the asset's title to the customer. Thus, this product combines three contracts: partnership, lease, and sale.

---

[1] See Chapter 9 for details of different adaptations in *Musharakah* financing.

The general process of diminishing *Musharakah*-based financing arrangement is as follows (See Fig. 6.1 for the illustration of the diminishing *Musharakah arrangement*):

Stage 1: Customer selected the asset to be acquired and applies for financing.
Stage 2: The bank and customer sign diminishing Musharakah contract and both parties contribute capital in the pre-agreed ratio.
Stage 3: The required asset is acquired which is mutually owned by the bank and customer.
Stage 4: The asset is leased back to the customer.
Stage 5: Customer uses the asset and in return pays periodic installments (usually on monthly basis) which cover rent for the period and periodic payments for the purchase of bank's share in the asset.
Stage 6: The title of the asset is transferred to the customer when he/she eventually become sole owner of the assets after buying the bank's share in the asset.

Running Musharakah

Running *Musharakah* is a variant of *Musharakah* which is based on the principle of *Shirkat ul Aqad*. The idea of the running *Musharakah* was presented by Mufti Taqi Usmani in his book (Usmani, 2002). This product was first applied in Pakistan by the Meezan bank in 2008–09 that is the premier Islamic bank of Pakistan operating under the Shariah supervision of Mufti Taqi Usmani himself (Ayub, 2016). It was predominantly introduced as an alternative to the running finance for corporate clients who were interested in a product that could offer the flexibility of withdrawing cash and returning it at any time, thus practically paying return only on the utilized portion of funds out of their maximum approved limit.

Under this model, bank and customer enter into a short-term *Musharakah* contract which allows the bank to invest in certain primary and operating business activities of the customer. The funds invested by bank can be utilized for any *Shariah* compliant operating activity of the

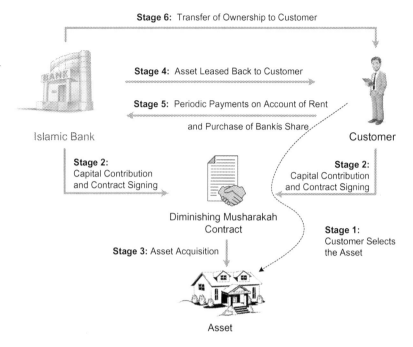

Fig. 6.1 Mechanism of diminishing *Musharakah*

business or any identifiable segment(s) thereof (e.g., a certain product line).[2] Moreover, customer is allowed to withdraw funds at choice up to a certain limit keeping in view the business needs, and deposit the idle funds at any time without submitting any additional document or altering the contract. Thus, the bank's investment is equivalent to the average balance of the customer's running *Musharakah* account maintained with the bank which is estimated on the daily product basis over the stipulated period of time (Fig. 6.2).

At the end of the transaction period, the bank and customer share the profit of the predefined operating activities or identifiable segment(s) of the business in the agreed ratio up to an agreed profit ceiling. That is, unlike pure *Musharakah* where actual profit of the business is shared among all partners, a maximum ceiling is decided in *running Musharakah*

---

[2] Other than the purchase of fixed assets.

6 THE APPLICATIONS OF PARTICIPATORY FINANCE

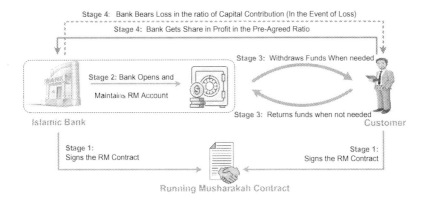

Fig. 6.2 Mechanism of Running *Musharakah*

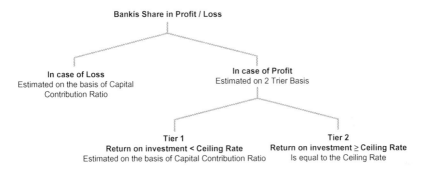

Fig. 6.3 Bank's share in the profit and loss in a RM-based arrangement

agreement for the distribution of profit. For this purpose, a two tier profit sharing ratio is agreed and the amount of profit over and above the ceiling rate, which is usually linked with the benchmark rate (KIBOR in Pakistan), is given to the customer as per the prior commitment. On the contrary in the event of loss, the bank has to share the losses relevant to the predefined activities or segment(s) of the business as per the ratio of its capital contribution. Figure 6.3 elaborates the procedure for estimation of the bank's share in the profit and loss.

6.2 Domains of Participatory Finance

Non-participatory modes dominate the asset side of Islamic banks in the major Islamic banking industries of the world while the share of participatory financing remains relatively low. In addition, the participatory modes of financing are rarely applied in their original form. There are some instances of banks using *Musharakah* in its pure form in Sudan. However, the practice of the participatory financing in the Islamic banking industries of other countries is predominantly based on the adapted variants of the *Musharakah*, particularly diminishing *Musharakah*. Illustration 6.1 presents the makeup of the financing portfolio of the Islamic industry of Pakistan to demonstrate the practice of participatory finance.

> **Illustration 6.1: The practice of Participatory finance in the Islamic banking industry of Pakistan**
> In Pakistan, Islamic banks provide *Shari'ah* compliant banking services including deposit, trade, and financing-related services to consumers, the small and medium sized enterprises (SMEs), corporations, and government. The leading Islamic banks are providing *Shari'ah* compliant financing solutions to meet (i) the consumer financing needs of general public, (ii) commodity operations financing needs of government departments, and (iii) project financing, long-term finance, export re-finance, import finance, working capital finance, documentary credit requirements, and trade finance needs of the corporations and SMEs.
> The statistics published by the State Bank of Pakistan indicate that *Musharakah*-based financing dominates the financing portfolio of the Islamic banking industry of Pakistan. The total share of *Musharakah*-based finance accounts to 52.6% of the overall financing of Islamic banking industry. Diminishing *Musharakah* retains the highest share (32.9%) in the overall financing portfolio of the Islamic banking industry of Pakistan Similarly, *Musharakah* has 19.7% share in the overall financing of Islamic banking industry. However, pure *Musharakah* is not applied by Islamic banks in Pakistan on the assets side. The 19.7% share of *Musharakah* in the statistics published by State Bank of Pakistan represents the de facto share of running *Musharakah*. Thus, the two variants of

Musharakah, including the diminishing *Musharakah* and running *Musharakah*, dominate the practice of Islamic banks operating in Pakistan. The following statistics presents the makeup of the financing portfolio of the Islamic industry of Pakistan.

Financing mix of Islamic banking industry of Pakistan (as of March 2021)

Modes	% Share
Murabahah	13.5
Ijarah	4.9
Musharakah	24.8
Mudarabah	0
Diminishing *Musharakah*	34.2
Salam	2.4
Istisna	8.9
Others	11.3
Total	100

Source Islamic Banking Bulletin March 2021 (SBP, 2021)

In many countries, Islamic banks offer participatory financing in various areas including working capital financing, consumer financing, commodity operations financing, and agriculture financing. The following subsections briefly elaborate how participatory financing is currently practiced in different areas of financing around the world.

Working Capital Financing

In Pakistan, Islamic banks offer a variety of *Shari'ah* compliant products to meet the working capital financing needs of SMEs and corporations. Various working capital finance products are available in the term structure and running *Musharakah* structure. Moreover, various specialized products are also offered by Islamic banks to cater the off balance sheet financing needs of multinational corporations (MNCs) and large corporations. The working capital finance products are based on different modes of financing including *Murabahah, Istisna, Tijarah, Musawamah, Bai Salam*, and Running *Musharakah*.

Running *Musharakah* is used as an alternative to conventional running finance structure. In the *running, Musharakah* arrangement bank invests funds in the business, usually for short term, on profit and loss sharing basis. These funds are utilized to meet the operational needs of a business. Unlike pure *Musharakah* where actual profit and loss of the business is shared among all partners, a ceiling rate is decided in *running Musharakah* for the distribution of profit. If the actual profit of the business is below the ceiling rate, the actual profit is shared with the bank in the ratio of capital contribution. However, if the profit exceeds the ceiling rate, bank's share of profit is calculated on the basis of the ceiling rate. The profit above the ceiling rate goes to the client while bank has no or a negligible claim on the additional profit. On the hand, in case of loss, the bank is responsible to share the loss in the ratio of capital contribution.

Consumer Financing

Islamic banks offer *Shari'ah* compliant financing facilities for a variety of consumer products including house financing, automobile financing, and durable goods financing facility based on different modes of financing including *Murabahah, Musawamah* and diminishing *Musharakah*. However, in many countries the consumer financing products of the major Islamic banks are predominantly based on the diminishing *Musharakah* model. The details of house financing and automobile financing are as follows:

(a) *House Financing*

In most of the countries, the house product of Islamic banks is based on the principle of diminishing *Musharakah*. In the house financing arrangement Islamic bank and the customer contribute a certain amount of financing which is utilized for purchasing, construction, or renovation of the property. Customer participates with the Islamic bank in the joint ownership of the property under consideration. The bank's share in the property is divided into ownership units. Customer promises (through undertaking to purchase) to buy the bank's share in the property gradually over a certain period of time. Customer uses the property and in return agrees to a periodic rent (usually monthly) to the bank for the use of home. Customer buys bank's ownership units every month. Therefore, the bank's ownership decreases in the property every month and vice versa. The rent is adjusted every month on the basis of bank's remaining ownership (units) in the property. Eventually, title to the property is completely transferred to the customer. That is, the customer becomes sole owner of the property while the bank's ownership diminishes. The illustration 6.2 illustrates the mechanism and tentative payment plan of a house financing project of an Islamic bank operating in Pakistan.

Illustration 6.2: The payment Plan of a Diminishing *Musharakah* based House Financing Scheme

Assume customer wants to acquire a house for personnel use using the house financing scheme of Islamic bank. The market value of the house is PKR 10 million and customer has 4 million rupees. Therefore, he/she requires 6 Million financing to purchase a house. The total tenure of the financing can be between 3 to 25 years and depends on the customer's choice. Customers usually decide the financing tenure keeping in view his/her required monthly installment. For illustration purpose, 20 years tenure is assumed to keep the monthly installment low.

Project details

Total price of house	PKR 10 Million
Banks contribution	PKR 6 Million
Customer's contribution	PKR 4 Million
Total Tenure	20 Years

The bank offers two types of payment plans the Unequal Monthly Installment Plan and the Step-Up Monthly Installments Plan. In the unequal, monthly installment plan the no of units are decided on the basis of number of months in the financing tenure. In each month, customer has to purchase one unit therefore the monthly rent decreases in each subsequent month due to reduction in the outstanding units. Following is the plan summary and the tentative payment schedule for this project using the Unequal Monthly Installment option.[3]

Plan summary (unequal monthly installment plan)

No. of units	120
Unit sale price	PKR. 50,000 Per Unit
Profit rate (rent)	14.79% Per Year
Monthly rent per unit	PKR. 616
Total starting rent	PKR. 73,950
Takaful contribution	0.298% Per Year
Takaful contribution in the starting month (= bank's contribution * Monthly Takaful Contribution)	PKR. 1490 (= 6,000,000 * 0.00298/12)
Starting month payment (= starting rent + price of one unit + takaful contribution)	PKR. 125,440 (= 73,950 + 50,000 + 1,490)

---

[3] The estimations are done using the payment calculator of the Meezan bank which is available on their official website.

Tentative payment schedule (unequal monthly installment plan)[a]

Months	Rent (PKR)	Unit price (PKR)	Takaful contribution (PKR)	Monthly payment (PKR)	Balance unit value (PKR)	Balance units
0					6,000,000	120
1	73,950	50,000	1490	125,440	5,950,000	119
2	73,334	50,000	1478	124,811	5,900,000	118
3	72,718	50,000	1465	124,183	5,850,000	117
4	72,101	50,000	1453	123,554	5,800,000	116
5	71,485	50,000	1440	122,925	5,750,000	115
6	70,869	50,000	1428	122,297	5,700,000	114
7	70,253	50,000	1416	121,668	5,650,000	113
8	69,636	50,000	1403	121,039	5,600,000	112
:	:	:	:	:	:	:
:	:	:	:	:	:	:
112	5546	50,000	112	55,658	400,000	8
113	4930	50,000	99	55,029	350,000	7
114	4314	50,000	87	54,401	300,000	6
115	3698	50,000	75	53,772	250,000	5
116	3081	50,000	62	53,143	200,000	4
117	2465	50,000	50	52,515	150,000	3
118	1849	50,000	37	51,886	100,000	2
119	1233	50,000	25	51,257	50,000	1
120	616	50,000	12	50,629	0	0
Total	4,473,975	6,000,000	90,145	10,564,120		

[a] For full payment schedule see Annexure 2

In the Unequal Monthly Installment Plan, the customer has to pay higher monthly installments in the starting months which gradually decrease with reduction in the outstanding units over time. Consequently, the monthly installment becomes relatively smaller in the last months. In Step-Up Monthly Installment Plan, on the contrary, the difference between the monthly installments of the starting and ending months is relatively low. This is because in this plan the number the units are kept relatively higher. The customer is required to purchase one unit each month in the first half of the project's life, while in the second half the customer has to purchase two units per months to reduce the difference between the monthly installments in the first and the second half of the project. Following is the plan summary and the tentative payment schedule for this project using the Step-Up Monthly Installment option.[4]

Plan summary (step-up monthly installment plan)

No. of units	180
Unit sale price	PKR. 33,333 per unit
Profit rate (rent)	14.79% per year
Monthly rent per unit	PKR. 411
Total starting rent	PKR. 73,950
Takaful contribution	0.298% per year
Takaful contribution in the starting month (= Bank's contribution * Monthly takaful contribution)	1490 (= 6,000,000 * 0.00298/12)
Starting month payment (= Starting Rent + Price of one unit + Takaful Contribution)	PKR. 108,773 (= 73,950 + 33,333 + 1490)

[4] See footnote 3.

Tentative payment schedule (step-up monthly installment plan)

Months	Rent (PKR)	Unit price (PKR)	Takaful contribution (PKR)	Monthly payment (PKR)	Balance unit value (PKR)	Balance units
0					6,000,000	180
1	73,950	33,333	1490	108,773	5,966,667	179
2	73,539	33,333	1482	108,354	5,933,333	178
3	73,128	33,333	1473	107,935	5,900,000	177
4	72,718	33,333	1465	107,516	5,866,667	176
5	72,307	33,333	1457	107,097	5,833,333	175
6	71,896	33,333	1449	106,678	5,800,000	174
7	71,485	33,333	1440	106,259	5,766,667	173
8	71,074	33,333	1432	105,840	5,733,333	172
:	:	:	:	:	:	:
:	:	:	:	:	:	:
112	7,395	66,667	149	74,211	533,333	16
113	6,573	66,667	132	73,372	466,667	14
114	5,752	66,667	116	72,534	400,000	12
115	4,930	66,667	99	71,696	333,333	10
116	4,108	66,667	83	70,858	266,667	8
117	3,287	66,667	66	70,020	200,000	6
118	2,465	66,667	50	69,181	133,333	4
119	1,643	66,667	33	68,343	66,667	2
120	822	66,667	17	67,505	0	0
Total	5,213,475	6,000,000	105,045	11,318,520		

(b) Automobile Financing

In majority of countries, the automobile financing product of the major Islamic banks is either based on the principle of *Ijarah* or *Murabahah*. However, few Islamic banks have based their car financing based on the principle of diminishing *Musharakah*.[5] The mechanism of the car financing is similar to the house financing, i.e., Islamic bank and the customer contribute a certain amount of financing which is utilized for purchase of a vehicle keeping in view the customer's requirements. Thus, customer participates with the Islamic bank in the joint ownership of the vehicle and promises to purchase bank's share gradually over a certain period of time. Moreover, customer uses the vehicle and in return agrees to a periodic rent (usually monthly) to the bank. However, unlike house financing the ownership of the car is not divided into distinct units. Rather, the monthly rent and the periodic payment for purchase of bank's share is adjusted in a way that the total payment remains constant throughout the financing period.

Commodity Operations Financing

In Pakistan, Islamic banks are also offering financing to government departments for commodity operations financing (COF). COF refers to the financing provided to government, public sector corporations, or private sector for procurement of commodities to support the prices of domestic products. Commodity operations financing can be used for the procurement of both soft and hard commodities. Hard commodities include the natural resources that need to be extracted or mined like oil, coil, gold, etc. On the other hand, soft commodities include the agricultural products and livestock such as wheat, cotton, corn, sugar, coffee, milk, beef, etc. In Pakistan, the commodity operations financing scheme aims at supporting the prices of domestic agricultural products, particularly wheat.

Previously, Islamic banks used to apply *Murabahah* mode for COF. However, recently running *Musharakah* has been introduced for COF because it is more flexible than the *Murabahah* mode of financing. The running *Musharakah* is based on the two tariff profit distribution system. In this system, the bank enters in to a restricted *Musharakah* with the client whereby commodities to be purchased and their buying and minimum selling rates are determined in advance. The selling price is usually set higher than the buying price. The difference between the buying and selling price is paid as a return to the bank. Therefore, bank

---

[5] E.g., Carsaaz product of Albarkah Islamic bank and Dubai Islamic Auto Finance product of Dubai Islamic Bank in Pakistan.

tries to ensure their expected profit by restricting the client to sell the assets/products of *Musharakah* at the predetermined or a higher price.

Thus, if the commodities are sold at a higher rate, banks get a negligible share in the additional profit. However, if government decides to sell the commodities at a price lower than the determined rate, the deficit is paid by the government form the subsidies account. Thus, the expected profit rate of the bank is predictable to much extent. Since, the main objective of the government is to support the prices of agriculture commodities through commodities operations. Therefore, government usually sells the commodities at a price lower than the buying price to support the local prices in the wake of encouraging local production and discouraging smuggling.

Domestic Trade Financing

In Sudan, some banks (e.g., Al Barakah Islamic Bank) use the *Musharakah* mode for financing the buying and selling of goods in the local market (Ahmad, 1993). For this purpose, bank signs *Musharakah* agreement with the customer for trade of local goods being specified by the customer and opens a special *Musharakah* account to manage the transactions. The bank and customer mutually contribute capital in a pre-agreed ratio to finance the cost of goods; however, the buying and selling of merchandise is the responsibility of entrepreneur. The profit of the venture is divided in the following manner:

a. The customer gets a pre-agreed percentage of net profit in return of the management of the trading activities.
b. The remaining amount is distributed shared by the bank and customer as per their investment ratio.
c. Similarly, the loss (if any) is also shared by both parties as per the ratio of their capital contribution.

Import Financing

In Sudan, Al Barakah Islamic Bank also uses *Musharakah* mode for financing the import of goods. The contract for the import of commodities is similar to the contract for trade of local merchandise. However, there are some nuances in the details:

a. Bank signs Musharakah contract with the importer on the request of importer to participate in the import and sale of certain foreign goods.
b. The contract specifies the commodities to be imported, the total cost of importing the goods in the appropriate currency, and the capital contribution and profit sharing ratio of the bank and the importer.
c. A special Musharakah account is created in the bank.
d. The importer pays a part of his/her contribution immediately after signing the contract, while the rest is paid after the invoices are received.
e. The bank opens Letter of Credit (L/C) to the importer and pays full amount to the exporter after receiving the shipment document.
f. The bank is also responsible to pay the insurance charges which are charged to the transaction account.

The matters related to import, clearance, and sale of the merchandise are managed by the importer. The net profit from the import proceeds is shared among both parties in the pre-agreed ratio while loss is shared as per their investment ratio.

Similarly, in Malaysia the Bank Islam Malaysia issues *Musharakah*-based Letter of Credit (L/C) for import financing. The mechanism of Musharakah-based L/C is as follows:

a. The customer shares the L/C requirements with the bank requests the bank to issue L/C.
b. The bank and customer negotiate the terms of reference for *Musharakah*-based L/C.
c. The customer deposits his/her contribution in the cost of goods imported.
d. The bank issues the L/C and pays the proceeds to the negotiating bank.
e. The bank subsequently handovers the related documents the customer.
f. The customer takes the goods in possession which are ultimately disposed of as per the agreement.
g. The resulting profit is shared in the pre-agreed ratio while loss if any shared in the ration of capital contribution.

Mudarabah *Based Financing*

The application of *Mudarabah* is very limited on the assets side. There are very few instances where Islamic banks allow *Mudarabah*-based financing to ventures. For example, in Indonesia, Bank Mandiri Syariah (BSM) applies *Mudarabah* financing whereby the bank finances the working capital requirement of a venture. The profit is divided in the pre-agreed ratio. Similarly, the Bank Syariah Bukopin (BSB) also offers *Mudarabah*-based financing in certain cases. However, it requires collateral that should worth 125% of the financing amount (Yustiardhi et al., 2020).

On the contrary, In Malaysia, *Mudarabah* is typically applied in the Profit-Sharing Investment Account (PSIA) under the Investment Account Platform (IAP) for mobilization of funds where bank acts as a *mudarib* and shares profit with PSIA holders. IAP is a stand-alone platform that was launched by Bank Negara Malaysia (The central Bank of Malaysia) and is managed by a consortium of six banks to channel funds invested by investors to viable ventures. Its major purpose is to establish a direct but viable link between investors and businesses seeking funds, with minimal involvement of bank.[6] Thus, the bank merely acts as a *mudarib* whose role is limited to the mobilization the funds from investors to different ventures through their financing facilities. However, the mobilization of funds on the financing side is predominantly done through exchange-based modes, while the application of equity-based financing is very limited.

6.3 Chapter Summary

Islamic banks are currently offering participatory financing via adapted variants in the major Islamic banking industries of the world. This chapter elaborates how Islamic banks apply participatory financing within the embedded contractual variants of *Musharakah* namely diminishing *Musharakah* and running *Musharakah*. This chapter covers several applications of participatory financing including working capital financing, consumer financing, commodity operations financing, local trade financing, import financing, and *Mudarabah*-based financing.

---

[6] For details of IAP see Chapter 8, Sect. 8.3.

References

Ahmad, A. (1993). *Contemporary practices of Islamic financing techniques.* Jeddah, Saudi Arabia: IRIT, Islamic Development Bank.

Ayub, M. (2016). Running Mushārakah by Islamic banks in Pakistan: Running from Mushārakah or moving back to square one (Editorial). *Journal of Islamic Business and Management, 6*(1), 7–18.

SBP. (2021). *Islamic banking bulletin - March 2021.* Islamic Banking Department, State Bank of Pakistan. http://www.sbp.org.pk/ibd/bulletin/bulletin.asp

Usmani, M. T. (2002). *An introduction to Islamic finance.* Kluwer Law International.

Yustiardhi, A. F., Diniyya, A. A., Faiz, F. A. A., Subri, N. S., & Kurnia, Z. N. (2020). Issues and challenges of the application of Mudarabah and Musharakah in Islamic bank financing products. *Journal of Islamic Finance, 9*(2), 26–41.

CHAPTER 7

Assessment and Mitigation of Risks in the Participatory Financing Arrangements

As discussed in Chapter 4, participatory modes of Islamic financing including *Musharakah* and *Mudarabah* are widely accepted as the ideal modes of financing among the jurists of Islamic banking and finance. However, paradoxically, these are not the most popular modes of financing in practice because the practice of these modes in Islamic banking is constrained by several factors. Therefore, Islamic banks are applying the adapted variants of *Musharakah*. Islamic banks adapt the participatory financing to make these fit for SME financing, corporate financing, consumer financing, and commodity operations financing within the embedded contractual variants of *Musharakah* namely diminishing *Musharakah* and running *Musharakah*, while pure *Musharakah* and *Mudarabah* are not applied in practice. Moreover, Islamic banks use extensive procedures for the assessment and mitigation of the underlying risks to ensure the viability of *Musharakah*-based financing arrangements. This chapter provides insights into the procedures adopted by Islamic banks for assessing and mitigating the underlying risks associated to the participatory financing, particularly the risk induced by asymmetric information including adverse selection and moral hazards.

7.1 Procedures for Assessment and Mitigation of Risks in Running *Musharakah*

Musharakah is a risky product because, being partner in the venture or a project, the bank is responsible to share the profit and losses arising out of venture. Therefore, Islamic banks are currently practicing running *Musharakah* on a limited scale, offering it to reliable clients for secure projects only. In Pakistan, running *Musharakah* is offered to (i) corporate sector and SMEs for working capital financing and (ii) government sector for commodity operations financing. Among corporations, only the blue chip organizations are allowed to use this product because in such business the chances of loss are negligible. Moreover, their operations are mostly transparent since they have to issue audited financial statements. Therefore, banks are less vulnerable to the inherent problems of the *Musharakah*, particularly the asymmetric information, adverse selection, and moral hazards.

On the other hand, its application in SME sector is very limited. This is because the current accounting and audit systems are weak. Businesses prepare many versions of financial statements to avoid taxation. Thus in the absence of a strong accounting system, the chances of asymmetric information are very high which may lead to adverse selection and moral hazards. For this purpose, Islamic banks are currently allowing working capital financing on running *Musharakah* basis only to leading SMEs that are willing to share their actual financial information with the banks.

Mechanism for the Assessment and Selection of Applicants

Besides offering *running Musharakah* to reliable and profitable business only, Islamic banks have devised an extensive mechanism for the assessment and selection of applicants and projects. All cases of SME and corporate financing including *running Musharakah* are handled in the selected business banking branches. The credit officer prepares each case of financing on the request of client after the checking the minimum eligibility of the client and sends it to the credit risk management department for further assessment. The case is approved by head office on the recommendation of credit risk management department.

Banks have set criteria for the assessment of businesses, whereby many factors are considered including their minimum eligibility, business cycle, current financial position, credit history, performance, experience in using the external financing, and prior experience with the bank, etc. This helps in reducing the adverse selection and moral hazards problems significantly. Table 7.1 Presents the list of documents to be submitted by small and medium enterprises for working capital financing.

The assessment is done in various phases by different departments. For example, risk management department is responsible to mitigate the risks in each case, while the credit department performs the credit risk assessment and assigns rating to the applicant. This rating is based upon client's previous history, balance sheets, turnover in accounts, import export history, and other factors. The case is then sent to the risk management department which is responsible to: (i) ensure whether the rating is assigned correctly and (ii) check the current market exposure of the clients to ensure their credit worthiness. Finally, the case is sent to the competent authority to decide whether the case should be approved.

Table 7.1 Documents required for working capital financing

Small enterprises	Medium enterprises
• Company profile • Request for financing • Last three years accounts signed by proprietor/partners/directors of the firm • Projections with assumptions (in case of long-term finance) • Memorandum and article of association (In case of private limited company) • Basic borrower fact sheet duly signed and stamped by proprietor/partners/directors • Personal net worth statement of proprietor/partners/directors • Stock report • Aging of receivables • Copy of CNIC of proprietor/partners/directors • Import/export business certificates from banks (If applicable) • Last one year bank statement • Form-H and partnership deed (in case of partnership firm) • Valuation report and legal opinion, etc	• Company profile • Request for financing • Audited accounts of last three years accounts • Projections with assumptions (in case of long-term finance) • Memorandum and article of association (in case of private limited company) • Basic borrower fact sheet duly signed and stamped by proprietor/partners/directors • Personal net worth statement of proprietor/partners/directors • Stock report • Aging of receivables • Copy of CNIC of proprietor/partners/directors • Import/export business certificates from banks (If applicable) • Last one year bank statement • Security/collateral documents • Valuation report and legal opinion, etc

Source Nouman et al. (2019)

Moreover, since banks usually do not have enough access to the internal information of the business. Furthermore, banks have limited expertise in the assessment of business. Thus, the lack of skilled human resource and limited access to information can make bank vulnerable to adverse selection and moral hazards problem. To avoid this problem, bank also seeks help from external bodies during the assessment process. For example, to ensure the profitability of a business, bank does income estimation in advance. However, if their income is not verifiable then the services of independent agencies are used for the income estimation of the applicant. Furthermore, the physical operations of the business are checked during the analysis process. The financial information is cross matched with the physical operations to ensure the reliability of the business.

Strategies for Risk Mitigation in Running Musharakah

Islamic banks allow *running Musharakah* in only certain situations keeping in view the business needs. Once reliability of a business gets ensured, the credit officer evaluates its business cycle to determine the most appropriate mode of financing. This helps in further reducing the chances of moral hazard because bank do not go for *running Musharakah* if the needs of the business can be fulfilled through other less risky modes of financing.

In the nutshell, in the first stage the case of each applicant is assessed systematically to determine whether this case should be considered for financing, while in the second stage the appropriate mode of financing is determined keeping in view the operating cycle and needs of the business. Figure 7.1 depicts the business assessment and product selection process employed by the banks after checking the minimum eligibility criteria.

Besides working capital financing, Islamic banks are also applying running *Musharakah* for commodity operations financing (COF). COF is a very attractive short term investment opportunity for Islamic banks because risk is very low in such investments. Furthermore, the size of each contract is very large (usually in billions). Therefore, it is more convenient to manage a single risk free project of multi-billion Rupees worth than several small risky projects.

On the other hand, Islamic banks are offering running *Musharakah* under commodity operations financing (COF) to government departments only. Thus, reliability of the clients is not an issue in the COF

7 ASSESSMENT AND MITIGATION OF RISKS ... 125

Fig. 7.1 The business assessment and mode selection process for the eligible firms (*Source* Nouman et al. [2019])

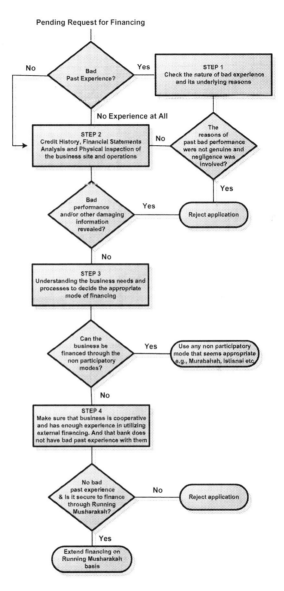

arrangements. However, banks have to do proper assessment to ensure the suitability of the project/commodities under consideration. For this, three important things are ensured in running *Musharakah*-based commodity operations financing: (i) the conversion of money into assets, (ii) identification of assets and estimation of revenue generated from these assets, and (iii) the assessment of revenue, i.e., whether the shared profit is earned from the sale of the underlying assets.

Compared to SMEs and corporations, government is more reliable and trustworthy. When running *Musharakah* is applied for COF, banks do not need to worry about the reliability of the client because these arrangements are done with the government bodies where each financing arrangement is backed by the sovereign guarantee of the federal government.[1] Therefore, there is no adverse selection issue in COF, while the moral hazards are very low.

Furthermore, there is no risk of default in such arrangements because government departments seldom default. Moreover, Guarantees issued against commodity operations are secured against the underlying commodity which are essentially self-liquidating on short term basis and thus should not create a long-term liability for the government.

Similarly, the risk of loss is also negligible in commodity operations financing. In the normal conditions, bank is responsible to share the losses, if any, in the ratio of its capital contribution. However, if government wants to sell the commodities at a price lower than the predetermined minimum selling price; the bank would not be responsible to bear the losses; rather the loss is covered through food subsidies by government.

7.2 Procedures for Assessment and Mitigation of Risks in Diminishing *Musharakah*

Islamic banks are offering *Shari'ah* compliant financing facilities for a variety of consumer products including house financing, car/automobile financing, and durable goods financing facility. The consumer financing, particularly the house and car/automobile financing, of the majority of

---

[1] These guarantees are issued against the commodity financing operations undertaken by TCP, PASSCO, and provincial governments. The outstanding stock of guarantees issued against commodity operations were Rs. 875 billion at end June 2018 (Ministry of Finance, 2018).

banks is based on the principle of diminishing *Musharakah*. Diminishing *Musharakah* is actually a *Musharakah* cum *Ijarah* arrangement whereby bank and client become joint owners of an asset. The asset is used by the client on *Ijarah* basis and pays rent to the bank for using the bank's share of property. Thus, diminishing *Musharakah* has features of both *Musharakah* (*Shirkat ul Milk*) and *Ijarah* modes of financing.

In diminishing *Musharakah*, since bank becomes joint owner of the asset, therefore, to reduce the underlying risks Islamic banks consider only reliable clients. Moreover, banks consider only those assets that are secure to finance. Furthermore, banks apply extensive risk management procedures such as obtaining legal opinion and buying a *Takaful* cover.

Procedures for Assessment of Risks in Diminishing Musharakah

Islamic banks consider only reliable clients and secure assets for diminishing *Musharakah* to reduce the underlying risks since bank becomes joint owner of the asset. Banks have defined proper criteria for assessment and selection of clients and the asset to be financed. Banks usually do three types of assessments including the personal assessment of the client, the financial assessment of the client, and the assessment of the underlying property/asset.

(a) *Personal assessment of the clients*

In the personal assessment bank assesses the person himself by considering his education, police track record, and financial track record. Moreover, his profession is also considered because it matters a lot. A minimum eligibility criterion has been defined for each type of customer Table 7.2 for house financing product, while Table 7.3 presents the eligibility criteria for car financing products of two banks operating in Pakistan.

In addition to the minimum eligibility criteria, a formal mechanism has been designed for the assessment of each client. In the first step, the concerned manager checks the minimum eligibility of the applicant seeking consumer financing. If the client meets the minimum eligibility criteria, his application is forwarded for detailed assessment. Bank's representatives visit the area where the client lives and work. They check the market reputation of the client and confirm the profession of the client. They may even confirm the conduct of the applicant in the society where

Table 7.2 Terms and conditions of the house financing scheme in Pakistan

	Purchase of new house/apartments		Construction of house/apartments		Renovation/improvement	
	Bank 1	Bank 2	Bank 1	Bank 2	Bank 1	Bank 2
Financing limit	PKR 0.5–50 million	PKR 40 million per client	PKR 0.5–50 million	PKR 40 million per client	PKR 0.5–10 million	PKR 5 million
Financing tenure	3–20 years	5–20 years	02 years (excluding construction period of max 12 months) to 20 years Maximum 25 years tenure for salaried and SEP customer	5–20 years	2–15 years	3–10 years
Bank investment ratio	Up to 75% for salaried/SEP/NRP Up to 65% for businesspersons	Up to 75%	Up to 75% for salaried/SEP/NRP Up to 65% for businesspersons	Up to 75%	Up to 30%	Up to 75%

SEP "self employed professionals" includes engineers, doctors, architects and auditors, *NRP* Non Resident Pakistanis
Source Nouman et al. (2019)

Table 7.3 Terms and conditions of the car financing scheme

	Bank 1	Bank 2
Bank investment ratio	Up to 85% of the car value	Up to 80% of the car value for new car Up to 75% of the market value assessed for used and imported car
Financing limit	Rs.100,000–5,000,000	Rs.350,000–5,000,000
Minimum age at the time of application		
• Salaried	• 21 years	• 22 years
• SEP/SEB	• 21 years	• 24 years
Maximum age at the time of finance maturity		
• Salaried	• 60 years	• 62 years
• SEP/SEB	• 65 years	• 65 years
Minimum monthly income		
• Salaried	• PKR 25,000	• PKR 35,000
• SEP/SEB	• PKR 25,000	• PKR 50,000
Minimum work experience		
• Salaried	• 3 Months	• Continuous working experience of 2 years with a minimum of 6 months with the current employer
• SEP/SEB	• 6 Months for SEP • 12 Months for SEB	• In business for a minimum continuous period of 3 years

SEP "self employed professionals" includes engineers, doctors, architects and auditors, *SEB* self employed businessman
Source Nouman et al. (2019)

he lives. In case of salaried person, the service card, joining date, and salary slips of the applicant are checked. Moreover, in some cases the employer is also contacted to confirm his profession. Table 7.4 presents the list of documents that have to be submitted by the applicant for car and house financing.

Furthermore, the credit history of the client is checked by consulting the electronic credit information Bureau (ECIB) report. The Credit Information Bureau department of State bank of Pakistan maintains a database in which credit history of every individual and business is maintained. This database has information on each person that has used

Table 7.4 Documents required for house and car financing[a]

House financing	Car financing
a. **Personal information:** • Copy of CNIC • 2 passport-sized colored photographs of applicant • Copy of rental documents (if applicable) • Copy of last paid utility bills (electricity/gas/telephone) • Bank statement—last 12 months • Copy of recent credit card bills b. **Income Information:** • Original or certified copy of recent pay slip • Employer's certificate including tenor/designation/salary • Professional association membership certificate/practice license (for self-employed professionals) • Property title documents (copies at initial stage and original before disbursement)	• Copy of primary applicant's CNIC • Copy of co-applicant's CNIC (if applicable) • 2 passport size photographs • Latest salary slip (for salaried) • Last 6 months bank statement • Bank certificate (if applicable) • Proof of three years in continuous business, e.g., letter of proprietorship/partnership deed/last 3 years tax returns with receipts (for business person) • Copies of any two latest paid utility bills of residence and business (for business and self-employed customers)

Source Nouman et al. (2019)
[a] Requirements may vary from bank to bank

the financing facility of any bank. The ECIB report is generated from this database and shows whether the person has defaulted in the past. Moreover, it also shows the repayment behavior of each person and entity.

(b) *The financial assessment of the clients*

In the financial assessment, the financial position of customer is estimated. For this purpose, bank estimates the monthly installment the client has to pay including the rentals, unit price, and insurance charges. Moreover, the monthly income of the customer and his monthly expenditure on the bare necessities like children schoolings, medical expenditures, and groceries, etc., is estimated. Finally, the monthly savings of the client are estimated by deducting expenditures from the income to check whether the client is able to pay the monthly installments. Bank has set standards for the minimum acceptable financial credibility of the clients, e.g., for few banks the acceptable level of income is the one that is at least two times higher than the installment the customer has to pay. If the bank feels that customer's saving is not enough to cover the installment, the client is asked to either increase his equity position so that the rental payments may get reduced, or increase the time period of financing to reduce the price of units (since the number of units increases with the increase in time period and the price of units decreases consequently).

(c) *Assessment of the asset to be financed*

The assessment of the asset/property to be financed involves (i) the estimation of the market value of the asset and (ii) detailed assessment of its underlying risks. Bank determines the market value of the asset though proper assessment in the market since financing is done on the basis of the estimated market value of the asset. In case of property, the property dealers of the particular area are involved in the estimation of its current market value. Moreover, the underlying risks are assessed by the team of experts. Furthermore, a team of legal experts also checks the legal aspects because the cases of property are very complicated.

Banks consider only secure assets for financing. For example, most of the banks do not finance those cars that are older than 5–7 years because these cars have many problems. Similarly, the properties in each region are divided into two zones: the positive zone and the negative zone. The positive zones include secure areas where property rights can easily be enforced, for example, Cantonment area, defense area, and secure townships. On the other hand, the properties in the neighborhoods, being transferred through inheritance, involve a high probability of disputes. Thus by considering properties in positive zones only, the bank significantly reduces risk.

Moreover, a formal mechanism has been devised for the assessment of assets. The assessment of the asset is done in various phases by trained persons. Moreover, different departments and teams of experts are involved in the assessment process. Illustration 7.1 presents the assessment process of one of the Islamic bank operating in Pakistan.

> **Illustration 7.1: The assessment process of an Islamic bank**
>
> In one of the Islamic banks, all cases of consumer financing are first sent to the consumer finance department (CFD). CFD after proper analysis sends the case the Risk Management Department (RMD). RMD, after thorough analysis, sends the case to the Credit Assessment Division (CAD) and Special Assets Management (SAM) department for further analysis. CAD checks the property documents and other legal requirements to secure the legal risk. On the other hand, SAM checks the credit history and payment behavior of the applicant to ensure whether it would be possible to recover funds from the applicant. After the approval of CAD and SAM, the case is sent to the Credit Committee for the final approval. The heads of the Islamic Assets, CAD, RMD, CFD, and Islamic banking division (IBD), etc., are the members of the Credit Committee.

Banks also seek help from external bodies during the assessment process. For this purpose, Islamic banks use the services of registered companies having expertise in property assessment. For example, the property assessment and its market value estimation is done through property evaluators who are registered members Pakistan Bank's Association (PBA), while income estimation is done, in certain cases, through approved income estimators. Similarly, banks may also seek legal opinion from the approved legal team. Moreover, manager's visit reports are also integral part of the assessment process. This report does not show market and post-sales values but demonstrates situation of a property, e.g., age and quality of construction, dimensions of the property, and road access to it. Finally, information from different sources is cross matched. In the nutshell, the case of each applicant is assessed systematically to determine the reliably of client and suitability of the asset under consideration. Figure 7.2 depicts the generalized assessment process employed by the Islamic banks for car financing and house financing schemes.

Strategies for Mitigation of Risks in Diminishing Musharakah

To mitigate the chances of loss in case of default, the asset being financed is mortgaged by the bank. Three types of mortgages including token mortgage, equitable mortgage, and registered mortgage are used by

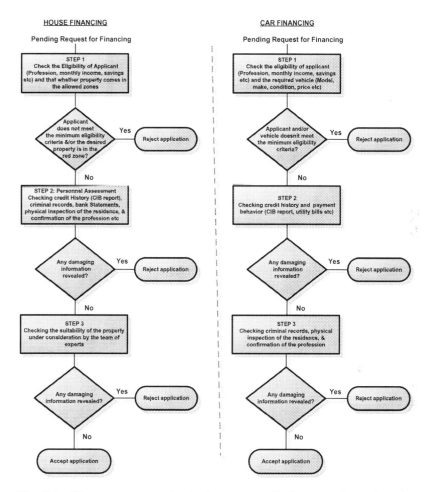

Fig. 7.2 The assessment and selection process for house and car financing (*Source* Nouman et al. [2019])

banks in different situations depending upon the level of risk. In equitable mortgage bank only keeps the title documents of the property in their custody. In the token, mortgage bank keeps the property documents in their custody and a contract is signed on a legal Stamp paper that bank has purchased the property and a certain amount (e.g., USD 5000) has been given as the token money for this purpose. Thus the bank becomes partner in this property. However, the title of the property is not transferred to the bank, thus the bank only has a lien on the property. On the other hand, the registered mortgage is the most secure form. In this form of mortgage, the title of the whole or a part of the property is transferred to the bank through registrar of deeds office.

Similarly, the bank uses the *Takaful* (Islamic alternative to insurance) coverage to reduce the accidental damages and losses from natural calamities. Both car financing and house financing involve *Takaful*. Moreover, to reduce the chances of loss in case of default, bank finances only a portion of asset. Similarly, in case of car financing bank uses trackers to reduce the chances of theft. These steps help in reducing the chances of loss significantly.

7.3 Chapter Summary

This chapter suggests that the financial environment of majority of the Islamic countries is characterized by weak regulatory framework, weak property rights, and weak judicial system. Thus, participatory financing schemes are prone to the agency problems including asymmetric information, adverse selection, and moral hazards besides several other inherent problems. Therefore, Islamic banks have introduced new variants of *Musharakah* through adaptation in the pure *Musharakah*. Moreover, they have devised alternative mechanisms to cope with these constraints and increase the viability of participatory financing.

Islamic banks are currently offering *Musharakah* financing to reliable clients for secure projects only. Moreover, they have devised extensive mechanisms for the assessment and mitigation of the underlying risks particularly the agency problems including asymmetric information, adverse selection, and moral hazards. These strategies have enabled Islamic banks to mitigate the inherent risks in the *Musharakah*-based financing particularly the risk of adverse selection and moral hazards. Consequently, the viability of participatory financing has increased in practice.

References

Ministry of Finance. (2018). *Debt Policy Statement 2018–19*. Debt Policy Coordination Office, Ministry of Finance.
Nouman, M., Ullah, K., & Jan, S. (2019). Variants of participatory financing for risk assessment and mitigation in Islamic banking. *Business & Economic Review, 11*(4), 1–28.

PART III

The Adaptations and Innovations in Participatory Finance

CHAPTER 8

Experiments with Participatory Financing

This chapter presents several case studies from different regions of the world to highlight the experiments by Islamic ban in participatory financing. The first case study presents the experience of Iran in dealing with participatory finance and the steps undertaken to increase the viability and application of participatory finance instruments including *Musharakah* and *Mudarabah*. The second case study presents the experience of the Sudanese Islamic Bank (SIB) that took the initiative of financing the needs of the handicapped rural agriculture sector of Sudan in innovative ways. This case study unveils innovative participatory products that were effectively applied to finance the needs of poorest and the most deprived sector of the country.

The third case study presents the experience of a state-owned Islamic bank that undertook one of the first real *Musharakah* project in Pakistan. This case study conceptualizes the constraints and challenges faced by the bank during the course of this project and how bank dealt with these. The final case study presents the story of an innovative participatory finance product in Malaysia using a stand-alone platform termed as the Investment Account Platform (IAP). This case study reveals how bank can facilitate and promote participatory financing with minimum involvement in its underlying risks and uncertainties.

© The Author(s), under exclusive license to Springer Nature
Singapore Pte Ltd. 2023
M. Nouman and K. Ullah, *Participatory Islamic Finance*,
https://doi.org/10.1007/978-981-19-9555-2_8

8.1 Iranian Experiments with Participatory Finance

A drastic change in the operations of the banking industry was witnessed in Iran in the last two decades of the twentieth century. This change was initiated by first the nationalization of its entire banking and insurance system in 1979 followed by the merger of 16 saving and loan associations and 36 banks into three specialized and six commercial banks.[1] Later on in 1983, the Law for Usury (Interest)-Free Banking operations were introduced which required the banks to shift their operations from being interest-based to interest-free.

Soon after the application of the Law of Interest-Free Banking operations, the Agricultural Bank of Iran (ABI) initiated the transition from the conventional modes of finance to the *Shariah* compliant modes. This shift over was characterized by a well-diversified portfolio of Shariah compliant instruments ranging from high-risk participatory products to low-risk non-participatory instruments. Consequently, the transition was not only smooth but also resulted in improving the efficiency of ABI's operations which is evident from the bank's impressive recovery rate on Islamic financing ranging between 95 and 99% in 1996.

This remarkable transition from conventional to Islamic financing was a result of an extensive drive undertaken by ABI's management in late 1980s and early 1990s to enhance the bank's efficiency, boost profitability, and improve service quality. This drive was characterized by several initiatives for: (i) enhancing monitoring and supervision, (ii) cutting down the processing and operating costs, and (iii) investments in research and development.

These initiatives, particularly investments in monitoring and supervisions, enabled the ABI to build strong and long lasting relationship with partners based on trust. Through improved supervision bank was able to learn about viable investment opportunities in different areas and regions of agriculture. In addition, it was able to develop better understanding of the moral and entrepreneurial characteristics of its partners. This expertise was then used over time to improve project selection and selection of best suited farmers for *Musharakah*-based financing. In addition, the improved and continuous monitoring and supervision also enabled the bank to acquire the up-to-date information to deal with the problem

---

[1] This case study is based on insights from Sadr and Iqbal (2002).

of asymmetric information which ultimately helped the bank in reducing the uncertainties and the moral hazards associated with the participatory financing contracts.

The capability of the ABI to cope with the adverse selection and moral hazard was evident from its experience in the provinces that were destroyed by Iraqi troops during the eight-year Iran–Iraq war. In these provinces, all the records and files of ABI got destroyed due to the destruction of the ABI's buildings by the Iraqi troops. Consequently, when these units resumed their operations after the war, the bank had neither record of the contracts nor written claim over any of their partners. However, interestingly the all the clients (i.e., partners) willingly provided the bank with their own copy of the contract and related records to help the bank in working out and collecting its claims. This experience helped the bank in conceptualizing the level of trustworthiness of its partners and ultimately paved the way for shifting from non-participatory financing to participatory financing arrangements.

In the wake of reducing the processing cost and the processing time of the contracts, the bank also started the revision of the contracts' procedural codes. For this purpose, a task force was formed which was responsible to design new procedures in such a way that not only the cost is reduced but also the customer's time consumed in preparing the necessary documentation and/or visiting the bank is also reduced. For this purpose, the time required to conclude a contract and steps involved in each contract were optimized using time and motion studies for each type of contract. Table 8.1 and Figs. 8.1 and 8.2 depict the number of steps reduced from the codes of procedures during 1990–1995 for each mode of financing (Fig. 8.1) and the time saved in each contract (Fig. 8.1). The time starts when a farmer visits the bank's branch to apply for financing and extends till the end when application gets the final decision after processing in different departments. On the other hand, the process involves various steps including the economic assessment, transfer of fund to the applicant, project supervision, transfer of the assets/venture to the partners after the completion, and settlements of the claims.

It is evident from the Figs. 8.1 and 8.2 that ABI was able to achieve the highest optimization in case of *Musharakah* financing where the time required to complete a transaction was reduced by 36%, while the average number of steps involved in a *Musharakah* contract were reduced by 138 steps (41%). In addition to the process optimization, efforts were also

Table 8.1 Average number of steps and time consumed to conduct a transaction

	Number of steps			Time consumed (minutes)		
	1990	1995	Saving (%)	1990	1995	Saving (%)
Forward purchase	229	135	41	557	406	27
Installment sale (raw materials)	272	182	33	668	506	24
Installment sale (machinery)	266	222	17	731	586	20
Musharakah	339	201	41	1171	749	36

Source Sadr and Iqbal (2002)

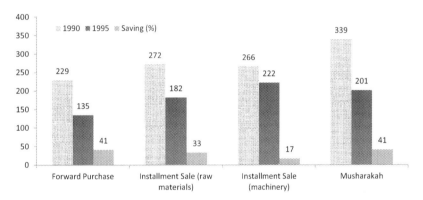

Fig. 8.1 Saving in number of steps

made to reduce the cost of *Musharakah* financing and relax its eligibility criteria. For this purpose, in 1989, those tenants who had the government distributed lands were made eligible for *Musharakah*-based financing. Consequently, all the tenants of registered lands and the official lessees of the non-registered lands became eligible to apply for participatory financing. Similarly, in 1990, the task force suggested to eliminate the requirement of registering the *Musharakah* contract in the Notary Public Office to save the considerable cost and time of the bank's partner. In addition, the task force allowed the *Musharakah* contract for financing the operating costs and short-term activities of farmers and the collateral requirements for *Musharakah* were also reduced significantly. These

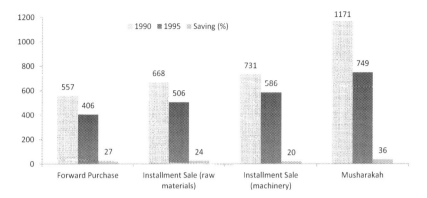

Fig. 8.2 Saving in time required (in minutes) to complete a transaction

efforts induced the sudden increase in the demand for *Musharakah*, making it the most dominant mode of financing in financing portfolio of ABI. Consequently, the composition of the ABI's financing (assets) portfolio changed drastically with a substantial shift from non-participatory financing to *Musharakah*-based financing (see Tables 8.2 and Fig. 8.3).

In the nutshell, the paradigm shift in the financing portfolio of ABI was induced by the initiatives taken by the bank to boost the efficiency of its operations and reducing the problems of asymmetric information, adverse selection, and moral hazards through enhanced supervision and monitoring. In addition, several other initiatives also helped in increasing the applicability and viability of *Musharakah*-based financing including application of *Musharakah* for financing the short-term needs of the farmers, relaxing the collateral requirements and eligibility criteria to broaden its client base, and reduction in the procedural requirements to save time and cost of the clients. These initiatives not helped in increasing participatory financing but also in making the financing portfolio of ABI more balanced compared to the financing portfolio of other banks which remained predominantly static during the same time period. Figure 8.4 compares the growth of *Musharakah* and *Mudarabah*-based financing in ABI and other Islamic banks operating in Iran.

Two types of *Musharakah* arrangements are used as a mode of finance in ABI and other Islamic banks operating in Iran namely equity partnership and civil partnership. Equity partnership involves participation of bank in productive projects through purchase of stocks and shares in a

Table 8.2 Percentage share of different modes in the financing portfolio of the Agriculture Bank of Iran (ABI)

% age share	1984	1985	1986	1987	1988	1989	1990	1991	1992	1993	1994	1995	1996
Installment sale	35.4	30.7	28.5	28.4	30.8	33.6	36.5	42.4	25.7	21.7	20.6	17.1	16.7
Qard-ul-Hassanah	55.2	57	58.1	57.4	51.6	43.8	33.1	17.2	17.6	16.4	12.7	8.7	7.7
Musharakah	0	0.8	0.4	0.5	0.7	1.2	4	16.4	38.3	42.4	41.8	44.8	48.1
Mudarabah	1.8	0.1	0.1	0.1	0.2	0.4	6.9	9.3	9.3	10.5	16	17.3	18.7
Forward Purchase	6.3	8.6	9.6	9.4	10.2	12.6	12.1	12.1	8.5	8.7	8.7	11.8	8.6
Jualah	1.3	2.8	3.3	4.2	6	8.3	7.3	2.3	0.6	0.1	0.1	0.1	0
Hire Purchase	0	0	0	0	0.5	0.1	0.1	0.3	0	0.2	0.1	0.2	0.2
Total	100	100	100	100	100	100	100	100	100	100	100	100	100
Total financing (Billion Riyals)	150.8	199.5	201.9	279.9	382.6	444.3	626.4	956.9	1076.4	1752.1	2363.7	3361.9	3695.2

Source Sadr (1999)

8 EXPERIMENTS WITH PARTICIPATORY FINANCING   143

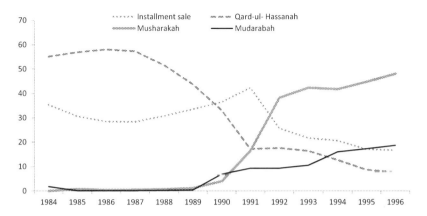

Fig. 8.3 Growth of participatory financing in ABI

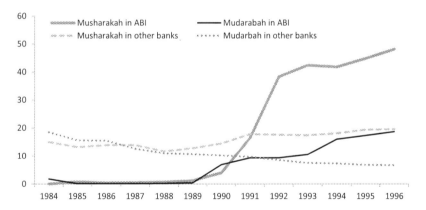

Fig. 8.4 Growth of participatory financing in Iran: ABI versus other banks

company. The civil partnership, on the other hand, involves the ownership of several owners in a single asset in such a way that the share of each partner remains indistinguishable. Thus, their shares being intermingled, each partner has claim over the partnership assets up to his/her share in the partnership.

Similarly, the partners in a civil partnership can be real or juridical persons who can own cash and/or non-cash partnership shares. Thus civil partnership can be defined as 'the mixing of cash and/or non-cash partnership shares of several real or juridical persons, in a profit-seeking partnership venture based on an agreement, such that the pre-determined share of each partner in the common asset remains indistinguishable' (Yasseri, 2002, p. 163). However, unlike the equity partnership, the civil partnership does not require the formation of a company for the management of business affairs. Consequently, this partnership does not acquire a juridical identity separate from its owners (i.e., the partners). Similarly, each partner is allowed to sell or transfer his share to anyone without taking consent from the rest of the partners. However, he is bound to offer his share to the other partners before selling it the third party.

The civil partnerships were initiated under the Article 7 of the Usury-Free Banking Law of 1983 which allows the banks to enter into partnership contracts with clients. The civil partnerships in which bank becomes partner, the managing non-bank partners are authorized financially to commit the joint venture only up to the common capital of the partnership. Consequently, bank's liability exceeds beyond its share in the partnership capital. Moreover, banks do not participate in the management of business affairs. Rather they delegate this right to the non-bank partners. Therefore, to control the moral hazards and agency problems the bank has the right to insist upon and require the non-bank partners to share the losses that may incur during the course of the business. Furthermore, the bank may require the non-bank partners to provide with collateral security and loss-recovery commitments to protect the common capital from the potential abuse and misuse by the managing partners. In addition, the bank has the right to monitor and supervise the business operations from the start till termination/completion to ensure the viability and success of the joint venture.

8.2 Sudanese Experiments with Participatory Financing

Sudan has a predominantly agriculture-based economy whose about 75% of population mainly depends on agriculture. Similarly, agriculture has around 60% contribution in the GDP and 90% share in the total exports of Sudan. However, the agriculture sectors had several issues until the recent past. Particularly, the rural agriculture, despite being the most important contributor in the agriculture output, was seriously handicapped. The small farming subsector was deprived of the financial services from the conventional financial institutions.[2]

Until 1990, the ceiling of financing provided to agriculture sector by nearly all commercial banks was at most 5%. Even the specialized government-run bank, the Agriculture Bank of Sudan (ABS), also failed to meet the financing needs of the small farmers in the rural areas. The failure of the ABS model was characterized by several factors including: the lack of comprehensive financing options, the existence of collateral and/or guarantees requirements that were difficult to arrange for small farmers, high cost of financing, cumbersome and slow procedures, and involvement of interest which was not acceptable to a majority of farmers due to religious norms.

Though the banking system of Sudan was fully Islamized in 1983, the commercial Islamic banks had very little involvement in agriculture and rural development financing till 1990. The Sudanese Islamic Bank (SIB) which was a nationalized Islamic bank took the initiative to finance the needs of handicapped rural agriculture subsector through several pilot projects across the country that were aimed at financing and delivering inputs and facilities directly to the small-scale farmers. Consequently, SIB became the pioneering and leading Islamic bank in Sudan with significant attention to financing agriculture and rural development.

SIB established a full-fledged rural development department, at its headquarters, staffed with well-qualified and highly experienced bankers and technical staff. This department successfully embarked upon several innovations for fulfilling the financing needs of small enterprises, rural agriculture sector, and productive households in efficient ways. It realized that the agriculture financing should in fact address the whole biological system that has certain requirements which needs to be delivered in the required amount at the right time. Therefore, they designed/introduced a comprehensive package for the small farmers to be delivered at their farm gate which included not only finance but also inputs, extension services, marketing advice, and storage facilities.

They also realized that the major constraint to rural agriculture financing was the collateral requirement of the conventional banks. To resolve this problem, SIB adopted *Musharakah* mode for financing the

---

[2] This case study is based on insights from Osman (1999).

needs of this sectors because it does not require any collateral or guarantees. In this model, the bank enters into actual partnership with the farmer whereby the farmer's contributes his land, management, labor, and part of the running expense. On the other hand, bank is responsible to provide most of the inputs, e.g., improved seeds, pesticides, fertilizers, and a part of the running expenses. Moreover, bank owns machinery, e.g., tractors, spraying equipment, harrows, and water pumps, etc., which is rendered to the farmer at the actual cost price. Above these bank also provides consultancy services. For this purpose, the bank deploys veterinary and agriculture experts who work closely with the partner farmers from the start of the project till harvesting.

SIB even went one step further and indulged in the storage and marketing of some the crops. SIB took this initiative because farmers normally lose a lot of value of the crop by selling it at the time of harvest when prices are usually at their lowest. SIB continued the relationship with the farmer through the storage and marketing stage again via *Musharakah* arrangement. In this model, the bank pays 50% of the crop's prevailing price at the time of harvest to meet his urgent needs, thus becoming partner in the crop. The crop is then stored in storage house under the dual control of SIB and the farmer. The transportation and storage cost is paid by the bank and the crop is sold at the time of higher prices. At the completion of the project, the famer charges 50% of the net profit for management while the rest of the net profit is equally divided between the farmer and bank. So in toto famer gets 75% share, while bank get 25% share of the net profit.

Agriculture financing was also extended through co-irrigation projects. In this project, SIB installs irrigation pumps and accessories on the farm and authorizes the famer to operate it. The SIB bears expenses related to the running maintenance and spare parts. Farmer pays a pre-agreed proportion of the harvest (usually 25%) in return to the bank. These projects also entail the option of additional financing for other inputs, e.g., pesticides, seeds, and fertilizers, etc. These inputs are usually financed through Murabahah.

Besides these projects SIB also initiated several other projects using other Islamic modes of financing, e.g., *Murabahah* and *Bai Muajal* (deferred payment). The experience of SIB proves that financing through Islamic modes proves to be a viable alternative which has the capability of financing the poorest sector without over-burdening it with guarantees and collateral requirements. These rural agriculture projects were so successful that in some projects return to farmers on the invested capital ranged from 93 to 1239% only in six months. Besides very high return on investment, most of the projects have even revealed nearly 100% recovery rate.

8.3 Pakistani Experiments with Participatory Financing

In Pakistan, Islamic banking is predominantly based on non-participatory modes. Therefore, very limited instances have been witnessed from inception of Islamic banking in Pakistan till date where Islamic banks have engaged in participation-based financing in real sense. Islamic banking industry reports a significant increase in *Musharakah* financing in the recent years but that is in fact running *Musharakah* which is the *Shariah* compliant alternative to the conventional running financing which cannot be termed as *Musharakah* in real sense (The case of the spur of running *Musharakah* in Pakistan is presented in the next chapter). This section presents the case study of the one of the first real *Musharakah* contracts initiated by an Islamic bank in Pakistan and conceptualizes the risks and constraints faced by the bank during the course of this project. [3]

The Bank of Khyber (BOK) is a state owned bank which operates mainly as a conventional bank. However, it also has Islamic banking operations which are managed through its Islamic banking branches. The Islamic banking department of BOK was approached by a well-reputed local entrepreneur with the proposal of a joint *Musharakah*-based project for the construction of apartments. In the first step, bank signed a Memorandum of Understanding (MoU) with the entrepreneur. The MoU was followed by a formal request to the Bank's Shariah Board secretariat for preparation of policy document for the proposed *Musharakah* contract. This document was then sent to the Board of Directors of the Bank for approval and to the State Bank of Pakistan thereafter for their feedback. This contract, being first of its kind, entailed high risk because neither bank nor customer had expertise. Therefore, bank was extremely careful at each step.

---

[3] This case study is based on insights from Jan, Ullah, and Jabeen (2018).

After the formation of the policy and approval of the *Musharakah* product from State bank of Pakistan, the entrepreneur initiated the application for *Musharakah* financing. The entrepreneur was asked to provide personal guarantees and submit documents related to previous experience and details of his business accounts. The complete file along with the proposal was submitted to the Head Office Credit Committee (HOCC) for approval. The HOCC raised the objection on how the project may be approved without prior guarantee of the return. This objection was raised because the HOCC of the bank, being mainly a conventional bank with Islamic banking windows, was headed by a person with experience and background in conventional banking. Consequently, the Shariah Board had to strive through several meetings to educate the HOCC members on the execution and operation of *Musharakah* and convince them to approve the case.

After an approval form the HOCC, in the first step the capital and profit sharing ratio was mutually determined. An 80:20 ratio for capital contribution was decided where entrepreneur was responsible to invest 20%, while bank agreed to invest 80% of the required capital. In total PKR, 43.083 million capital was required for the project therefore bank agreed to invest 34.46 million rupees. Similarly, a 60:40 ratio was decided for profit distribution whereby entrepreneur, being responsible for managing all construction activities, would get 60% while bank would get 40% of the net profit. In case of losses, each party was responsible to bear losses in the ratio of capital contribution (i.e., 80: 20). A timeline of two years from the date of first disbursement of funds was set for the completion of the project. Moreover, Takaful coverage was obtained from a bank approved reputable *takaful* company to cover the risks of accidents and natural calamities including fire and earthquakes, etc.

In the second step, a joint *Musharakah* investment account was opened and an initial equity of 13.475 million, which was jointly contributed to the ratio of capital contribution, was deposited in this account for the acquisition of the land after satisfying all the necessary pre-requisites. These pre-requisites included land valuation by SBP approved property evaluator, visit report of the bank's professional property evaluator, evaluation of the title documents and market value of the land, and assessment of the transparency of the transaction. The payment to the original landowner(s) was paid through cross payment order. Though the land was jointly owned by the bank and entrepreneur, it was transferred in the name of the bank to meet the prudential regulations.

In the third step, an architect was hired for designing the building. Moreover, services of professional builders were hired to manage the construction work. The entrepreneur, being an active partner, was responsible to monitor the progress and quality of the construction work. Moreover, to ensure the smooth running of the project, a committee was formed by the bank to authorize and supervise the requisition of raw materials and monitor the overall budget of the project. Table 8.3 presents the project specification.

After initializing the construction, the bank proposed that the flats should be advertised for sale in advance and the proceeds from sales should be utilized in the construction to reduce the investment by partners. Interestingly, as soon as the project was advertised, an overwhelming response was received from the customers and all apartments got booked. 13.907 million rupees were received as proceeds from the advanced sales, while the rest was to be received through installments. A *Musharakah* collection account was created to manage the proceeds from sales. The project generated total revenue of 56.465 million rupees and net profit of 13.382 million. The return on investment for bank was 23% per annum which was the highest return the bank had ever earned from any kind of financing. Consequently, bank was able to distribute higher returns to depositors in the market. Table 8.4 presents summary of the project's investments and outcomes.

After the successful competition of the project, BOK decided to launch another *Musharakah*-based construction project with the same entrepreneur. However, based on experience from the previous project, the bank decided to build luxury apartments in the expectation of even higher returns. For this purpose, land adjacent to the previous project was acquired. The bank also decided to adopt an aggressive marketing

Table 8.3 Details of the project

Land	14,974 square feet (55 Marla)
Covered area	31,405 square feet
Building plan	02 blocks
	Multistory (ground plus 3/4)
Specification of each flat	03 bedrooms with attached baths, drawing room, one dressing room, lounge, kitchen, servant room and store

Source Jan et al. (2018)

Table 8.4 Investments and returns of the project

Total investment	PKR 43.083 million
Capital sharing ratio	80:20
	Bank's contribution 80%
	Entrepreneur's contribution 20%
Share of partners in the capital	Bank's share PKR 34.46 million
	Entrepreneur's share PKR 08.623 million
Total revenue generated	PKR 56.465 million
Net profit	PKR 13.382 million
Profit sharing ratio	60:40
	Entrepreneur's share 60%
	Bank's share 40%
Share of partners in the profit	Bank's share @40% PKR 5.353 million
	Entrepreneur's share @60% PKR 08.029 million

strategy to attract advanced bookings in the wake of reducing investment by partners. However, in the meanwhile, the city (where project was initiated) saw a sudden surge in the law-and-order problem due to sever terrorist attacks. Consequently, the real estate business of the city went into a severe recession where the investors started selling their properties at very low prices to shift their investments to secure regions.

Thus, bank failed to initiate same level of interest in the market. However, the bank continued with the construction with the hope of improvement in the law and order situation and market conditions. After completing 80% of the construction, the bank made an attempt to promote the sale of apartments through flexible installments. However, despite an aggressive marketing campaign, the strategy failed to induce interest of customers. Meanwhile, another problem arise which created an immense pressure on this project. A new government in the province was elected due to which a new board of directors (BOD) of the bank was elected. The top management and the new BOD of the bank were against bold investment decisions due to the prevailing market and law and order conditions. Consequently, the project was put on hold to stop further investment in a project which has very little prospects of sale in near future.

However, the partner entrepreneur wasn't satisfied with this decision since he wanted to liquidate his investment. He was willing to sell his share in the market incase bank was not willing to purchase. After thorough assessment of the different options, the bank decided to purchase his share which raised bank's investment to PKR 56.008 million. This project was auctioned few years later in 2015 in nominal terms. Interestingly, bank was able to earn 10 million rupees in this project. However, given the uncertainty underlying this project and the time and effort involved in it, the bank wasn't satisfied with this project.

8.4 Malaysian Experiments with Participatory Financing

As discussed in this chapter several factors induce uncertainty in the operation and viability of participatory financing arrangements. Due to the underlying risk of participatory finance, very few risk-sharing options were available at Islamic banks in Malaysia. To cope with the issue of scarcity of risk-sharing financing options the central bank of Malaysia, Bank Negara Malaysia (BNM), took an initiative in 2015 to develop a participatory finance product using a stand-alone platform. To reduce the underlying risks, the product, termed as Investment Account Platform (IAP), was designed in a way that the bank's involvement was kept a minimum. This was done by using the platform as a direct link between the financiers (equity providers) and the finance (the entrepreneurs/businesses), where banks merely acts as the facilitator.

IAP was launched in Malaysia on 17 February 2016 by BNM through a consortium of four Islamic Banks namely Maybank Islamic Berhad, Bank Muamalat Malaysia Berhad, Bank Islam Malaysia Berhad, and Affin Islamic Bank Berhad. The consortium was later joined by Bank Simpanan Nasional and Bank Kerjasama Rakyat Malaysia Berhad. Thus IAP is a multi-bank platform where several banks have formed a consortium to channel funds invested by investors to finance viable ventures through investment account (IA) products. Its major purpose is to establish a direct but viable link between investors and businesses seeking funds, with minimal involvement of bank. Under this, scheme investor specifies the choice of ventures where funds may be channeled to and the terms and conditions of the investment including the eligibility criteria and the investment mandate. The transactions under IAP and the role of banks are regulated by the Islamic Financial Services Act 2013 (IFSA) and Development Financial Institutions Act 2002 (DFIA). However, the funds placed under IAP are not guaranteed by the deposit insurance corporation.

Thus, the platform facilitates efficient intermediation by the banks to match financing requirement of ventures with investment from retail and

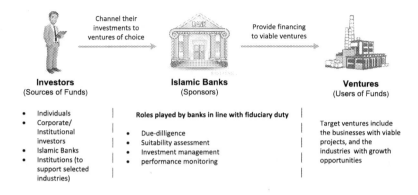

Fig. 8.5 The functioning of IAP

institutional investors. Significant roles are undertaken by the member banks including thorough assessment and selection of viable ventures for financing, suitability assessment on individual investors, and continuous monitoring of the ventures' post-financing performance. Thus, the role of banks is same *Mudarib* who mobilize the funds from investors to different ventures through their financing facilities. However, the financing is not based merely on participation bases (i.e., equity-based); rather it can also be non-participatory or the hybrid of the two. In fact, the mobilization of funds on the financing side is predominantly done through exchange-based modes, while the application of equity-based financing is very limited. Thus, the returns to investors are based on performance of the financed ventures depending upon the nature of financing. Figure 8.5 illustrates the functioning of the IAP.

8.5   Turkiye's Experiments with Participatory Financing

The case of Turkiye is interesting and different as its participation approach to Islamic finance is more political as it names every Islamic finance contract as participation, irrespective of the levels of actual participation of financial institutions and individual customers therein. Turkiye has a rich historical relevance to Islamic finance as the great Ottoman Caliphate has provided rich archival record for avoiding interest and establishing participatory finance. Most popularly, the *Waqf*-based institutions of Ottoman Caliphate are noteworthy and contemporary practice still take analogies for building contemporary *waqf*-based participatory institutions.

The Turkiye's finance sector is influenced by its secular traditions since the start of the modern Republic in 1923. The secular influence on the financial sector is predominantly induced by the secular reforms introduced between 1920 and 1930 (Hardy, 2012). Both theory and practice, however, shows that in Turkiye there is a great appetite for the participation banking that has grown even more after financial crises in 2001 and 2008 (Hardy, 2012). Most of the participation banks such as Kuvat Turk Bank, Al-baraka Turk Bank, Vakif Katilm, and Zari Katilm use various Islamic finance contracts to establish participation banking.

The regulatory structure of Turkiye is different from other countries, as here the central bank and regulator are two different entities, which provide central banking services and regulation, respectively. The participation banking and finance is regulated and supervised partly through the association of participation banks, where a central shariah board issues *Fatawas* from time to time. This decentralized structure makes the participation banking more efficient and prominent than the conventional banks in the country (Eyceyurt Batir et al., 2017).

The participation banking in Turkiye has helped in enhancing financial inclusion as the population with strong religious sentiments was excluded from the interest-based finance. Participation banks have helped these individuals to channelize their capital into more productive industries (Aysan et al., 2013). In addition, during recent history, the participation banking has shown more stability in terms of profitability, liquidity, riskiness and asset quality. Also in asset quality, it remained similar to its conventional counterpart (Aktaş, 2013). More recently, Turkish Banks have moved to participation in Gold banking too and perhaps that would further enhance its experience and share in the overall participation banking.

8.6 Chapter Summary

This chapter presents four case studies to highlight the experiments by Islamic banks in participatory financing. The first case study presents the experience of the Agriculture Bank of Iran (ABI) in dealing with participatory finance and the steps undertaken by the bank to increase the viability and application of participatory finance instruments including *Musharakah* and *Mudarabah*. This case study also provides thought provoking evidence of prevalence of the moral commitments and ethical values which have resulted in the successful completion of participatory financing arrangements despite the fact that the arrangements were characterized by the asymmetrical information.

The second case study presents the experience of the Sudanese Islamic Bank (SIB) that took the initiative of financing the needs of handicapped rural agriculture sector of Sudan in innovative ways. The bank identified loopholes in the financing models of other banks and came up with an array of innovative products, most of which were participatory in nature. These innovative products were predominantly comprehensive packages which included not only finance but also inputs, extension services, marketing advice, and storage facilities. Interestingly, though these products were offered to the poorest and the most deprived sector of the country, the bank witnessed nearly 100% recovery rate besides a substantial income and relief to the customers.

The third case study presents the experience of a state-owned Islamic bank that undertook one of the first real *Musharakah* project in Pakistan. This project was jointly initiated by the bank and a local entrepreneur for the construction of apartments on *Musharakah* basis. The project was so successful that it gave the highest return the bank had ever earned from any kind of financing. Therefore, the bank initiated another project with the same partner. However, due to sudden changes in the market conditions, the second project didn't go according to the plan. This case study conceptualizes the constraints and challenges faced by the bank during the course of this project and how bank dealt with these.

The fourth case study presents the story of an innovative participatory finance product in Malaysia using a stand-alone platform, this platform, termed as the Investment Account Platform (IAP), was initiated by the central bank of Malaysia through a consortium of several local banks to channel investors' funds to the business sector. This case study reveals how bank can facilitate and promote participatory financing with minimum involvement in its underlying risks and uncertainties. Finally, the case of Turkiye's participation banking is presented. Turkiye's case is unique as participation finance is a political name used for every kind of Islamic finance contract, irrespective of the levels of participation involved in the real arrangements.

REFERENCES

Aktaş, M. (2013). Stability of the participation banking sector against the economic crisis in Turkey. *International Journal of Economics and Financial Issues, 3*(1), 180–190.

Aysan, A., Dolgun, M., & Turhan, M. (2013). Assessment of the participation banks and their role in financial inclusion in Turkey. *Emerging Markets Finance and Trade, 49*(SUPPL. 5), 99–111. https://doi.org/10.2753/REE 1540-496X4905S506

Eyceyurt Batir, T., Volkman, D. A., & Gungor, B. (2017). Determinants of bank efficiency in Turkey: Participation banks versus conventional banks. *Borsa Istanbul Review, 17*(2), 86–96. https://doi.org/10.1016/j.bir.2017.02.003

Hardy, L. (2012). The evolution of participation banking in Turkey. *Online Journal on Southwest Asia and Islamic Civilization*, Winter, 1–15.

Jan, S., Ullah, K., & Jabeen, Z. (2018). Musharakah in constructing housing flats. *Journal of Islamic Business and Management, 8*(S), 239–249.

Osman, B. B. (1999). The experience of the Sudanese Islamic bank in partnership (Musharakah) financing as a tool for rural development among small farmers in Sudan. *Arab Law Quarterly, 14*(3), 221–230.

Sadr, K. (1999). The experience of the Sudanese Islamic bank in partnership (Musharakah) financing as a tool for rural development among small farmers in Sudan: The role of Musharakah financing in the agricultural bank of Iran. *Arab Law Quarterly, 14*(3), 245–256.

Sadr, K., & Iqbal, Z. (2002). Choice between debt and equity contracts and asymmetrical information: Some empirical evidence. In M. Iqbal & D. T. Llewellyn (Eds.), *Islamic Banking and Finance: New perspectives on profit-sharing and risk* (pp. 139–154). Edward Elgar.

Yasseri, A. (2002). Islamic banking contracts as enforced in Iran. In M. Iqbal & D. T. Llewellyn (Eds.), *Islamic Banking and Finance: New perspectives on profit-sharing and risk* (pp. 155–167). Edward Elgar.

CHAPTER 9

Adaptation in Participatory Islamic Finance to Constraints and Its Outcomes

This chapter presents the curious case of the Islamic banking industry of Pakistan that has revealed a sudden and a significant increase in *Musharakah*-based financing after 2013 and the adaption process that has induced this meaningful change. The chapter begins with the description of this paradigm shift in the financing portfolio of the overall Islamic banking industry that is characterized by an unexpected surge in the *Musharakah*-based financing and a shift away from *Murabahah*-based financing. This discussion is followed by a brief discussion on the evolution of Islamic baking in Pakistan, and how the evolutionary banking model provides grounds for this paradigm shift.

This discussion is followed by a detailed discussion on the obscured adaptation in the Islamic participatory financing products to the prevailing constraints, and how these adaptations have paved the way for this sudden surge in participation-based financing in Pakistan. For this purpose, this chapter explores the adaptations in *Musharakah*-based working capital financing, consumer financing, and commodity operations financing in the Islamic banking industry of Pakistan, and presents the Constraints, Adaptation, and Outcomes (CAO) framework of participatory finance.[1] The first construct of this framework conceptualizes the constraints to the participatory financing and their typology. The second construct outlines

---

[1] For details on how this framework was empirically developed see Nouman (2019).

© The Author(s), under exclusive license to Springer Nature Singapore Pte Ltd. 2023
M. Nouman and K. Ullah, *Participatory Islamic Finance*, https://doi.org/10.1007/978-981-19-9555-2_9

157

the typology of adaptation to conceptualize the structural variations in participatory financing products in response to the constraints. While the third construct represents the typology of the outcomes of adaptation to conceptualize how effectively adaptation resolves the key constraints to participatory financing.

9.1 The Curious Case of *Musharakah* Spur in Pakistan

In Pakistan Islamic bank had a consistent tendency to avoid profit and loss sharing from inception till 2013 due to the factors discussed in Chapter 8. Therefore, their operations were by far based the non-participatory modes of financing. However, Islamic banking industry of Pakistan showed considerable progress in terms of the application of participatory financing after 2013. Consequently, the assets side of the balance sheet of Islamic banks operating in Pakistan transformed swiftly, whereby the share of *Murabahah* financing in the overall financing mix of Islamic banks dropped from the 39.7% in December 2012 to 13.7% by December 2020 (see Table 9.1 and Fig. 9.1). On the other hand, the share of *Musharakah* financing grew from 0.8 to 22.7% within less than a decade (December 2012 to December 2020).

Table 9.1 Financing mix of Islamic banking industry of Pakistan (percentage share)

Modes	Dec-12	Dec-13	Dec-14	Dec-15	Dec-16	Dec-17	Dec-18	Dec-19	Dec-20
Murabahah	39.7	40.6	30.1	24.5	15.8	13.2	13.6	12.9	13.7
Ijarah	9.3	7.7	7.7	6.6	6.8	6.4	6.2	5.7	4.8
Musharakah	0.8	6.7	11	14	15.6	22	19.9	19.8	22.7
Mudarabah	0.2	0.2	0.1	0	0	0	0	0	0
Diminishing Musharakah	36.2	30.8	32.6	31.7	34.7	30.7	33.3	34.1	33.6
Salam	3	4	4.5	5.3	4.4	2.8	2.4	2.6	1.9
Istisna	6.5	5.6	8.3	8.6	8.4	8.2	9.1	9.5	8.3
Others	4.3	4.4	5.6	9.3	14.3	16.7	15.5	15.4	15
Total	100	100	100	100	100	100	100	100	100

Source State Bank of Pakistan (2012–2020)

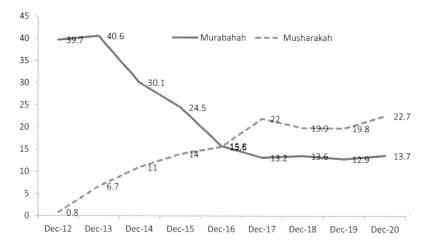

Fig. 9.1 Shift in the share of *Musharakah* and *Murabahah*-based financing

The major reason behind the shift in the financing portfolio of the Islamic banking industry of Pakistan can be contributed to the adaptation in the structure of *Musharakah* financing. Islamic banks have adapted the standard *Musharakah* mode of financing to create a variety of financial services in different contexts. This adaptation has allowed Islamic banks to offer several new participatory financing products to cope with the growing demands of the modern industry. The adaptation in *Musharakah*-based financing is explained in Sect. 9.3.

9.2 Detour: Adaptability of the Islamic Banking in Pakistan

This section takes a slight detour to conceptualize the evolution of Islamic banking in Pakistan, and how the evolutionary banking model provides grounds for this paradigm shift. Adaptation is not a novel phenomenon in the Islamic banking industry of Pakistan. Islamic banking has been evolving from the inception to resolve constraints and sustain. In fact, the present Islamic banking system is an outcome of the continuous adaptation in the obscure Islamic banking system introduced in Pakistan in the early 1980s. The adaptability of Islamic banking stems from the transition of the Islamic banking system from revolutionary framework to the evolutionary framework. Government of Pakistan adopted the revolutionary regulatory framework in the early 1980s to abruptly Islamize the country's banking system. Under a revolutionary framework a centrally designed structure is applied to the overall industry which has to be followed firmly to establish a desired planned system. However, Islamic banking failed in this framework due to several constraints including the lack of flexibility in the new banking system to meet the ever-changing needs of the dynamic market, lack of mechanisms to ensure the *Shari'ah* compliance, the deficient infrastructure, and the inability of the stakeholders to play their roles in the new system.

After having the dissatisfactory outcome of the evolutionary framework, Pakistan adopted an evolutionary framework, and the Islamic banking system was re-launched in 2003. The current evolutionary framework allows continuous adaptation in the Islamic banking products to cope with the ever-changing environment, remain competitive in the local and global market, and achieve *Shari'ah* compliance. Within the current dynamic framework State Bank of Pakistan (SBP) as regulator allows Banks to design services and adapt them with in *Shari'ah* boundaries to meet the diversified needs of the market. The Islamic banking departments of SBP issues model contracts and minimum prudential regulations while the rest of the service design process lies in the hands of Banks.[2]

9.3 Constraints, Adaptation, and Outcomes (CAO) Framework of Participatory Islamic Finance

The shift in the financing portfolio of the Islamic banking industry of Pakistan is predominantly induced by the recent adaptations in the service design of *Musharakah* financing. Adaptation refers to the process of altering the contents or structure of a service product into context which can better be achieved through enactment of various positive list, negative list, and range varieties in the product structures, to enable the product sustainability in new contexts. Managers adapt to cope with the changing environment through the design of a matching structure and choice of an appropriate strategy.

---

[2] See Nouman et al. (2022). For detailed discussion on the factors that have induced the recent spur of participatory finance in Pakistan.

Islamic banks operating in Pakistan continuously adapt their services to remain competitive and resolve constraints. The menu of their services grows with the emergence of new needs in the market and changing market conditions. New services are introduced by altering the designs of the earlier services through inclusion and exclusion in service components[3] which ultimately lead to the adaptation in the products and scope of Islamic banks.

Islamic banks operating in Pakistan have adapted the standard *Musharakah* mode of financing to create a variety of financial services in different contexts. This adaptation has allowed Islamic banks to offer several new products to cope with the growing demands of the modern industry and resolve the constraints to the pure *Musharakah*-based financing. Moreover, it has induced the spur of *Musharakah*-based financing in the Islamic banking industry of Pakistan.

Islamic banks are currently offering the adapted variant of *Musharakah* in three key areas including working capital financing, consumer financing, and commodity operations financing. Therefore, adaptations in these three areas of financing including (i) working capital financing (WCF), (ii) consumer financing (CF), and (iii) commodity operations financing (COF) are presented to explore:

i. Why Islamic banks have adapted *Musharakah* mode of financing?
ii. How have they adapted it? And
iii. What are the outcomes of *Musharakah* adaptation?

This chapter answers these questions by presenting the Constraints, Adaptation, and Outcomes (CAO) framework of participatory finance[4] to

---

[3] Inclusion in service refers to introducing new options, facilities, and benefits in the existing services, while exclusion in service refers to the withdrawal of the unattractive features of the existing services.

[4] We proposed the CAO framework is proposed in Nouman (2019). This framework was developed in three steps. In the first step, the Qualitative Content Analysis was applied for the analysis of data (which was collected through in-depth interviews, personal observations, and documents) in each case study using the NVivo software. The analysis of individual case studies using QCA helped in developing inductively two a posteriori frameworks including (*i*) the typology of adaptation and (*ii*) the typology of the outcomes in each case, respectively. In the second step, the adaptation and outcomes typologies of both cases were synthesized, through cross-case synthesis, to come up with a generalized typology of adaptation and outcomes respectively. This was important because these

conceptualize the adaptation in *Musharakah* and its role in resolving the constraints to *Musharakah* financing. Table 9.2 presents the details of the selected *Musharakah*-based products, while Fig. 9.2 presents the CAO framework.

Table 9.2 Details of the selected *Musharakah*-based products

Case study	Description	Current Financing Mode
Working Capital Financing (WCF)	WCF refers to a variety of financing products offered by Islamic banks to meet the working capital financing needs of SMEs and corporations. Various WCF products are available in the term structure and running *Musharakah* structure. Moreover, various specialized products are also offered by Islamic banks to cater the off balance sheet financing needs of multinational corporations and large corporations. Banks can apply *Murabahah, Istisna, Tijarah, Musawamah, Bai Salam*, and Running *Musharakah* for WCF	Running *Musharakah*
Consumer Financing (CF)	CF refers to a variety of *Shari'ah* compliant consumer financing products offered by Islamic banks. The CF products include house financing, car/automobile financing, and durable goods financing facility for purchasing consumer durable goods, such as air conditioners, refrigerators, generators; banks can apply *Murabahah, Musawamah*, and diminishing *Musharakah* modes for CF	Diminishing *Musharakah*
Commodity Operations Financing (COF)	COF refers to financing provided either to government, public sector corporations or private sector for procurement of commodities. In Pakistan the government initiates commodity operations to support the prices of domestic agricultural products (particularly wheat). Banks can apply *Murabahah* and running *Musharakah* for COF	Running *Musharakah*

emergent frameworks had nuances at the micro-level in each case. While in the third step, the participatory finance constraints framework presented in Chapter 5, and the generalized typologies of adaptation and outcomes were then synthesized to develop a novel Constraints, Adaptation, and Outcomes (CAO) framework. See Nouman (2019) for detailed discussion on why and how this framework was developed.

9 ADAPTATION IN PARTICIPATORY ISLAMIC FINANCE ... 163

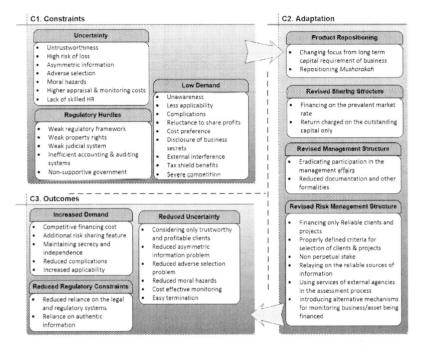

Fig. 9.2 Constraints, Adaptation, and Outcomes (CAO) framework of participatory finance (*Source* Nouman, 2019)

The first construct of the CAO framework provides insight into the constraints to participatory financing to answer the question 'why Islamic banks have adapted *Musharakah* mode of financing.' Similarly, the second construct conceptualizes the adaptation in *Musharakah*, this construct answers the question of 'how participatory financing has been adapted?'. While the third construct conceptualizes the outcomes of adaptation in *Musharakah*. This construct answers the question 'how adaptation resolves the constraints to participatory finance?' The constructs of the CAO framework are discussed in the following subsections.

Constraints to Musharakah *Financing*

The first construct of CAO framework conceptualizes the constraints to participatory finance. This construct is based on the constraints framework presented in Chapter 5. This framework indicates that there are several constraints to participatory financing which put *Musharakah* and *Mudarabah* on less advantageous position compared to the non-participatory financing arrangements and lead to the banks' lower preference for the participatory financing. These constraints can be broadly classified into three categories namely (a) uncertainty, (b) low demand, and (c) regulatory constraints.

a. Uncertainty

Uncertainty entails the factors in the contemporary business settings, prevailing social setting, and the bank's internal environment that underpin uncertainty in the viability of participatory financing arrangements. These factors include lack of reliability and trustworthiness in the society, lack of skilled HR, higher costs associated to the project appraisal and monitoring, risk-averse depositors, and agency problems including the asymmetric information, adverse selection, and moral hazard problems.

b. Low demand

Similarly, there are several the inherent characteristics of participatory modes of financing and few external factors which lead to the *lower demand* for participatory financing compared to the non-participatory financing. These factors include the less applicability of participatory financing, complications in structuring and dealing with such arrangements, higher cost, lack of secrecy and independence, external interference in the business affairs, unfair treatment in taxation, severe competition, and lack of understanding and familiarity in the society.

c. Regulatory constraints

On the other hand, the *regulatory constraints* indicate that the current regulatory structure restrains the viability of participatory financing in several ways. The major regulatory constraints include: non-supportive regulatory framework, restrictive prudential regulations, weak property rights, weak judicial systems, inefficient auditing and accounting systems, lack of liquid and deep secondary markets, and lack of government support.

Since most of these constraints are beyond the control of banks, therefore, the banks operating in Pakistan have adopted the adaptation strategy whereby they have adapted the design of the Musharakah contract keeping in view the market demands. Thus constraints have triggered the process of adaptation in the participatory financing within the Islamic banking industry of Pakistan. Section 9.2 describes the typology of adaptations in *Musharakah*.

Adaptation in Musharakah

The second construct of the CAO framework suggests that banks have adapted the design of pure *Musharakah* arrangement to cope with the constraints through inclusion and exclusion of service components. Consequently, different variants of *Musharakah* have emerged including Running *Musharakah* (RM) and Diminishing *Musharakah* (DM). At the macro-level, this construct indicates that four structural reforms are inherent in the *Musharakah* adaptation across the selected case studies including (a) product repositioning, (b) revised sharing structure, (c) revised management structure, and (d) revised the risk management structure.

a. **Product Repositioning**

The first component of *Musharakah* adaptation is *product repositioning*. Islamic banks have repositioned *Musharakah* by: (i) changing focus from long-term equity financing to non-perceptual/short-term capital requirements of clients, and (ii) restructuring *Musharakah* to make these fit for SME financing, corporate financing, consumer financing, and commodity operations financing within the embedded contractual variants of *Musharakah*, namely diminishing *Musharakah* and running *Musharakah*.

i. *Changing focus from long-term equity financing to non-perceptual/short-term capital requirements of clients*

Pure *Musharakah* is originally applied in two forms including *Shirkat ul Aqad* and *Shirkat ul Milk*. *Shirkat ul Aqad* involves joint ownership of a business enterprise while *Shirkat ul Milk* involves joint ownership of an asset. Thus, pure *Musharakah* is originally a long-term financing mode whereby financier either invests funds in the form of equity to become perpetual partner in the business (*Sahirkat ul Aqad*), or becomes joint owner of an asset (*Shirkat ul Milk*). However, adaptation has allowed Islamic banks to reposition *Musharakah* to meet the non-perceptual/short-term capital requirements of clients.

ii. *Restructuring Musharakah to make these fit for SME financing, corporate financing, consumer financing, and commodity operations*

Presently, running *Musharakah* (RM) is used to support the day-to-day operational needs of SMEs and corporations, and financing needs of government for commodity operations, while diminishing *Musharakah* (DM) is used to support the consumer financing needs.

Among the consumer finance products the house financing and car/automobile financing[5] are based on DM which has emerged from *Shirkat-al-Milk*. In house financing arrangement Islamic bank and the customer contribute a certain amount of financing which is utilized for purchasing, construction, or renovation of the property. Consequently, customer and Islamic bank becomes joint owner of property whereby the bank's share in the property is divided into ownership units. Customer uses the property and in return pays a periodic rent (usually monthly) to the bank. Moreover, he/she promises (through undertaking to purchase) to buy the bank's share in the property gradually over a certain period of time. Therefore, the bank ownership decreases in the property every month and vice versa. The rent is adjusted every month on the basis of bank's outstanding ownership (units) in the property. Eventually, bank's ownership diminishes and title to the property is completely transferred

---

[5] The car financing product of most of the major Islamic banks is based on the principle of *Ijarah*. However, few Islamic banks have based their car financing based on the principle of diminishing *Musharakah*.

to the customer. In such arrangements loss, if any, shall be borne by the bank and customer in the proportion of their respective investments. On the other hand, the mechanism of the car financing is similar to the house financing; however, unlike house financing the ownership of the car is not divided into distinct units. Moreover, the monthly rent is adjusted in a way that it remains constant throughout a year.

On the other hand, the running *Musharakah* (RM) product has been introduced as an alternative for running finance and conventional commodity operations financing. In case of working capital financing arrangement, financing is extended to support the day-to-day operational needs of a business. Conventional running finance is a revolving credit arrangement whereby a maximum limit is determined by the business and the financier. Business is allowed to withdraw any amount to the extent of allowed limit and can return the extra funds at any time. The business has to pay interest only on the amount that has actually been withdrawn, and a commitment fee on the unused portion of the agreed limit. RM is a *Shari'ah* compliant alternative to running finance product where bank shares the profit and losses of the business instead of charging interest and commitment fee.

Similarly, Islamic banks also use running *Musharakah* for financing the commodity operations. Under such arrangement, bank usually provides funds to government departments for the procurement of domestic agricultural products, particularly wheat. The selling price is determined in advance. The selling price is usually set higher than the purchasing price because the difference between the selling price and the buying price is paid to the bank as a profit.

In the nutshell, *Musharakah* has been restructured as RM to meet the short-term financing needs of large corporations and SMEs, and financing needs of government departments for the commodity operations. Moreover, it has been restructured as DM to meet the needs of consumers for the financing of fixed assets.

b. Revised Sharing Structure

The second component of adaptation is the *revised sharing structure*. The revised sharing structure involves two underlying adaptations including (i) financing on the prevalent market rate and (ii) charging return on the outstanding capital only.

i. *Financing on the prevalent market rate*

In case of pure *Musharakah*, business has to share the real profit with the financier. In adapted variants, however, the bank's share in profit is adjusted to the prevalent market rate by putting a cap on it. For example, in case of working capital financing, a ceiling is determined for bank's share of profit that is usually benchmarked with the Karachi Inter Bank Offered Rate (KIBOR). If the profit of the business is below the ceiling rate, the actual profit is shared with the bank in the ratio of capital contribution. However, if the profit exceeds the ceiling rate, bank's share of profit is calculated on the basis of the ceiling rate while the profit above the ceiling rate goes to the client. Bank usually does not have claim on the additional profit; however, in certain situations it may get only a negligible share in the profit above the ceiling rate, e.g., up to 1% of the profit above KIBOR.

Similarly, in case of commodity operations financing (COF), the bank's profit share is determined in advance which is usually close to the KIBOR. This is done by determining the minimum buying and selling price of the commodity under consideration. However, if government decides to sell the commodities at a lower rate, the deficit in the buying and selling rate has to be paid by the government in the form of subsidies. On the other hand, if commodities are sold at higher than the minimum selling rate, bank gets a negligible portion of the additional profit. Thus the bank's share of profit is benchmarked to the prevalent market rate.

On the other hand, profit and loss sharing cannot be applied in the consumer asset financing since it involve fixed/durable assets which are usually handed over to the clients for their personal usage. To cope with this issue bank leases the asset being financed to client on *Ijarah* basis. In return client has to pay periodically a predetermined rent for the bank's share of asset. To remain competitive Islamic banks charge rent on the prevailing market rate by benchmarking it with the KIBOR.

ii. *Charging return on the outstanding capital only*

The second inherent adaptation in the revised sharing structure is *charging return on the utilized portion of capital*. In *Musharakah* arrangement each partner gets share in the profit in the pre-agreed ratio regardless of the fact that whether his capital is utilized or not. However, in case of adapted variants, banks get profit on the utilized portion of capital only. For example, when RM is utilized for working capital financing and commodity operations financing, the client has the option to return surplus funds at any time. The bank's share in the profit is determined on the daily outstanding capital basis. Similarly, in case of DM the bank's share in the property is divided into units and rent per unit is determined. Customer has to pay rent for the bank's outstanding units and has to purchase a certain number of units every month. The rent is adjusted accordingly with the decrease in the bank's ownership. Thus, both in RM and DM, the profit is paid on the utilized portion of capital only.

c. Revised Management Structure

The third component of the adaptation is *revised management structure*. Islamic banks have adapted the management structure of *Musharakah* for RM and DM by: (i) eradicating participation in management and (ii) relaxing the documentation requirements and other formalities.

i. *Eradicating participation in management*

In pure *Musharakah* all partners have the right to participate in the management affairs except the sleeping partners. However, in a RM arrangement bank does not participate in the management affairs. Similarly, in DM arrangement fixed assets are involved instead of business venture which are handed over to the client on the *Ijarah* basis. Thus, the client is independent in using the asset and the bank usually does not participate or interfere in the usage of the asset.

ii. *Reduced documentation requirements and other formalities*

Unlike pure *Musharakah*, bank does not have access to internal accounts in RM arrangement. Rather, the financial statements are used for the estimation of profit or losses incurred during a period which consequently reduces the documentation requirement and other formalities. Thus, RM has lower documentation requirements compared to pure *Musharakah* and other modes of financing. Similarly, management of the consumer financing arrangements is very simple, involving no formalities and complexities. Customer uses the asset being financed and pays a predetermined rent to the bank. Thus, the documentation requirements and other formalities are negligible in the consumer financing.

d. Revised Risk Management Structure

The fourth component of adaptation is the *revised risk management structure*. Islamic banks have revised their risk management structure by introducing extensive risk management practices for running *Musharakah* (RM) and diminishing *Musharakah* (DM). The revised risk management structure of DM and RM is characterized by six adaptations including (i) non-perpetual stake, (ii) financing only reliable clients and projects, (iii) devising extensive mechanisms for the assessment and selection of clients and projects, (iv) using services of external agencies in the assessment process, (v) relying on the reliable sources of information, and (vi) introducing alternative mechanisms for monitoring business/asset being financed.

i. *Non-perpetual stake*

Unlike pure Musharakah, banks do not take perpetual stake in the asset/venture being financed through the adapted variants of Musharakah. For example, in RM arrangement, banks do short-term investment in the form of working capital financing and commodity operations financing to meet the short-term capital requirements of businesses and government departments respectively. Similarly, in case of DM banks have non-perpetual stake in the assets being financed because the bank's ownership in the asset diminishes gradually over an agreed period of time and the client eventually becomes sole owner of the asset.

ii. *Financing only dependable clients and projects*

Islamic banks consider only reliable clients and projects for participatory financing. Since RM is a risky product, therefore, Islamic banks are currently offering RM-based working capital financing to reliable businesses only including blue-chip corporations and top performing SMEs, and to government departments for commodity operations financing. Similarly, Islamic banks are considering only reliable clients and secure assets in the DM arrangements to reduce the underlying risks. Furthermore, to mitigate the chances of loss, in case of default, the asset being financed is mortgaged by the bank. Moreover, the bank uses the *Takaful* (Islamic insurance) coverage to reduce the accidental damages and losses from natural calamities.

iii. *Devising extensive mechanisms for the assessment and selection of clients and projects*

Banks have devised an extensive mechanism for the assessment and selection of projects/assets. For example, in case of RM banks have set criteria for the assessment of different businesses including corporations, small enterprises, and medium enterprises whereby many factors are considered including their minimum eligibility, credit history, current financial position, performance, business cycle, experience in using the external financing, and their prior experience with the bank. On the contrary, reliability of the clients is not an issue in the commodity operations financing arrangements because it is offered to only government departments.[6] However, banks have to do proper assessment to ensure the suitability of the project/commodities under consideration.

In case of DM the assessment is done in two phases. In the first phase the client is assessed to judge his/her payment behavior and ability. A minimum eligibility criterion has been defined for each type of customer and a formal mechanism has been designed for the assessment of each client. For example, in the first step personal assessment of the client is done where bank assesses the person himself, his education, profession, police track record, CIB track record, and financial track record to judge his payment behavior. In the second step, bank performs the financial assessment of the client to judge his/her payment ability. In the financial assessment bank estimates the monthly installment the client has to pay, his monthly income and monthly expenditure on the bare necessities like children schoolings, medical expenditures, groceries, etc. to determine whether the client would be able to pay the monthly installments.

---

[6] When running *Musharakah* is applied for commodity operations financing, the risk is extremely low. The default risk is zero because government never defaults. Similarly, the risk of loss is also negligible because if the selling price is lower than the deficit would be paid from the food subsidies.

In the second phase the asset under consideration is assessed to ensure its suitability for financing. A formal mechanism has been devised for the assessment of asset. The assessment of the asset is done in various steps by specialized personnel. Moreover, different departments are involved in the assessment process.

iv. *Using services of external agencies in the assessment process*

Banks also seek help from external bodies during the assessment process. For example, banks use the services of the State Bank of Pakistan (i.e., Credit Information Bureau [CIB]) for the credit history of the clients. Moreover, bank may also use the services of registered external agencies for income estimation of the clients. Similarly, in case of DM, banks may use the services of registered property dealers for the estimation of market value of the property, and the services of registered property evaluators to ensure the suitability of the property.

v. *Using reliable sources of information*

Islamic banks rely on reliable sources of information. In case of running *Musharakah*, they use audited versions of the financial statements to ensure the authenticity of the financial information shared by the corporations and government departments. On the other hand, in case of consumer financing banks use different sources of information, authenticate the information being provided by the client, and cross match information from different sources to ensure authenticity of information. For example, in case of DM property evaluation is done by done by property evaluators who are registered members of Pakistan Bank's Association (PBA). Similarly, manager's visit report is also an integral part of the assessment process. The bank matches the manager visit report, property evaluation report and the title documents to ensure that the information in all these documents is consistent.

vi. *Alternative mechanisms for monitoring the business/assets being financed*

Being a sleeping partner in RM and DM-based arrangements, Islamic banks do not participate directory in the management affairs. There fore, they have devised alternative mechanisms for monitoring the business/assets being financed. For example, in the case of working capital financing a running *Musharakah* finance model is developed in advance keeping in view the data provided by the business. In the running *Musharakah* model, a calculation sheet is developed which is used to estimate expected profit, in advance, by looking at the past three years historical financial figures including financial history, inventories, etc. The bank monitors the financial performance of the business using this model by comparing the actual performance with the expected performance.

On the other hand, in case of commodity operations financing software is used for tracking the inflows and outflows of the concerned commodities in the warehouse. Due to software the actual income and expense allocation has become very easy. In all the new warehouses software is being used which maintains the record of all inflows and outflows. The inflows and outflows are determined by recording value of the assets at the time of arrival of asset in the warehouse and at the time of disbursement from the warehouse. The difference between these two determines the everyday sales. The expense and the fixed cost are also easy to determine for example salary of the people working there, etc. Previously, these were difficult to determine because bank had to rely on the files or registers maintained by the department which are now replaced by computer software. Similarly, in case of DM the asset being financed (especially car) is monitored by the bank. For this purpose tracking device is installed to track the car being financed by the bank. Moreover, the properties are monitored through proper personal visits by bank's agents.

Outcomes of Adaptation

The third construct of CAO framework indicates that the constraints to participatory finance have resolved significantly as the outcome of adaptation. Analysis of the case studies and the cross-case synthesis suggest three major outcomes of the *Musharakah* adaptation including (a) increased demand, (b) reduced uncertainty, and (c) reduced regulatory constraints.

a. **Increased Demand**

The adaptation in real *Musharakah* has helped in resolving most of the constraints that hamper the demand for participatory financing. The following factors have contributed to increasing demand for participatory financing in Pakistan:

i. *Competitive financing cost*

The first factor contributing toward the increased demand is the competitive financing cost. One of the most dominant factors contributing to the lower demand for *Musharakah* is its high cost of financing. One of the basic reasons for this problem is the requirement of *Musharakah* to share the actual profit of the business. Clients do not want to disclose or share their actual profits with the bank, because they may end up paying a very high cost of financing than the prevalent market rate. Secondly, conventional banks provide financing to businesses on a pre-determined rate without having any concern with the actual profit. Therefore, clients are reluctant to use *Musharakah*-based financing, because they can get financing at a comparatively lower rate from conventional banks or by using non-participatory modes of Islamic finance.

To resolve this issue the profit distribution ratio of running *Musharakah* (RM) is linked to KIBOR, contrary to the pure *Musharakah* arrangement where actual profit of the business is shared among the partners. Thus, in a RM arrangement financier gets capital at the prevalent market rate. Similarly, in diminishing *Musharakah* (DM) arrangement rent is charged because profit and loss sharing is not possible in consumer asset financing. The rent is linked to the benchmark rate, i.e., the KIBOR to ensure that client gets capital at the prevalent market rate.

ii. *Additional risk-sharing feature*

The cost of financing in RM arrangement is not only competitive but also offers additional benefits. Unlike non-participatory-based and conventional financing schemes, RM offers an additional risk-sharing feature. In a RM arrangement, if the actual profit is higher than the ceiling (KIBOR) rate, bank gets share up to the ceiling rate, while the profit above ceiling rate goes to the entrepreneur. However, bank gets share on the actual profit ratio if actual profit is lower than the ceiling rate. Furthermore, if business incurs losses, bank is responsible to share losses of the business in the ratio of capital contribution. This adaptation has provided a competitive edge to RM over the non-participatory modes of Islamic finance, and conventional financing. Moreover, it has led to resolve the demand issue.

Similarly in case of DM, being joint owner of the asset, bank is responsible to bear the risks. For example, if the asset (e.g., vehicle), being financed via DM, goes under an accident, the bank does not charge any rent during the time span in which the asset is under maintenance. For example, if the repair requires two months, customer will not pay the rent of those two months.

iii. *Maintaining secrecy and independence*

Many businesses avoid participatory financing to avoid external interference. Moreover, they do not want to disclose their business secrets. In a RM arrangement though bank becomes partner in the business, however, the secrecy issue does not persist. The 'no participation in management affairs feature' of RM and the 'reliance on the financial statements for information' help in resolving this issue and maintaining the secrecy and independence of the business.

On the other hand, the issue of secrecy does not arise in case of DM because focus has been changed from business financing to consumer asset financing. In a DM arrangement though bank becomes partner in the asset, however, the interference issue also does persist because bank hands over the asset being financed to the client on the *Ijarah* basis. The client is independent in using the asset and bank normally does not participate or interfere in the usage of the asset:

iv. *Reduced complications*

Pure *Musharakah* is considered as a complicated product because it is difficult to structure and deal with due to extensive documentation and other formalities. As discussed in the preceding section the documentation and other formalities have been reduced in RM arrangement. This has helped in reducing the complications in RM arrangement, making it a very simple product to structure and deal with compared to other financing schemes. For example, in case of commodity operations financing the government departments were pushing the Islamic banks to develop a structure in which (i) the documentation requirement is low, and (ii) they get advantage in case of early repayment. Both of these issues got resolved in running *Musharakah*. Thus these are two important reasons due to which they have converted their entire commodity operations from *Murabahah* financing to *Musharakah* financing.

Similarly, in case of DM, once the asset is being financed the customer has to pay installment covering the principal amount and rent every month. Thus the management of the financing arrangement is very simple for both bank and client involving no formalities and complexities.

v. *Increased applicability*

Pure *Musharakah* is acclaimed to have lower applicability in the modern complicated business world due to its lack of flexibility. The adaptation in pure *Musharakah* has helped in increasing the applicability of RM arrangement since it suits the needs of modern businesses. For example, RM is a very effective tool for working capital financing, running finance, and commodity operations financing. Previously, mainly conventional banks were involved in the commodity operations financing while Islamic banks had a negligible share because they lacked flexible products that could effectively meet the requirements of government departments. However, with the introduction of running *Musharakah*, Islamic banks have also got a significant share in the commodity operations financing.

Similarly, the demand for working capital financing via RM has increased because banks have provided a good alternative for demand finance or running finance. If *Tijara* or *Istisna* mode is used for this purpose, it involves a restriction that client has to produce finished products for the bank and will sell these products as the agent of the bank. Most of the companies are reluctant to use *Istisna* because they do not want to put themselves in such formalities. On the contrary, RM does not require such formalities.

In the nutshell, the issue of low demand for *Musharakah* has resolved because it has been adapted keeping in view the market needs. First, the cost of MF has become competitive because Islamic banks have become able to offer *Musharakah* financing on the prevalent market rate due to the revised sharing structure. Second, Islamic banks have got a competitive edge over the conventional running finance product due to the inherent additional risk-sharing feature of the RM. Third, the secrecy and independence of the business are ensured in RM due to it no participation in management feature. Fourth, the structuring and operation of *Musharakah arrangements* have become very simple due to reduced complications and formalities. Finally, the applicability of *Musharakah* has increased significantly because RM has been developed keeping in view the industry needs.

b. Reduced Uncertainty

There are several factors that induce uncertainty in the participatory financing. For example, there is a lack of trustworthiness in the market. Moreover, *Musharakah* arrangements have agency problems including asymmetric information, adverse selection, and moral hazards. To cope with these problems Islamic banks have devised extensive risk management structure. For example, Islamic banks try to play safely and consider only reliable clients and secure projects. RM is currently offered to only secure businesses, including top performing SMEs and leading blue-chip firms, for working capital financing, and to government departments for commodity operations financing.

Similarly, in case of DM, banks consider only secure assets for financing. Furthermore, Islamic banks rely on the reliable sources of information and have developed an extensive mechanism for the evaluation and selection of clients and projects. These extensive risk management procedures enable the banks to reduce the problems of asymmetric information, adverse selection, and moral hazards. Furthermore, Islamic banks use the Takaful coverage to reduce the risk of accidental losses. Similarly, to reduce the chances of loss in case of default, bank finances only a portion of asset and mortgages the assets being financed. While in case of vehicle financing bank uses trackers to reduce the chances of theft. These steps help in reducing the chances of loss significantly.

Similarly, since banks usually do not have enough access to the internal information of the clients/businesses. Furthermore, banks have limited expertise in the assessment of the ventures and assets. Thus, the lack of skilled human resource and limited access to information can make bank vulnerable to adverse selection and/or moral hazards problem. To avoid this problem banks are using services of professional agencies for the assessment of the ventures/assets to be financed. Furthermore, once reliability of a business/asset is ensured, bank selects the appropriate mode of financing keeping in view the needs of the business. This helps in reducing, further, the chances of moral hazards because bank does not go for participatory financing if the needs of the business can be fulfilled through other less risky modes of financing.

In addition, participatory financing is blamed for having high monitoring cost. Therefore, they have devised alternative cost-effective mechanisms for monitoring the business/assets being financed. Thus, the issue of higher monitoring cost has reduced significantly. Similarly, the product repositioning adaptation has also proved helpful in reducing uncertainty. *Musharakah* basically involves long-term equity-based financing. In RM on the other hand, focus has been shifted to the day-to-day operational needs of the business and short-term capital requirements of government departments. This adaptation has helped in reducing uncertainty significantly along with other benefits because RM arrangement is easy to structure and terminate contrary to pure *Musharakah* arrangement.

Thus, if bank feels that performance of the business is not up to the par, they can withdraw their investment easily since they do not have long-term stake in the business. Similarly, bank has non-perpetual stake in the DM arrangements. Moreover, the ownership of bank diminishes automatically at the end of the financing period and the title of the asset is transferred to the client. Thus the termination of the DM arrangement is very easy.

In the nutshell, the uncertainty underlying the participatory financing has reduced significantly in several ways due to the adaptation. First, Islamic banks are now able to attract and select reliable clients and suitable projects. Second, the asymmetric information problem has reduced significantly. Third, the adverse selection problem has reduced significantly due to reduction in the asymmetric information problem and development of proper evaluation and selection procedure. Fourth, the moral hazards have reduced significantly due to selection of reliable clients and suitable projects. Fifth, the cost of mentoring has reduced significantly. Finally, the structuring and termination of MF has become very easy thus bank can inject capital or withdraw its investment very easily.

c. **Reduced Regulatory Constraints**

The third component of outcomes is the reduced regulatory constraints. The constraints framework indicates that there are several factors in the regulatory environment of developing countries that restraint the application and successful operation of participatory financing. For example, the current regulatory environment of most developing countries including Pakistan is characterized by weak regulatory framework, inefficient judicial system, and weak property rights. Furthermore, there is a lack of government support in the promotion of participatory financing. However, the adaptation in *Musharakah* has allowed Islamic banks to cope with the regulatory constraints by devising alternative mechanisms to cope with these regulatory constraints and increase its viability. For example:

i. *Reduced reliance on the regulatory and judicial system for the resolution of disputes*

Islamic banks have reduced their reliance on the regulatory and judicial system for the resolution of disputes and protection of their property rights by playing with utmost care. To avoid disputes Islamic banks finance only the secure clients and undisputed assets. That is why Islamic banks are allowing RM to only blue-chip companies for working capital financing and to government departments for commodity operations financing. Similarly, in case of DM, Islamic bank tries to secure itself from disputes and legal formalities through mortgage, legal documentation, and declarations form the clients. Furthermore, bank also secures the right of liquidating the property in case of default through written agreement in advance. Moreover, bank uses the services of legal experts who evaluate the legal complexities in each case and advice the bank to take preemptive measures in advance.

ii. *Relying on authentic information*

The current accounting and auditing system is weak. Businesses prepare many versions of financial statements to avoid taxation. Thus, in the absence of a strong accounting system, bank becomes vulnerable to asymmetric information problem, which may lead to adverse selection and moral hazards problem. To avoid this problem banks ensure the authenticity of the information shared by the clients with the bank. For this purpose Islamic banks are currently allowing RM to leading SMEs (that are willing to share their actual financial information with the banks), government departments, and blue-chip firms. The blue-chip corporations follow accounting standards and publish audited financial statements. Therefore, their activities are comparatively transparent. Thus, by selecting blue-chip firms the issue of weak accounting system is resolved significantly.

Similarly, in case of government financing banks use audited versions of the financial statements to ensure the authenticity of the financial information shared by the government departments. On the other hand, in case of DM, the product repositioning has helped in reducing this constraint significantly. Moreover, Islamic banks are relying on the reliable sources of information and the information from different sources is cross matched to ensure the authenticity of the information. This adaptation helps in reducing reliance on the current accounting systems for information, and reducing the asymmetric information and adverse selection problems significantly.

In the nutshell, Islamic banks evade the chances of disputes by selecting reliable clients and less risky assets. Hence, they reduce their reliance on the current legal system for the resolution of disputes. Similarly, the adapted management structure and the extensive risk management structure help in reducing reliance on the current accounting and legal system for information and reducing the asymmetric information and adverse selection problems significantly. Consequently, the adaptation has not only reduced the uncertainty underlying the participatory financing but has also helped in reducing the regulatory constraints up to some extent.

9.4 Chapter Summary

This chapter seeks to theorize the obscured adaptation in the Islamic participatory financing products to the prevailing constraints and the key outcomes of this adaptation. For this purpose this chapter explores the adaptations in *Musharakah*-based working capital financing, consumer financing, and commodity operations financing in the Islamic banking industry of Pakistan, and presents the Constraints, Adaptation, and Outcomes (CAO) framework of participatory finance. By developing a pragmatic CAO framework, this chapter not only highlights the typology of adaptation through which Pakistani Islamic banks have achieved innovative output and problem-solving capabilities within participatory financing products; but it also develops a theoretical basis, the researchers and service designers can use to device novel adaptation strategies to meet specific problem-solving and innovation goals.

The Constraints, Adaptation, and Outcomes (CAO) framework suggests that constraints have triggered the process of adaptation in the participatory financing within the Islamic banking industry of Pakistan. Moreover, adaptation has allowed Islamic banks to cope with the constraints to participatory financing and offer several innovative financing products to meet the growing demands of the modern industry. Thus, the major reason behind the spur of participatory financing in the Islamic banking industry of Pakistan can be attributed to the recent adaptations in the service design of *Musharakah* financing, through enactment of varieties in the product structures, to enable the product sustainability in new contexts.

This framework suggests that Islamic banks have moved from the lower level of adaptation called the *unstable state* to the higher level of adaptation called the *stable state*. According to Chakravarthy (1982) the firms in the unstable state, called the "defenders," try to buffer themselves from the environment because they are extremely vulnerable to environmental changes. Such firms are characterized by narrow product-market domains. Moreover, they seldom allow major adjustments in their operations, structures, or technologies. Such firms create stability through actions and decisions that reduce their interactions with environment. It is possible for defenders to achieve good financial performance in the short run. However, their long-term viability is severely vulnerable and constrained. These firms adapt by simply ignoring the environmental demands or events. On the other hand, in the stable state the organization, called an "analyzer," is open to the environment and adapts itself with the changing environment. Such firms have devised extensive mechanisms that enable the firm to imitate the best of the products and markets developed by others.

References

Chakravarthy, B. S. (1982). Adaptation: A metaphor for strategic management. *Academy of Management Review*, 7(1), 35–44.

Nouman, M. (2019). *Constraints, adaptation, and outcomes framework of particpatory financing in Islamic banking.* (PhD), Institute of Management Sciences, Peshawar Pakistan.

Nouman, M., Ullah, K., & Jan, S. (2022). Domains and motives of Musharakah spur in the Islamic banking industry of Pakistan. *The Singapore Economic Review*, 67(1), 381–409. https://doi.org/10.1142/S0217590819500620

State Bank of Pakistan. (2012–20). *Islamic Banking Bulletin.* Islamic Banking Department, State Bank of Pakistan.

Annexures

Annexure A: Details of the Systematic Literature Review Approach

Since, the authors aimed to highlight the major factors hindering the application of participatory financing and produce a coherent view by synthesizing different explanations of constrains to participatory financing. Insights from the extant literature were employed using a systematic review approach. According to Tranfield et al. (2003) a systematic review *"provide[s] collective insights through theoretical synthesis"* (p. 220). Systematic reviews aim to *"answer a specific question, to reduce bias in the selection and inclusion of studies, to appraise the quality of the included studies, and to summarize them objectively"* (Petticrew, 2001, p. 99).

A number of articles in the management sciences field appearing in the top ranking journals employ the systematic review approach (see for example Farashahi et al., 2005; Knoben & Oerlemans, 2006; Pittaway et al., 2004). The present study follows the same approach for the first objective of the study. Moreover, this approach is applied and justified on the following grounds:

> *First*, According to Geraldi et al. (2011) systematic review was traditionally employed in areas such as medicine to sum up findings based on quantitative and positivistic researches. However, the management research having diverse nature (Bryman, 1995), follows

differnt logic (Tranfield et al., 2003). Therefore, the quantitative analysis of the diverse sample of publication can result in the ontological and epistemological issues (Geraldi et al., 2011). Moreover, it may lead to the loss of the richness of the qualitative studies (Petticrew, 2001). The systematic review approach has "*methodologies that are more flexible*" (Petticrew, 2001, p. 98), accounting for the different conceptualisations and epistemologies. Moreover, it employs the qualitative reasoning of the reviewed studies (Geraldi et al., 2011).

Second, according to Petticrew (2001) good quality systematic reviews are superior over the traditional narrative review in the following ways:

- Systematic reviews always strive to answer a clear research question or evaluate a stated hypothesis,
- Excellent quality systematic reviews strive to locate all relevant studies,
- Such reviews have an explicit criterion for deciding which studies to be included which helps in limiting the reviewer's selection bias,
- These examine the methods employed in the selected studies in a systematic manner to assess the quality of the studies. Moreover, it examines the potential biases and differences in the studies' results, and
- Conclusions of such studies are based on the methodologically sound studies.

Third, the first objective of the study is to integrate the diverse literature to develop a holistic framework by synthesizing different explanations provided for the underutilization of participatory financing in the extant literature. Thus systematic review being "a *method of locating, appraising, and synthesizing evidence*" (Petticrew, 2001) proves to be the most appropriate approach in this regard.

Finally, the constraints framework serves as a pre-empirical framework to be extended into the post-empirical CAO framework (in Chapter 9). Therefore, it was necessary to employ a flexible methodology for literature review that could help in reducing bias in the searching, selection, and analysis of the relevant literature. Since systematic reviews aim to "*answer a specific question, to reduce bias in the selection and inclusion of studies, to appraise the quality of the included studies, and to summarize them objectively*" (Petticrew, 2001, p. 99). Therefore, systematic review provides sound ground for the development of a reliable constraints framework.

Sample Selection
The systematic review strives to locate all relevant studies (Petticrew, 2001). For this purpose systematic review entails well defined criteria for searching and identifying the extant literature (Armitage & Keeble-Ramsay, 2009). Furthermore, it require an explicit criteria for deciding which studies to be included in the sample to reduce the selection bias (Petticrew, 2001; Petticrew & Roberts, 2006). To ensure that the search process employed in this study had been comprehensive enough and the selected sample is fairly representative of the literature the following literature review methodology has been employed:

> The Web of Science was used as a starting point of the search. Relevant papers containing the keywords: *Musharakah*, *Mudarabah*, participatory financing, participation, partnership, profit and loss sharing, pain share gain share, and risk sharing were identified using this database. Additionally, databases including Elsevier (ScienceDirect), Wiley Online Library, Jstor, SpringerLink, Taylor & Francis, and Emerald etc. were also searched using the above keywords. Moreover, archives of the key peer-reviewed scholarly journals on Islamic finance were explored to identify relevant publications. The in press articles were not considered.

The initial sample was refined through the following steps:

> *Step 1: Focus on the academic papers.* Among the downloaded articles only the academic papers were considered. Many databases provide this option automatically by defining the article type.
> *Step 2: Focus on Islamic finance.* Based on the analysis of the articles' abstracts, the sample was refined to publications explicitly related to Islamic finance. Publications that clearly did not aim at contributing to the participatory financing in Islamic finance at least in a broad sense were excluded from the sample, for example articles that were clearly focused on different knowledge areas such as agriculture and manufacturing industries.

Step 3: Focus on the rare utilization of participatory financing. Since this review paper is focusing on issues in participatory financing. Only those articles were considered that at least in a broad sense focus on the issue of the rare utilization of participatory financing.

Step 4: Checking completeness. To ensure that we do not miss a substantial number of relevant papers we cross-checked with the content of the selected papers by backward and forward chaining. Starting with our selected papers downloaded from the sources mentioned above, we added to our list of relevant papers by *backward chaining* i.e., following up on the list of references found in those selected papers. The same was done for the new papers identified via backward chaining. This helped us expand our literature from present into the past. For *forward chaining* we took each of our selected articles one by one and explored what other articles cite the particular article. The same process was repeated for the new identified articles as well. This process also known as 'citation searching' helps expand literature from past into present. Cross-checking via backward and forward chaining helped us identify a large number of additional articles complying with the selection criteria defined in steps 1–3. Few articles were not accessible because of deferent reasons. These articles were accessed by corresponding directly to their authors.

To reduce the likelihood of missing relevant studies, many books authored by the seminal authors and relevant edited books have also been consulted. Most of the books were available online while few had to be purchased from the local market. Similarly, for relevant conference papers, the key conferences on Islamic finance were identified and their proceedings were explored. After cross-checking our sample grew to 101 relevant research studies complying with the selection criteria defined in steps 1–3. Table 3.1 presents the breakup of the relevant studies identified till step 4.

Step 5: The final filter. Finally, the sample was reduced to those research studies that explicitly focus on problems in the participatory financing arrangements or the constraints faced by Islamic financial institutions in adopting participatory financing arrangements while investing. This reduced our sample to 91 research publications meeting the selection criteria. Table A.1 presents the classification of these publications on the basis of their nature. Similarly, Table A.2 presents the year wise classification of the selected publications.

Table A.1 Overview of the number and the type of selected publications in the refining steps 4 and 5

Refining step	Books	Chapters of edited books	Journal articles	IMF Working papers	Conference papers	Total
4	15	14	66	3	10	108
5	11	14	55	3	8	91

Table A.2 Overview of the Final Sample of selected publications (Step 5)

Publication Year		Type of Paper[a]	
1983–1989	3	Theoretical	25
1990–1996	8	Qualitative	3
1997–2003	29	Quantitative	43
2004–2010	26	Qual and Quant	3
2011–2017	25	Literature Review	5

[a] Excluding books

Analysis of the Literature

The present study applies the qualitative evidence synthesis (QES) for the analysis of the selected studies and development of the constraints framework. Paterson (2012) defines QES as 'the synthesis or amalgamation of individual qualitative research reports that relate to a specific topic or focus in order to arrive at new or enhanced understanding about the phenomenon under study'. The QES entails an interpretative process by which 'the constituent study texts can be treated as the multivocal interpretation of a phenomenon, just as the voices of different participants might be in a single qualitative study' (Zimmer, 2006). The QES provides a broad overview of a body of research, therefore it has the ability to reveal more powerful explanations that are provided in the individual studies (Hannes & Lockwood, 2012). Hence, synthesis often leads to the increased level of abstraction and generalizability of the research findings (Sherwood, 1999).

Several methods can be applied for the synthesis of the qualitative evidence including thematic synthesis, framework synthesis, narrative synthesis, grounded theory, and meta-analysis (Hannes & Lockwood, 2012). The present study adopts the thematic synthesis method. The thematic synthesis follows a highly structured approach for the selection, organizing, and tabulation of the primary research data. It mainly entails listing the findings of selected studies and then combining them into similar descriptors or themes to develop a general description of the problem at hand (Hannes & Lockwood, 2012). The thematic synthesis 'uses thematic analysis techniques, as well as adaptations from grounded theory and meta-ethnography, to identify themes across primary research studies. Synthesis component entails an iterative process of inductively grouping themes into overarching categories that capture the similarities, differences, and relationships between the themes' (Paterson, 2012, p. 17). The developers of the thematic synthesis view 'informing practice or policy' as the intended outcome of the thematic synthesis (see for example Harden et al., 2004; Thomas et al., 2003, 2007).

The present study follows the approach developed by Marston and King (2006) for analyzing and synthesizing the selected studies. In this method the selected research papers and books as treated as documents, and are analyzed using the established qualitative research techniques: Analysis of the selected publications followed three steps. The first two steps were concerned with the identification; while the third step involved the classification of the major factors restraining the adaptation of participatory financing.

- In the first step the selected 91 publications were independently reviewed and coded. Codes represent the constraints explicitly appearing in the selected publications.
- In the second step the dozens of codes that emerged in the first step were refined through constant comparisons within and between codes to ensure that they accurately reflect the constraints to participatory financing. A total of 24 constraints to participatory financing were identified from the codes extracted in the first step with the overlapping items either eliminated or combined. Table A.3 reports the constraints to participatory financing.
- In the last step link between the constraints were identified, grouping them into the broad overall themes. The constraints identified in the second step were classified into three distinct categories including: uncertainty, low demand, and regulatory constraints. Our intention was to develop the typology of constraints by connecting the

Table A.3 Factors restraining the application of participatory financing

Contributors	Constraints
Abdalla (1999), Adnan and Muhamad (2008), Ascarya (2010), Ascarya and Yumanita (2006), Farooq and Ahmed (2013), Greuning and Iqbal (2007), Hanif and Iqbal (2010), Kayed (2012), Khan (2010), Khan and Bhatti (2008), Khan (1989), Mansoori (2011), Nouman and Ullah (2014), Sadique (2010a, 2010b), Shaikh (2011), Siddiqi (1991), Siddiqi (2006)	Untrustworthiness
Abdalla (1999), Abdul-Rahman and Nor (2016), Abou-Ali (2002), Ahmed (2008a, 2008b), Ajija et al. (2012), Al-Harran (1999b), Ascarya (2010), Ascarya and Yumanita (2006), El-Gamal (2005), Farooq and Ahmed (2013), Hasan (2002), Iqbal et al. (1998), Iqbal and Molyneux (2005), Iqbal (1997), Kayed (2012), Khan (2010), Khan and Bhatti (2008), Khan (1995), Khan and Ahmed (2001), Mansoori (2011), Mirakhor and Zaidi (2007), Nienhaus (1983), Nouman and Ullah (2014), Roy (1991), Sadique (2010a, 2012), Samad et al. (2005), Warde (1999, 2000), Yasseri (2002), Zaher and Hassan (2001)	Lack of skilled HR
Farooq and Ahmed (2013), Iqbal (1997), Nouman and Ullah (2014), Siddiqi (1991), Zaher and Hassan (2001)	Weak accounting procedures
Ahmed (2008b), Ajija et al. (2012), Al-Harran (1999b), Ascarya (2010), Ascarya and Yumanita (2006), Kayed (2012), Khan and Bhatti (2008), Nouman and Ullah (2014), Zaher and Hassan (2001)	Unawareness

(continued)

Table A.3 (continued)

Contributors	Constraints
Abdalla (1999), Abdul-Rahman and Nor (2016), Adnan and Muhamad (2008), Ahmed (2008a), Ajija et al. (2012), Akacem and Gilliam (2002), Al-Harran (1999a), Alam and Parinduri (2017), Ariffin et al. (2015), Ascarya (2010), Ascarya and Yumanita (2006), Ayub (2007), Bacha (1997), Boumediene (2011), Chong and Liu (2009), Dar and Presley (2000), Dusuki (2007), El-Komi and Croson (2013), Farooq and Ahmed (2013), Farooq (2007), Greuning and Iqbal (2007), Hanif and Iqbal (2010), Hasan (2002), Huda (2012), Iqbal and Mirakhor (2011), Kayed (2012), Khalil et al. (2002), Khan (2010), Khan and Bhatti (2008), Khan (1995), Mansoori (2011), Mansour et al. (2015), Marizah and Nazam (2016), Mirakhor and Zaidi (2007), Nouman and Ullah (2014), Othman and Masih (2015), Sadique (2010a, 2010b), Sadr and Iqbal (2002), Samad et al. (2005), Shaikh (2011), Sundararajan and Errico (2002), Warde (1999), Yasseri (2002)	Higher risk
Ascarya (2010), Ayub (2007), Dar et al. (1999), Dar and Presley (2000), Farooq (2007), Khan (1995), Nouman and Ullah (2014), Samad et al. (2005), Shaikh (2011)	Less applicability
Abdul-Rahman and Nor (2016), Abedifar et al. (2015), Ahmad (1993), Ajija et al. (2012), Alam and Parinduri (2017), Ariffin et al. (2015), Ascarya (2010), Dusuki (2007), Farooq and Ahmed (2013), Farooq (2007), Khan (1995), Nouman and Ullah (2014), Sadique (2010a, 2010b, 2012), Sundararajan and Errico (2002), Warde (2000)	Complications
Ayub (2007), Iqbal and Mirakhor (2011), Mansoori (2011)	Protection of depositors' interest
Dar et al. (1999), Dar and Presley (2000), Dusuki (2007), Farooq (2007), Iqbal (1997), Khan (1995), Nouman and Ullah (2014), Siddiqi (2006), Zaher and Hassan (2001)	Shallow secondary market

Contributors	Constraints
Abedifar et al. (2015), Al-Muharrami and Hardy (2013), Ascarya (2010), Chong and Liu (2009), Dar and Presley (2000), Greuning and Iqbal (2007), Iqbal and Mirakhor (2011), Khan and Bhatti (2008), Marizah and Nazam (2016), Nouman and Ullah (2014), Sadique (2010a)	Risk averse depositors
Abalkhail and Presley (2002), Abdul-Rahman et al. (2014), Abdul-Rahman and Nor (2016), Abou-Ali (2002), Adnan and Muhamad (2008), Aggarwal and Yousef (2000), Ahmed (2008b), Ahmed (2002), Al-Muharrami and Hardy (2013), Al-Suwailem (1998), Ascarya (2010), Åström (2011), Bacha (1995), Baldwin et al. (2002), Bashir (1996), Boumediene (2011), Chong and Liu (2009), El-Din (1992, 2008), El-Gamal (2005), El-Komi and Croson (2013), Farooq (2007), Greuning and Iqbal (2007), Haque and Mirakhor (1986), Hassan and Kayed (2009), Huda (2012), Iqbal and Llewellyn (2002), Iqbal and Molyneux (2005), Iqbal and Mirakhor (2011), Jouaber and Mehri (2012), Karim (2002), Khalil et al. (2002), Khan (2010), Khan and Bhatti (2008), Khan (1995), Khan (1989), Mansour et al. (2015), Marizah and Nazam (2016), Nagaoka (2010), Nouman and Ullah (2014), Othman and Masih (2015), Sadique (2010a, 2010b), Sadr (1999), Sadr and Iqbal (2002), Sarker (1999), Sundararajan and Errico (2002), Warde (2000)	Asymmetric information

(continued)

Table A.3 (continued)

Contributors	Constraints
Abalkhail and Presley (2002), Abdul-Rahman et al. (2014), Abdul-Rahman and Nor (2016), Abedifar et al. (2015), Abou-Ali (2002), Aggarwal and Yousef (2000), Al-Suwailem (1998), Ariffin et al. (2015), Ascarya (2010), Åström (2011), Bacha (1995), Baldwin et al. (2002), Bashir (1996), Boumediene (2011), Dusuki (2007), El-Din (1992), El-Gamal (2005), El-Komi and Croson (2013), Farooq (2007), Huda (2012), Iqbal and Llewellyn (2002), Iqbal and Molyneux (2005), Jouaber and Mehri (2012), Khalil et al. (2002), Khan (2010), Khan and Bhatti (2008), Khan (1995), Khan and Ahmed (2001), Mansoori (2011), Mansour et al. (2015), Nagaoka (2010), Nouman and Ullah (2014), Pryor (2007), Sadr (1999), Sadr and Iqbal (2002), Sarker (1999), Siddiqi (1983), Siddiqi (2006)	Adverse selection

Contributors	Constraints
Abalkhail and Presley (2002), Abdul-Rahman et al. (2014), Abdul-Rahman and Nor (2016), Abedifar et al. (2015), Abou-Ali (2002), Adnan and Muhamad (2008), Aggarwal and Yousef (2000), Ahmed (2008a, 2008b), Ahmed (2002), Akacem and Gilliam (2002), Al-Muharrami and Hardy (2013), Al-Suwailem (1998), Ariffin et al. (2015), Ascarya (2010), Åström (2011), Ayub (2007), Bacha (1995, 1997), Baldwin et al. (2002), Bashir (1996), Boumediene (2011), Chong and Liu (2009), Dar et al. (1999), Dar and Presley (2000), Dusuki (2007), El-Din (2008), El-Gamal (2005), El-Komi and Croson (2013), Farooq (2007), Hanif and Iqbal (2010), Haque and Mirakhor (1986), Hasan (2002), Hassan and Kayed (2009), Huda (2012), Iqbal and Llewellyn (2002), Iqbal and Molyneux (2005), Iqbal and Mirakhor (2011), Jouaber and Mehri (2012), Kayed (2012), Khalil et al. (2002), Khan (2010), Khan and Bhatti (2008), Khan (1995), Khan and Ahmed (2001), Khan (1989), Kuran (1995), Mansoori (2011), Mansour et al. (2015), Marizah and Nazam (2016), Mirakhor and Zaidi (2007), Nagaoka (2010), Nouman and Ullah (2014), Othman and Masih (2015), Pryor (2007), Rethel (2011), Sadique (2010a, 2010b, 2012), Sadr (1999), Sadr and Iqbal (2002), Samad et al. (2005), Sarker (1999), Shaikh (2011), Siddiqi (1983), Siddiqi (2006), Sumarti, Fitriyani, and Damayanti (2014), Sundararajan and Errico (2002), Usmani (2002), Warde (1999, 2000), Yousef (2004), Zaher and Hassan (2001)	Moral hazards
Abdalla (1999), Ahmed (2008b), Amrani (2012), Dar and Presley (2000), El-Din (1992), Farooq and Ahmed (2013), Khan and Bhatti (2008), Sadique (2010a), Shaikh (2011)	Reluctance to share profit

(continued)

Table A.3 (continued)

Contributors	Constraints
Abedifar et al. (2015), Chong and Liu (2009), Dar et al. (1999), Dar and Presley (2000), Dusuki (2007), Farooq (2007), Hanif and Iqbal (2010), Khan (2010), Khan (1995), Nienhaus (1983), Othman and Masih (2015), Pryor (2007), Roy (1991), Sadique (2010a, 2010b), Samad et al. (2005), Sarker (1999)	Severe competition
Abalkhail and Presley (2002), Abdalla (1999), Abdul-Rahman et al. (2014), Abdul-Rahman and Nor (2016), Abedifar et al. (2015), Ahmed (2008a), Akacem and Gilliam (2002), Al-Muharrami and Hardy (2013), Alam and Parinduri (2017), Ariffin et al. (2015), Chong and Liu (2009), El-Gamal (2005), El-Komi and Croson (2013), Farooq (2007), Greuning and Iqbal (2007), Haque and Mirakhor (1986), Huda (2012), Iqbal et al. (1998), Iqbal and Llewellyn (2002), Iqbal and Mirakhor (2011), Khalil et al. (2002), Khan and Bhatti (2008), Khan (1989), Marizah and Nazam (2016), Mirakhor and Zaidi (2007), Nagaoka (2010), Nouman and Ullah (2014), Othman and Masih (2015), Sadique (2010a, 2010b), Sadr (1999), Sadr and Iqbal (2002), Sarker (1999), Siddiqi (2006)	Higher appraisal and monitoring costs
Amrani (2012), El-Din (1992), Iqbal et al. (1998), Nienhaus (1983), Sadique (2010a)	Cost preference
Ahmed (2008b), Ajija et al. (2012), Khan and Bhatti (2008), Khan (1995), Nouman and Ullah (2014), Samad et al. (2005), Shaikh (2011), Usmani (2002)	Disclosure of business secrets
Ahmed (2008a, 2008b)	External interference
Abdul-Rahman et al. (2014), Dar et al. (1999), Dar and Presley (2000), Dusuki (2007), Farooq (2007), Khan (2010), Warde (1999)	Weak properly rights

Contributors	Constraints
Abdul-Rahman et al. (2014), Alam and Parinduri (2017), Ariffin et al. (2015), Ascarya (2010), Ascarya and Yumanita (2006), Farooq and Ahmed (2013), Haque and Mirakhor (1986), Hasan (2002), Hassan and Kayed (2009), Huda (2012), Iqbal and Molyneux (2005), Iqbal (1997), Kayed (2012), Khan and Bhatti (2008), Khan (1995), Khan and Ahmed (2001), Mansour et al. (2015), Nouman and Ullah (2014), Othman and Masih (2015), Rethel (2011), Roy (1991), Sadique (2010b), Shaikh (2011), Siddiqi (1991), Siddiqi (2006), Sundararajan and Errico (2002), Warde (1999), Yousef (2004), Zaher and Hassan (2001)	Weak regulatory and legal framework
Ascarya (2010), Ascarya and Yumanita (2006), Farooq and Ahmed (2013), Hassan and Kayed (2009), Kayed (2012), Nouman and Ullah (2014), Roy (1991), Usmani (2002, 2007), Warde (1999)	Non-supportive government
Abdul-Rahman et al. (2014), Ahmed (2008b), Dar et al. (1999), Dar and Presley (2000), Dusuki (2007), Farooq and Ahmed (2013), Farooq (2007), Hanif and Iqbal (2010), Khan (2010), Khan and Bhatti (2008), Khan and Ahmed (2001), Nouman and Ullah (2014), Sadique (2010a, 2010b), Shaikh (2011)	Tax shield benefits
Hanif and Iqbal (2010), Iqbal et al. (1998), Kayed (2012), Khalil et al. (2002), Khan and Bhatti (2008), Khan and Ahmed (2001), Mansoori (2011), Nouman and Ullah (2014), Shaikh (2011), Siddiqi (1991)	Inefficient accounting and audit systems

rather abstract concepts into the broader sets of constraints for better conceptualization and policy implications. Since the literature was divergent, with diverse studies focused on few specific issues. This helped us integrate the extant literature and produce a coherent view about constraints to participatory financing.

REFERENCES

Abalkhail, M., & Presley, J. R. (2002). How informal risk capital investors manage asymmetric information in profit/loss-sharing contracts. In M. Iqbal & D. T. Llewellyn (Eds.), *Islamic banking and finance: New perspectives on profit-sharing and risk* (pp. 111–134). Edward Elgar.

Abdalla, M. G.-E. (1999). Partnership (Musharakah): A new option for financing small enterprises? *Arab Law Quarterly, 14*(3), 257–267.

Abdul-Rahman, A., Latif, R. A., Muda, R., & Abdullah, M. A. (2014). Failure and potential of profit-loss sharing contracts: A perspective of New Institutional, Economic (NIE) Theory. *Pacific-Basin Finance Journal, 28*, 136–151.

Abdul-Rahman, A., & Nor, S. M. (2016). Challenges of profit-and-loss sharing financing in Malaysian Islamic banking. *Malaysian Journal of Society and Space, 12*(2), 39–46.

Abedifar, P., Ebrahim, S. M., Molyneux, P., & Tarazi, A. (2015). Islamic banking and finance: Recent empirical literature and directions for future research. *Journal of Economic Surveys, 29*(4), 637–670.

Abou-Ali, S. (2002). Comments: How informal risk capital investors manage asymmetric information in profit/loss-sharing contracts. In M. Iqbal & D. T. Llewellyn (Eds.), *Islamic banking and finance: New perspectives on profit-sharing and risk* (pp. 135–138). Edward Elgar.

Adnan, M. A., & Muhamad. (2008). Agency problems in mudarabah financing: The case of Sharia (Rural) banks, Indonesia. In M. Obaidullah & H. S. H. A. Latiff (Eds.), *Islamic finance for micro and medium enterprises* (pp. 107–130). Islamic Research & Training Institute, Islamic Development Bank.

Aggarwal, R. K., & Yousef, T. (2000). Islamic banks and investment financing. *Journal of Money, Credit and Banking, 32*(1), 93–120.

Ahmad, A. (1993). *Contemporary practices of Islamic financing techniques*. IRIT, Islamic Development Bank.

Ahmed, G. A. (2008a). The implication of using profit and loss sharing modes of finance in the banking system, with a particular reference to equity participation (partnership) method in Sudan. *Humanomics,* 24(3), 182–206.

Ahmed, G. A. (2008b). Islamic micro-finance practice with a particular reference to financing entrepreneurs through equity participation contracts in Sudanese banks. In M. Obaidullah & H. S. H. A. Latiff (Eds.), *Islamic finance for micro and medium enterprises* (pp. 75–105). Islamic Research & Training Institute, Islamic Development Bank.

Ahmed, H. (2002). Incentive-compatible profit-sharing contracts: A theoretical treatment. In M. Iqbal & D. T. Llewellyn (Eds.), *Islamic banking and finance: New perspectives on profit-sharing and risk* (pp. 40–54). Edward Elgar.

Ajija, S. R., Annisa, E., & Hudaifah, A. (2012). *How do Islamic banks optimize profit and loss sharing arrangements?*. Paper presented at the Fourth Research Forum inIslamic Banking Bank Indonesia.

Akacem, M., & Gilliam, L. (2002). Principles of Islamic banking: Debt versus equity financing. *Middle East Policy,* 9(1), 124–138.

Al-Harran, S. (1999a). Introduction: Cases in Islamic finance. *Arab Law Quarterly,* 14(3), 193–202.

Al-Harran, S. (1999b). New strategic alliances between Islamic financial institutions, international university students and entrepreneurs to implement Musharakah financing to meet the challenges of the 21st century *Arab Law Quarterly,* 14(3), 268–281.

Al-Muharrami, S., & Hardy, D. C. (2013). *Cooperative and Islamic banks: What can they learn from each other?* (International Monetary Fund Working Paper, WP/13/184).

Al-Suwailem, S. (1998). Venture capital: A potential model of Musharakah *Journal of King Abdulaziz University: Islamic Economics,* 10, 3–20.

Alam, N., & Parinduri, R. A. (2017). Do Islamic banks shift from mark-up to equity financing when their contracting environments are improved? *Applied Economics Letters,* 24(8), 545–548.

Amrani, F. (2012, June 28-29). *Financing cost and risk sharing in Islamic finance: A new endogenous approach.* Paper presented at the 29th International Symposium on Money, Banking and Finance, Nantes-France.

Ariffin, N. M., Kassim, S. H., & Razak, D. A. (2015). Exploring application of equity-based financing through Mushārakah Mutanāqiṣah in

Islamic banks in Malaysia: Perspective from the industry players. *International Journal of Economics, Management and Accounting, 23*(2), 241–261.

Armitage, A., & Keeble-Ramsay, D. (2009). The rapid structured literature review as a research strategy *US-China Education Review, 6*(4).

Ascarya. (2010). The lack of profit-and-loss sharing financing in Indonesia's islamic banks revisited. *Review of Indonesian Economic and Business Studies, 1*(1), 57–80.

Ascarya, & Yumanita, D. (2006). *The lack of profit and lost sharing financing in Indonesian Islamic banks: Problems and alternative solutions.* Paper presented at the INCEIF Islamic Banking and Finance Educational Colloquium, KL Convention Center, Kuala Lumpur, Malaysia.

Åström, Z. H. O. (2011). *Enhancing the structure of Islamic banking by lessening the asymmetric information pertaining to profit and loss sharing instruments.* Paper presented at the 8th International Conference on Islamic Economics and Finance, Qatar National Convention Center, Qatar.

Ayub, M. (2007). *Understanding Islamic finance.* John Wiley & Sons Ltd.

Bacha, O. I. (1995). Conventional versus mudarabah financing: An agency cost perspective. *Journal of Islamic Economics, 4*(1&2), 33–49.

Bacha, O. I. (1997). Adapting mudarabah financing to contemporary realities: A proposed financing structure. *The Journal of Accounting, Commerce & Finance, 1*(1), 26–54.

Baldwin, K., Dar, H. A., & Presley, J. R. (2002). On determining moral hazard and adverse selection in the Islamic firm. In H. Ahmad (Ed.), *Theoretical foundations of Islamic economics* (Vol. 1, pp. 145–166). IRTI, Islamic Development Bank.

Bashir, A. H. M. (1996). Investment under profit-sharing contracts: The adverse selection case. *Managerial Finance, 22*(5/6), 48-58.

Boumediene, A. (2011). Is credit risk really higher in Islamic banks? *The Journal of Credit Risk, 7*(3), 97–129.

Bryman, A. (1995). *Research methods and organization studies.* Allen & Unwin Pty.

Chong, B. S., & Liu, M.-H. (2009). Islamic banking: Interest-free or interest-based? *Pacific-Basin Finance Journal, 17*, 125–144.

Dar, H. A., Harvey, D. I., & Presley, J. R. (1999). *Size, profitability, and agency in profit and loss sharing in Islamic banking and finance.* Paper presented at the Second Harvard University Forum on Islamic Finance: Islamic Finance into the 21st Century, Cambridge, Massachusetts.

Dar, H. A., & Presley, J. R. (2000). Lack of profit loss sharing in Islamic banking: Management and control imbalances. *International Journal of Islamic Financial Services, 2*(2), 3–18.

Dusuki, A. W. (2007). The ideal of Islamic banking: A survey of stakeholders' perceptions. *Review of Islamic Economics, 11*(Special Issue), 29–52.

El-Din, S. I. T. (1992). Debt and equity in a primary financial market: A theory with Islamic implications. *JKAU: Islamic Economics, 4*, 3–34.

El-Din, S. I. T. (2008). Income ratio, risk-sharing, and the optimality of mudarabah. *The Journal of King Abdulaziz University, Islamic Economics, 21*(2), 37–59.

El-Gamal, M. A. (2005). Islamic bank corporate governance and regulation: A call for mutualization. *Rice University*.

El-Komi, M., & Croson, R. (2013). Experiments in Islamic microfinance. *Journal of Economic Behavior & Organization, 95*, 252–269.

Farashahi, M., Hafsi, T., & Molz, R. (2005). Institutionalized norms of conducting research and social realities: A research synthesis of empirical works from 1983 to 2002. *International Journal of Management Reviews, 7*(1), 1–24.

Farooq, M., & Ahmed, M. M. M. (2013). Musharakah financing: Experience of Pakistani banks. *World Applied Sciences Journal, 21*(2), 181–189.

Farooq, M. O. (2007). Partnership, equity-financing and Islamic finance: Whither profit-loss sharing? *Review of Islamic Economics, 11*(Special Issue), 67–88.

Geraldi, J., Maylor, H., & Williams, T. (2011). Now, let's make it really complex (complicated): A systematic review of the complexities of projects. *International Journal of Operations & Production Management, 31*(9), 966–990.

Greuning, H. V., & Iqbal, Z. (2007). Banking and the risk environment. In S. Archer & R. A. A. Karim (Eds.), *Islamic finance: Regulatory challenge* (pp. 11–36). John Wiley and Sons.

Hanif, M., & Iqbal, A. M. (2010). Islamic financing and business framework: A survey. *European Journal of Social Sciences, 15*(4), 475–489.

Hannes, K., & Lockwood, C. (Eds.). (2012). *Synthesizing qualitative research: Choosing the right approach*. John Wiley & Sons, Ltd.

Haque, N. U., & Mirakhor, A. (1986). *Optimal profit-sharing contracts and investment in an interest-free Islamic economy* (International Monetary Fund Working Paper, WP/86/12).

Harden, A., Garcia, J., Oliver, S., Rees, R., Shepherd, J., Brunton, G., & Oakley, A. (2004). Applying systematic review methods to studies of people's views: An example from public health. *Journal of Epidemiology in Community Health, 58*, 794–800.

Hasan, Z. (2002). Mudaraba as a mode of finance in Islamic banking: Theory, practice and problems. *The Middle East Business and Economic Review, 14*(2), 41–53.

Hassan, M. K., & Kayed, R. N. (2009). The global financial crisis, risk management and social justice in Islamic finance. *ISRA International Journal of Islamic Finance, 1*(1), 33–58.

Huda, A. N. (2012). The development of islamic financing scheme for SMEs in a developing country: The Indonesian case. *Procedia-Social and Behavioral Sciences, 52*, 179–186.

Iqbal, M., Ahmad, A., & Khan, T. (1998). *Challanges facing Islamic banking* (Vol. 1). Islamic Research and Training Institute.

Iqbal, M., & Llewellyn, D. T. (2002). Introduction. In M. Iqbal & D. T. Llewellyn (Eds.), *Islamic banking and finance: New perspectives on profit-sharing and risk*. Edward Elgar.

Iqbal, M., & Molyneux, P. (2005). *Thirty years of Islamic banking: History, performance and prospects*. Palgrave Macmillan.

Iqbal, Z. (1997, June). Islamic Financial Systems. *Finance & Development*, 42–45.

Iqbal, Z., & Mirakhor, A. (2011). *An introduction to Islamic finance: Theory and practice* (2nd ed.). John Wiley & Sons (Asia) Pte. Ltd.

Jouaber, K., & Mehri, M. (2012). *A theory of profit sharing ratio under adverse selection: The case of islamic venture capital*. Paper presented at the 29th International Conference of the French Finance Association (AFFI).

Karim, A. A. (2002). Incentive-compatible constraints for Islamic banking: Some lessons from Bank Muamalat. In M. Iqbal & D. T. Llewellyn (Eds.), *Islamic banking and finance: New perspectives on profit-sharing and risk* (pp. 95–108). Edward Elgar.

Kayed, R. N. (2012). The entrepreneurial role of profit-and-loss sharing modes of finance: theory and practice. *International Journal of Islamic and Middle Eastern Finance and Management, 5*(3), 203–228.

Khalil, A. F. A. A., Rickwood, C., & Murinde, V. (2002). Evidence on agency-contractual problems in mudarabah financing operations by Islamic banks. In M. Iqbal & D. T. Llewellyn (Eds.), *Islamic banking and finance: New perspectives on profit-sharing and risk* (pp. 57–92). Edward Elgar.

Khan, F. (2010). How 'Islamic' is Islamic banking? *Journal of Economic Behavior & Organization, 76*, 805–820.

Khan, M. M., & Bhatti, M. I. (2008). *Developments in Islamic banking: The case of Pakistan*. Hampshire, New York: Palgrave Macmillan.

Khan, T. (1995). Demand for and supply of PLS and mark-up funds of Islamic banks: Some alternative explanations *Islamic Economic Studies, 3*(1), 1–46.

Khan, T., & Ahmed, H. (2001). *Risk management: An analysis of issues in Islamic financial industry*. Islamic Research and Training Institute-Islamic Development Bank.

Khan, W. M. (1989). Towards an interest-free Islamic economic system. *Journal of King Abdulaziz University: Islamic Economics, 1*, 3–38.

Knoben, J., & Oerlemans, L. A. G. (2006). Proximity and inter-organizational collaboration: A literature review. *International Journal of Management Reviews, 8*(2), 71–89.

Kuran, T. (1995). Further reflections on the behavioral norms of Islamic economics *Journal of Economic Behavior and Organization, 27*, 159–163.

Mansoori, M. T. (2011). Is "Islamic banking" Islamic? Analysis of current debate on Sharī'ah legitimacy of Islamic banking and finance. *Islamic Studies, 50*(3/4), 383–411.

Mansour, W., Abdelhamid, M. B., & Heshmati, A. (2015). Recursive profit-and-loss sharing. *Journal of Risk, 17*(6), 21–50.

Marizah, M., & Nazam, D. (2016). Islamic corporate financing: Does it promote profit and loss sharing? *Business Ethics: A European Review, 25*(4), 482–497.

Marston, C., & King, E. (2006). Factors that shape young people's sexual behaviour: A systematic review. *The Lancet, 368*, 1581–1586.

Mirakhor, A., & Zaidi, I. (2007). Profit-and-loss sharing contracts in Islamic finance. In K. Hassan & M. Lewis (Eds.), *Handbook of Islamic banking* (pp. 49–63). Edward Elgar Publishing.

Nagaoka, S. (2010). Reconsidering mudarabah contracts in Islamic finance: What is the economic wisdom (hikmah) of partnership-based instruments? *Review of Islamic Economics, 13*(2), 65–79.

Nienhaus, V. (1983). Profitability of Islamic PLS banks competing with interest banks: Problems and prospects. *Journal of Research in Islamic economics, 1*(1), 37–47.

Nouman, M., & Ullah, K. (2014). Constraints in the application of partnerships in Islamic banks: The present contributions and future directions. *Business & Economic Reivew, 6*(2), 47-62.

Othman, A. N., & Masih, M. (2015). Do profit and loss sharing (PLS) deposits also affect PLS financing? Evidence from Malaysia based on DOLS, FMOLS and system GMM techniques. Munich Personal RePEc Archive (MPRA Paper No. 65224) from MPRA http://mpra.ub.uni-muenchen.de/65224/

Paterson, B. L. (2012). It looks great but how do I know if it fits?: An introduction to meta-synthesis research. In K. Hannes & C. Lockwood (Eds.), *Synthesizing qualitative research: Choosing the right approach*. John Wiley & Sons, Ltd.

Petticrew, M. (2001). Systematic reviews from astronomy to zoology: Myths and misconceptions. *British Medical Journal, 322*(13), 98–101.

Petticrew, M. A., & Roberts, H. (2006). *Systematic reviews in the social sciences*. Blackwell.

Pittaway, L., Robertson, M., Munir, K., Denyer, D., & Neely, A. (2004). Networking and innovation: A systematic review of the evidence. *International Journal of Management Reviews, 5/6*(3&4), 137–168.

Pryor, F. L. (2007). The economic impact of Islam on developing countries. *World Development, 35*(11), 1815–1835.

Rethel, L. (2011). Whose legitimacy? Islamic finance and the global financial order. *Review of International Political Economy, 18*(1), 75–98.

Roy, D. A. (1991). Islamic banking. *Middle Eastern Studies, 27*(3), 427–456.

Sadique, M. A. (2010a). Islamic banks' dilemma between ideals and practice: Debt or equity *Global Journal of Management and Business Research, 10*(2), 147–150.

Sadique, M. A. (2010b). *Transition of Islamic banks from debt-based modes to equity-based financing: Issues and prospects*. Paper presented at the International Conference on Islamic Banking & Finance: Cross Border Practices & Litigations, International Islamic University Malaysia.

Sadique, M. A. (2012). *Capital and profit sharing in Islamic equity financing: Issues and prospects*. The Other Press.

Sadr, K. (1999). The role of Musharakah financing in the agricultural bank of Iran *Arab Law Quarterly, 14*(3), 245–256.
Sadr, K., & Iqbal, Z. (2002). Choice between debt and equity contracts and asymmetrical information: Some empirical evidence. In M. Iqbal & D. T. Llewellyn (Eds.), *Islamic banking and finance: New perspectives on profit-sharing and risk* (pp. 139–154). Edward Elgar.
Samad, A., Gardner, N. D., & Cook, B. J. (2005). Islamic banking and finance in theory and practice: The experience of Malaysia and Bahrain. *The American Journal of Islamic Social Sciences, 22*(2), 69–86.
Sarker, M. A. A. (1999). Islamic business contracts, agency problem and the theory of the Islamic firm. *International Journal of Islamic Financial Services, 1*(2).
Shaikh, M. A. (2011). Contemporary Islamic banking: The issue of Murābahah. *Islamic Studies, 50*(3/4), 435–448.
Sherwood, G. (1999). Meta-synthesis: Merging qualitative studies to develop nursing knowledge. *International Journal of Human Caring, 3*, 37–42.
Siddiqi, M. N. (1983). *Issues in Islamic banking*. The Islamic Foundation.
Siddiqi, M. N. (1991). Some economic aspects of mudarabah: Review of Islamic economics. *Journal of the International Association for Islamic Economics, 1*(2), 21–34.
Siddiqi, M. N. (2006). Islamic banking and finance in theory and practice: A survey of state of the art *Islamic Economic Studies, 13*(2), 1–48.
Sumarti, N., Fitriyani, V., & Damayanti, M. (2014). A mathematical model of the profit-loss sharing (PLS) scheme *Procedia—Social and Behavioral Sciences, 115*, 131–137.
Sundararajan, V., & Errico, L. (2002). *Islamic financial institutions and products in the global financial system: Key issues in risk management and challenges ahead* (International Monetary Fund Working Paper, WP/02/192).
Thomas, J., Kavanagh, J., Tucker, H., Burchett, H., Tripney, J., & Oakley, A. (2007). *Accidental injury, risk-taking behaviour and the social circumstances in which young people live: A systematic review*. University of London; EPPI-Centre, Social Science Research Unit, Institute of Education.
Thomas, J., Sutcliffe, K., Harden, A., Oakley, A., Oliver, S., Rees, R., Brunton, G., & Kavanagh, J. (2003). *Children and healthy eating:*

A systematic review of barriers and facilitators. University of London; EPPI-Centre, Social Science Research Unit, Institute of Education.

Tranfield, D., Denyer, D., & Smart, P. (2003). Towards a methodology for developing evidence-informed management knowledge by means of systematic review. *British Journal of Management, 14*(3), 207–222.

Usmani, M. T. (2002). *An introduction to Islamic finance*. Kluwer Law International.

Usmani, M. T. (2007). *An introduction to Islamic finance*. Maktaba Ma'ariful Qur'an.

Warde, I. (1999). *The revitalization of Islamic profit-and-loss sharing*. Paper presented at the Third Harvard University Forum on Islamic finance: Local challenges, global opportunities, Cambridge, Massachusetts.

Warde, I. (2000). *Islamic finance in the global economy*. Edinburgh University Press.

Yasseri, A. (2002). Islamic banking contracts as enforced in Iran. In M. Iqbal & D. T. Llewellyn (Eds.), *Islamic banking and finance: New perspectives on profit-sharing and risk* (pp. 155–167). Edward Elgar.

Yousef, T. M. (2004). The murabaha syndrome in Islamic finance: Laws, institutions and politics. In C. Henry & R. Wilson (Eds.), *The politics of Islamic finance*. Edinburgh University Press.

Zaher, T. S., & Hassan, M. K. (2001). A comparative literature survey of Islamic finance and banking. *Financial Markets, Institutions & Instruments, 10*(4), 155–199.

Zimmer, L. (2006). Qualitative meta-synthesis: A question of dialoguing with texts. *Journal of Advanced Nursing, 53*, 311–318.

Annexure B: Tentative Payment Schedule with Unequal Monthly Payments

Months	Rent (PKR)	Unit price (PKR)	Takaful contribution (PKR)	Monthly payment (PKR)	Balance unit value (PKR)	Balance units
0					6,000,000	120
1	73,950	50,000	1490	125,440	5,950,000	119
2	73,334	50,000	1478	124,811	5,900,000	118
3	72,718	50,000	1465	124,183	5,850,000	117
4	72,101	50,000	1453	123,554	5,800,000	116
5	71,485	50,000	1440	122,925	5,750,000	115
6	70,869	50,000	1428	122,297	5,700,000	114
7	70,253	50,000	1416	121,668	5,650,000	113
8	69,636	50,000	1403	121,039	5,600,000	112
9	69,020	50,000	1391	120,411	5,550,000	111
10	68,404	50,000	1378	119,782	5,500,000	110
11	67,788	50,000	1366	119,153	5,450,000	109
12	67,171	50,000	1353	118,525	5,400,000	108
13	66,555	50,000	1341	117,896	5,350,000	107
14	65,939	50,000	1329	117,267	5,300,000	106
15	65,323	50,000	1316	116,639	5,250,000	105
16	64,706	50,000	1304	116,010	5,200,000	104
17	64,090	50,000	1291	115,381	5,150,000	103
18	63,474	50,000	1279	114,753	5,100,000	102
19	62,858	50,000	1267	114,124	5,050,000	101
20	62,241	50,000	1254	113,495	5,000,000	100
21	61,625	50,000	1242	112,867	4,950,000	99
22	61,009	50,000	1229	112,238	4,900,000	98
23	60,393	50,000	1217	111,609	4,850,000	97
24	59,776	50,000	1204	110,981	4,800,000	96
25	59,160	50,000	1192	110,352	4,750,000	95
26	58,544	50,000	1180	109,723	4,700,000	94
27	57,928	50,000	1167	109,095	4,650,000	93
28	57,311	50,000	1155	108,466	4,600,000	92
29	56,695	50,000	1142	107,837	4,550,000	91
30	56,079	50,000	1130	107,209	4,500,000	90
31	55,463	50,000	1118	106,580	4,450,000	89
32	54,846	50,000	1105	105,951	4,400,000	88
33	54,230	50,000	1093	105,323	4,350,000	87
34	53,614	50,000	1080	104,694	4,300,000	86
35	52,998	50,000	1068	104,065	4,250,000	85
36	52,381	50,000	1055	103,437	4,200,000	84
37	51,765	50,000	1043	102,808	4,150,000	83

(continued)

(continued)

Months	Rent (PKR)	Unit price (PKR)	Takaful contribution (PKR)	Monthly payment (PKR)	Balance unit value (PKR)	Balance units
38	51,149	50,000	1031	102,179	4,100,000	82
39	50,533	50,000	1018	101,551	4,050,000	81
40	49,916	50,000	1006	100,922	4,000,000	80
41	49,300	50,000	993	100,293	3,950,000	79
42	48,684	50,000	981	99,665	3,900,000	78
43	48,068	50,000	969	99,036	3,850,000	77
44	47,451	50,000	956	98,407	3,800,000	76
45	46,835	50,000	944	97,779	3,750,000	75
46	46,219	50,000	931	97,150	3,700,000	74
47	45,603	50,000	919	96,521	3,650,000	73
48	44,986	50,000	906	95,893	3,600,000	72
49	44,370	50,000	894	95,264	3,550,000	71
50	43,754	50,000	882	94,635	3,500,000	70
51	43,138	50,000	869	94,007	3,450,000	69
52	42,521	50,000	857	93,378	3,400,000	68
53	41,905	50,000	844	92,749	3,350,000	67
54	41,289	50,000	832	92,121	3,300,000	66
55	40,673	50,000	820	91,492	3,250,000	65
56	40,056	50,000	807	90,863	3,200,000	64
57	39,440	50,000	795	90,235	3,150,000	63
58	38,824	50,000	782	89,606	3,100,000	62
59	38,208	50,000	770	88,977	3,050,000	61
60	37,591	50,000	757	88,349	3,000,000	60
61	36,975	50,000	745	87,720	2,950,000	59
62	36,359	50,000	733	87,091	2,900,000	58
63	35,743	50,000	720	86,463	2,850,000	57
64	35,126	50,000	708	85,834	2,800,000	56
65	34,510	50,000	695	85,205	2,750,000	55
66	33,894	50,000	683	84,577	2,700,000	54
67	33,278	50,000	671	83,948	2,650,000	53
68	32,661	50,000	658	83,319	2,600,000	52
69	32,045	50,000	646	82,691	2,550,000	51
70	31,429	50,000	633	82,062	2,500,000	50
71	30,813	50,000	621	81,433	2,450,000	49
72	30,196	50,000	608	80,805	2,400,000	48
73	29,580	50,000	596	80,176	2,350,000	47
74	28,964	50,000	584	79,547	2,300,000	46
75	28,348	50,000	571	78,919	2,250,000	45
76	27,731	50,000	559	78,290	2,200,000	44
77	27,115	50,000	546	77,661	2,150,000	43

(continued)

(continued)

Months	Rent (PKR)	Unit price (PKR)	Takaful contribution (PKR)	Monthly payment (PKR)	Balance unit value (PKR)	Balance units
78	26,499	50,000	534	77,033	2,100,000	42
79	25,883	50,000	522	76,404	2,050,000	41
80	25,266	50,000	509	75,775	2,000,000	40
81	24,650	50,000	497	75,147	1,950,000	39
82	24,034	50,000	484	74,518	1,900,000	38
83	23,418	50,000	472	73,889	1,850,000	37
84	22,801	50,000	459	73,261	1,800,000	36
85	22,185	50,000	447	72,632	1,750,000	35
86	21,569	50,000	435	72,003	1,700,000	34
87	20,953	50,000	422	71,375	1,650,000	33
88	20,336	50,000	410	70,746	1,600,000	32
89	19,720	50,000	397	70,117	1,550,000	31
90	19,104	50,000	385	69,489	1,500,000	30
91	18,488	50,000	373	68,860	1,450,000	29
92	17,871	50,000	360	68,231	1,400,000	28
93	17,255	50,000	348	67,603	1,350,000	27
94	16,639	50,000	335	66,974	1,300,000	26
95	16,023	50,000	323	66,345	1,250,000	25
96	15,406	50,000	310	65,717	1,200,000	24
97	14,790	50,000	298	65,088	1,150,000	23
98	14,174	50,000	286	64,459	1,100,000	22
99	13,558	50,000	273	63,831	1,050,000	21
100	12,941	50,000	261	63,202	1,000,000	20
101	12,325	50,000	248	62,573	950,000	19
102	11,709	50,000	236	61,945	900,000	18
103	11,093	50,000	224	61,316	850,000	17
104	10,476	50,000	211	60,687	800,000	16
105	9860	50,000	199	60,059	750,000	15
106	9244	50,000	186	59,430	700,000	14
107	8628	50,000	174	58,801	650,000	13
108	8011	50,000	161	58,173	600,000	12
109	7395	50,000	149	57,544	550,000	11
110	6779	50,000	137	56,915	500,000	10
111	6163	50,000	124	56,287	450,000	9
112	5546	50,000	112	55,658	400,000	8
113	4930	50,000	99	55,029	350,000	7
114	4314	50,000	87	54,401	300,000	6
115	3698	50,000	75	53,772	250,000	5
116	3081	50,000	62	53,143	200,000	4
117	2465	50,000	50	52,515	150,000	3

(continued)

(continued)

Months	Rent (PKR)	Unit price (PKR)	Takaful contribution (PKR)	Monthly payment (PKR)	Balance unit value (PKR)	Balance units
118	1849	50,000	37	51,886	100,000	2
119	1233	50,000	25	51,257	50,000	1
120	616	50,000	12	50,629	0	0
Total	4,473,975	6,000,000	90,145	10,564,120		

Annexure C: Tentative Payment Schedule with Step-Up Monthly Payments

Months	Rent (PKR)	Unit price (PKR)	Takaful contribution (PKR)	Monthly payment (PKR)	Balance unit value (PKR)	Balance units
0					6,000,000	180
1	73,950	33,333	1490	108,773	5,966,667	179
2	73,539	33,333	1482	108,354	5,933,333	178
3	73,128	33,333	1473	107,935	5,900,000	177
4	72,718	33,333	1465	107,516	5,866,667	176
5	72,307	33,333	1457	107,097	5,833,333	175
6	71,896	33,333	1449	106,678	5,800,000	174
7	71,485	33,333	1440	106,259	5,766,667	173
8	71,074	33,333	1432	105,840	5,733,333	172
9	70,663	33,333	1424	105,420	5,700,000	171
10	70,253	33,333	1416	105,001	5,666,667	170
11	69,842	33,333	1407	104,582	5,633,333	169
12	69,431	33,333	1399	104,163	5,600,000	168
13	69,020	33,333	1391	103,744	5,566,667	167
14	68,609	33,333	1382	103,325	5,533,333	166
15	68,198	33,333	1374	102,906	5,500,000	165
16	67,788	33,333	1366	102,487	5,466,667	164
17	67,377	33,333	1358	102,068	5,433,333	163
18	66,966	33,333	149	101,648	5,400,000	162
19	66,555	33,333	1341	101,229	5,366,667	161
20	66,144	33,333	1333	100,810	5,333,333	160
21	65,733	33,333	1324	100,391	5,300,000	159
22	65,323	33,333	1316	99,972	5,266,667	158
23	64,912	33,333	1308	99,553	5,233,333	157

(continued)

(continued)

Months	Rent (PKR)	Unit price (PKR)	Takaful contribution (PKR)	Monthly payment (PKR)	Balance unit value (PKR)	Balance units
24	64,501	33,333	1300	99,134	5,200,000	156
25	64,090	33,333	1291	98,715	5,166,667	155
26	63,679	33,333	1283	98,296	5,133,333	154
27	63,268	33,333	1275	97,876	5,100,000	153
28	62,858	33,333	1267	97,457	5,066,667	152
29	62,447	33,333	1258	97,038	5,033,333	151
30	62,036	33,333	1250	96,619	5,000,000	150
31	61,625	33,333	1242	96,200	4,966,667	149
32	61,214	33,333	1233	95,781	4,933,333	148
33	60,803	33,333	1225	95,362	4,900,000	147
34	60,393	33,333	1217	94,943	4,866,667	146
35	59,982	33,333	1209	94,524	4,833,333	145
36	59,571	33,333	1200	94,104	4,800,000	144
37	59,160	33,333	1192	93,685	4,766,667	143
38	58,749	33,333	1184	93,266	4,733,333	142
39	58,338	33,333	1175	92,847	4,700,000	141
40	57,928	33,333	1167	92,428	4,666,667	140
41	57,517	33,333	1159	92,009	4,633,333	139
42	57,106	33,333	1151	91,590	4,600,000	138
43	56,695	33,333	1142	91,171	4,566,667	137
44	56,284	33,333	1134	90,752	4,533,333	136
45	55,873	33,333	1126	90,332	4,500,000	135
46	55,463	33,333	1118	89,913	4,466,667	134
47	55,052	33,333	1109	89,494	4,433,333	133
48	54,641	33,333	1101	89,075	4,400,000	132
49	54,230	33,333	1093	88,656	4,366,667	131
50	53,819	33,333	1084	88,237	4,333,333	130
51	53,408	33,333	1076	87,818	4,300,000	129
52	52,998	33,333	1068	87,399	4,266,667	128
53	52,587	33,333	1060	86,980	4,233,333	127
54	52,176	33,333	1051	86,560	4,200,000	126
55	51,765	33,333	1043	86,141	4,166,667	125
56	51,354	33,333	1035	85,722	4,133,333	124
57	50,943	33,333	1026	85,303	4,100,000	123
58	50,533	33,333	1018	84,884	4,066,667	122
59	50,122	33,333	1010	84,465	4,033,333	121
60	49,711	33,333	1002	84,046	4,000,000	120
61	49,300	66,667	993	116,960	3,933,333	118
62	48,478	66,667	977	116,122	3,866,667	116
63	47,657	66,667	960	115,284	3,800,000	114

(continued)

(continued)

Months	Rent (PKR)	Unit price (PKR)	Takaful contribution (PKR)	Monthly payment (PKR)	Balance unit value (PKR)	Balance units
64	46,835	66,667	944	114,445	3,733,333	112
65	46,013	66,667	927	113,607	3,666,667	110
66	45,192	66,667	911	112,769	3,600,000	108
67	44,370	66,667	894	111,931	3,533,333	106
68	43,548	66,667	877	111,092	3,466,667	104
69	42,727	66,667	861	110,254	3,400,000	102
70	41,905	66,667	844	109,416	3,333,333	100
71	41,083	66,667	828	108,578	3,266,667	98
72	40,262	66,667	811	107,740	3,200,000	96
73	39,440	66,667	795	106,901	3,133,333	94
74	38,618	66,667	778	106,063	3,066,667	92
75	37,797	66,667	762	105,225	3,000,000	90
76	36,975	66,667	745	104,387	2,933,333	88
77	36,153	66,667	728	103,548	2,866,667	86
78	35,332	66,667	712	102,710	2,800,000	84
79	34,510	66,667	695	101,872	2,733,333	82
80	33,688	66,667	679	101,034	2,666,667	80
81	32,867	66,667	662	100,196	2,600,000	78
82	32,045	66,667	646	99,357	2,533,333	76
83	31,223	66,667	629	98,519	2,466,667	74
84	30,402	66,667	613	97,681	2,400,000	72
85	29,580	66,667	596	96,843	2,333,333	70
86	28,758	66,667	579	96,004	2,266,667	68
87	27,937	66,667	563	95,166	2,200,000	66
88	27,115	66,667	546	94,328	2,133,333	64
89	26,293	66,667	530	93,490	2,066,667	62
90	25,472	66,667	513	92,652	2,000,000	60
91	24,650	66,667	497	91,813	1,933,333	58
92	23,828	66,667	480	90,975	1,866,667	56
93	23,007	66,667	464	90,137	1,800,000	54
94	22,185	66,667	447	89,299	1,733,333	52
95	21,363	66,667	430	88,460	1,666,667	50
96	20,542	66,667	414	87,622	1,600,000	48
97	19,720	66,667	397	86,784	1,533,333	46
98	18,898	66,667	381	85,946	1,466,667	44
99	18,077	66,667	364	85,108	1,400,000	42
100	17,255	66,667	348	84,269	1,333,333	40
101	16,433	66,667	331	83,431	1,266,667	38
102	15,612	66,667	315	82,593	1,200,000	36
103	14,790	66,667	298	81,755	1,133,333	34

(continued)

(continued)

Months	Rent (PKR)	Unit price (PKR)	Takaful contribution (PKR)	Monthly payment (PKR)	Balance unit value (PKR)	Balance units
104	13,968	66,667	281	80,916	1,066,667	32
105	13,147	66,667	265	80,078	1,000,000	30
106	12,325	66,667	248	79,240	933,333	28
107	11,503	66,667	232	78,402	866,667	26
108	10,682	66,667	215	77,564	800,000	24
109	9860	66,667	199	76,725	733,333	22
110	9038	66,667	182	75,887	666,667	20
111	8217	66,667	166	75,049	600,000	18
112	7395	66,667	149	74,211	533,333	16
113	6573	66,667	132	73,372	466,667	14
114	5752	66,667	116	72,534	400,000	12
115	4930	66,667	99	71,696	333,333	10
116	4108	66,667	83	70,858	266,667	8
117	3287	66,667	66	70,020	200,000	6
118	2465	66,667	50	69,181	133,333	4
119	1643	66,667	33	68,343	66,667	2
120	822	66,667	17	67,505	0	0
Total	5,213,475	6,000,000	105,045	11,318,520		

Index

A
AAFOI standard
  defined as, 12
AAOFI rules, 18
AAOFI standard, 18
Academia, 98
Accidental losses, 177
Accounting and Auditing
  Organization for Islamic Financial
  Institutions (AAOIFI), 104
Accounting system, 96, 122, 179, 180
Acquirement of wealth, 37
Acquisition of benefit, 32
Actual cost price, 146
Actual profit, 93
  of business, 110
Adaptation, 134, 157–161, 165–170, 173–176, 178, 180, 181, 188
  in Islamic banking, 160
  in *Musharakah*, 157, 159, 162, 163, 165, 179, 180
  of participatory financing, 188
Additional benefits, 174
Additional profit, 117

Additional risk-sharing feature, 174
'Adl (Justice), 33, 35
Adverse selection, 88, 91–93, 99, 121–124, 126, 134, 139, 141, 164, 177–180, 192
Affin Islamic Bank Berhad, 151
Agency problems, 77, 88, 92, 93, 99, 134, 144, 164, 177
Agency relationships, 93
Agency theory, 87
Agreement, 9, 16, 19, 21, 23, 27, 118, 144, 179
Agricultural products, 116
Agriculture, 15, 137, 138, 144–146
Agriculture Bank of Iran (ABI), 138, 142, 153
  efficiency, 138
Agriculture Bank of Sudan (ABS), 145
Agriculture-based economy, 144
Agriculture financing, 109, 145, 146
Agriculture industries, 185
Al-baraka Turk Bank, 153
Al-hayah, 50
Allah, 13–15, 30, 38, 39, 51

© The Editor(s) (if applicable) and The Author(s), under exclusive license to Springer Nature Singapore Pte Ltd. 2023
M. Nouman and K. Ullah, *Participatory Islamic Finance*,
https://doi.org/10.1007/978-981-19-9555-2

Allah Almighty, 31
Allocation of risk, 9
al-Maslahah, 30, 32
al Shari'ah, 33, 76
Ambiguity, 34
Analogical reasoning, 40
Ansar and *Muhajireen*, partners
    in agriculture, 13
    in commerce, 13
    in trade, 13
Application, 54, 66, 127, 138, 139, 179
    in Islamic banking industry, 90
    of contracts, 77
    of participatory financing, 87, 88, 90, 94, 96, 97, 103, 119, 158, 183, 189
    of *thubat*, 34
Areas of financing
    commodity operations financing (COF), 161
    consumer financing (CF), 161
    working capital financing (WCF), 161
Aspiration-oriented school, 48, 49
Aspiration-oriented Vs reality-oriented schools, 48
Assessment, 121–123, 126, 127, 130, 131, 134, 148, 150, 152, 170, 171
    of different businesses, 171
    of investment, 69
    of the ventures/assets, 177
Assessment bank, 171
Assessment of the ventures/assets, 178
Assessment process, 124, 131, 132, 170, 172
Asset financing, 168, 174, 175
Asset/property, 131
Asset(s), 6, 7, 9, 11, 12, 16–18, 20, 22, 25, 39, 64, 69–72, 104, 105, 108, 117, 119, 126, 127, 131, 132, 134, 143, 144, 153, 166, 168–173, 175–178
    assessment of, 131, 172
Assets and expenses, 6
Assets financing, 177
Asset side, 6, 7, 95, 104, 108, 158
Asset/venture, 139, 170
A's share
    divided between A and B, 23
    under the *Mudarabah* agreement, 23
Associated risks, 92
Asymmetric information, 43, 88, 91–93, 96, 99, 121, 122, 134, 139, 141, 164, 177–180, 191
Automobile financing, 110, 115
Avoiding Gharar, 42
Avoiding Interest, 39
Avoiding Qimar (Maysir), 44
Axioms, 58

B
Bai Salam, 109
Bank, 4, 5, 7–9, 56, 63, 64, 66, 67, 70–72, 75, 92–95, 97, 104–106, 110, 111, 116–119, 122–124, 126, 127, 130–134, 137–141, 143–154, 160, 164–180
    borrower at a predetermined higher price, 10
    commodities via parallel *Salam* contracts, 10
    delivered goods, 10
    furnish a security, 10
    higher price to earn profit, 10
    originated from Islamically acceptable sources, 8
    principles of *Shari'ah*, 8
    provided credit without charging interest, 10
    right to use the asset, 9

share the profit, 106
Bank assesses, 171
Bank feels, 178
Bank finance, 134, 177
Bank guarantees, 72
Bank Holding Company Model, 7
Banking, 76, 95, 138, 145
Banking crises, 72
Banking culture, 98
Banking industry, 138
Banking laws, 97
Banking model, 7, 76
Banking services, 108, 153
Banking system, 5, 7, 63, 65, 66, 70, 76, 160
Banking venture, 86
Bank Investment Ratio, 128, 129
Bank invests, 110
Bank Islam Malaysia, 118, 151
Bank Kerjasama Rakyat Malaysia, 151
Bank leases, 168
Bank (lessor) purchases, 9
Bank Mandiri Syariah (BSM), 119
Bank Muamalat Malaysia, 151
Bank Negara Malaysia (The central Bank of Malaysia), 119, 151
Bank of Khyber (BOK), 147
Bank ownership, 166
Bank partners, 77, 144
Bank risks, 72
Bank's agents, 173
Banks contribution, 111, 112, 114
Bank's debt, 75
Bank's efficiency, 138
Bank's funds, 97
Banks get profit, 169
Bank shares, 97, 167
Bank's insolvency, 72
Bank's interests, 94
Bank's internal environment, 89, 164
Bank's investment, 106, 151
Bank's liability, 72, 144

Bank's net worth, 72
Bank's outstanding ownership (units), 166
Bank's outstanding share in the asset, 104
Bank's ownership, 9, 110, 111, 169, 170
Bank's ownership diminishes, 166
Bank's point of view, 93
Bank's (principal) interest, 93
Bank's profit share, 110, 168
Bank's remaining ownership, 111
Bank's share, 104, 116, 166, 169
Bank's share in the asset, 104, 105
Bank's share in the property, 110
Bank's share in profit and loss, 107
Bank's share of asset, 168
Bank's Shariah, 147
Bank Simpanan Nasional, 151
Banks operating in Pakistan, 165
Banks to design services, 160
Banks using *Musharakah*, 108
Bank Syariah Bukopin (BSB), 119
Bank vs. business (borrower) relationships, 65
Behavior, 29, 55, 91
Behavioral/moral standard, 39
Behavioral premises, 91
Behavioral reforms, 37
Behavior of entrepreneur, 94
Behavior of surplus, 71
Belief system, 30
Benefiting partner(s), 11
Benefits of participatory modes of finance, 68, 86
Benevolence, 33
Benevolent act, 41, 42
BNM. *See* Bank Negara Malaysia
Borrower and the lender, 69
Borrower (*Mudarib*), 66
Borrower(s), 39–41, 53, 56, 66, 69, 70, 92, 93, 123

216   INDEX

Bounded rationality, 91, 92
Brotherhood, 13, 32, 41, 51, 52, 54, 57, 58, 64
Business, 13, 16–28, 39, 51–54, 57, 64, 69, 71, 75, 77, 78, 86, 93, 95, 99, 106, 107, 110, 119, 122–124, 129, 144, 148, 150, 151, 154, 167, 168, 173–179
  assessment of, 122, 124
  needs of, 124
Business activities, 6, 105
Business affairs, 164
Business arrangement, 11
Business assessment, 124, 125
Business/assets
  monitoring, 173
Business banking, 122
Business condition, 75
Business cycle, 171
Business enterprise, 12
Business environment, 77
Businesses and government, 170
Business ethics constraints, 90
Business failure, 69
Business financing, 175
Business law, 96
Business needs, 106
  view in, 124
Business operations, 95
Business practices, 37
Business profits, 95
Business risk, 72
Business/trade, 41
Business transaction, 34, 43
Business venture, 9, 67, 71, 169
Business ventures as equity, 70
Buyer, 9
Buyer pays full price, 10
Buying price, 116, 117, 167
Bylaws, 97

C
CAO framework, 162–165, 173, 181, 184
CAO framework of participatory finance, 163
Capital, 7–9, 17, 19, 21–23, 26, 28, 59, 72, 75, 117, 119, 144, 148, 153, 167–170, 174, 178
  creditworthiness or labor, 11
Capital and profit sharing ratio, 148
Capital basis, 169
Capital contribution, 17, 107, 110, 117, 118, 126, 148, 168, 175
Capital contributions by the partners, 9
Capital financing, 109, 119, 122–124, 161, 167–170, 173, 176, 177, 179, 180
Capital financing needs, 109
Capital goods, 86
Capital in the pre-agreed ratio, 105
Capitalism, 38, 69
Capital markets, 4
Capital movements, 5
Capital protection, 67, 87
Capital provision, 9
Capital sharing ratio, 23
  A's share, 23, 24
  B's share, 23, 24
Caption of *Shirkah*, 11
Car/automobile financing, 126, 166
Car financing, 116, 130
Cash payment, 39
Categories of constraints
  low demand, 164
  regulatory constraints, 164
  uncertainty, 164
Central bank of Malaysia, 151, 154
Challenges, 137, 154
Chances of disputes, 180
Chances of loss, 171, 177
Channeling savings, 6

INDEX   217

Charging interest, 40, 41, 45
Circulation of wealth, 33
Civil law, 96
Civil partnership, 141, 143, 144
Clarity, 34, 53
Classification, 186, 188
Clients/businesses, 177
Coffee, 116
Coherent constraints framework, 88, 90
Coherent framework, 77
Collateral requirements, 71, 140, 141, 146
Commerce, 41
Commercial activity, 13
Commercial banking, 6–8, 138, 145
  practiced, 7
Commercial/financial transaction, 45
Commercial enterprise, 12
Commercial Islamic banks, 145
Commercial risk, 44
Commercial transactions, 20
Commodities, contract for, 117, 118
Commodity, 17, 25, 40, 116, 117, 126, 168, 173
Commodity Operations Financing (COF), 103, 109, 116, 119, 121, 122, 124, 126, 157, 161, 162, 165, 168–171, 173, 176, 177, 179, 180
Commodity operations financing needs of government departments, 108
Common law, 96
Common values, 98
Communism, 38
Companion(s), 14, 15
Competitive financing, 174
Competitive financing cost, 174
Conditions, 16–21, 25, 150, 151, 154, 161
Conducive, 35, 92, 99

Consent, 16, 20, 22, 26, 144
Constraints, 52, 68, 85, 87–89, 96, 98, 104, 134, 137, 147, 154, 157–162, 165, 174, 180, 181, 186, 188, 196
Constraints, Adaptation, and Outcomes (CAO), 157, 160, 161, 180
Constraints framework, 89, 90, 98, 164, 179, 184, 185
Constraints to *Musharakah* financing, 164
Constraints to participatory financing, 77, 85–89, 157, 158, 163, 164, 173, 181, 196
Construction, 110, 132, 147–150, 154, 166
Construction activities, 7
Constructive form, 17
Constructive liquidation, 27
Consumer Finance Department (CFD), 132
Consumer Financing (CF), 103, 110, 121, 126, 157, 161, 162, 165, 170, 180
Consuming process, 72
Contemporary, 16, 34, 153
Contemporary business, 11, 90, 94
Contemporary business environment, 27, 49
Contemporary business settings, 89
Contemporary economic setting, 99
Contemporary financial needs, 94
Contemporary Islamic banking, 63, 76
Contemporary Islamic economics, 50
Contemporary practice, 43, 153
  of Islamic banking, 86
Contemporary social, 98
Contemporary social setting, 99
Contract for trade, 117
Contracting, 43

Contracting problems, 92
Contract(s), 9, 15–22, 25–27, 34, 39–45, 50, 53, 56, 59, 60, 64, 70, 73, 76, 92, 93, 98, 106, 118, 124, 133, 139, 160
Contracts of exchange, 34
Contractual choice, 94
Contractual obligations, 45
Contractual variants of *Musharakah*, 165
Contribution, 4, 17, 19, 22, 28, 40, 54, 55, 66, 118, 144
Control, 9, 21, 95, 146
Control of banks, 165
Control over the business, 9
Control right, 97
Control the adverse selection, 94
Control the entrepreneur, 97
Conventional and non-participatory financing, 75
Conventional banking, 5–8, 42, 45, 65, 94, 95, 98, 145, 147, 148, 153, 174, 176
  conducting business through *Shari'ah*, 8
  customers interested, 8
Conventional banking system, 6
Conventional counterparts, 4
Conventional debt, 78
Conventional financial institutions, 4, 145
Conventional financial system, 4
Conventional financing, 174, 175
Conventional fund, 8
Conventional institutions, 45
Conventional insurance, 45
Conventional interest, 59, 70, 72, 78
Conventional interest based banking system, 63
Conventional interest-based banks, 17
Conventional interest-based economies, 73
Conventional modes, 138
Conventional risk, 72
Conventional running finance, 110, 167, 176
Conventional system, 70, 73
Cooperation, 30, 41, 51, 52, 57–59, 65, 98
Co-ownership, 12
Corporate financing, 121, 165
Corporation, 42, 108, 109, 122, 126, 151, 170–172, 180
Corporations and SMEs, 167
Corruption, 32, 51, 96
Cost of capital, 93
Coupons, 44
Course of life, 33
Credit, 15, 18, 39, 73, 94, 122–124
Credit arrangement, 167
Credit Assessment Division (CAD), 132
Credit channel, 75
Credit Committee, 132
Credit creation, 67, 70
Credit creation or money creation, 70
Credit expansion, 73
Credit history, 78, 122, 129, 132, 171, 172
Credit Information Bureau (CIB), 129, 172
Credit multipliers, 70
Credit price, 40
Credit risk, 72
Credit risk assessment, 123
Credit risk management, 122
Creditworthiness, 71
Creditworthiness of the business, 69
Culture needs, 55
Culture of the world, 39
Curious Case of *Musharakah* Spur in Pakistan, 158
Currency, 17, 20, 22, 118
Customers (borrowers), 94

Customer's contribution, 111
Customs of society, 33

D

Daruriyyat (necessities/essentials), 32, 33
Debt servicing, 75
Deferred sale, 18, 43
Definition and Forms participation in Islam, 11
Degrees of risk, 3
Depositors, 7, 56, 66, 74, 91, 95, 149
Depositors as shareholders, 49, 71
Depositors as shareholders in the bank, 67, 70
Depositors interests, 97
Depositors in the bank, 72
Depositors/investors, 65
Depositors of Islamic banks, 91, 95
Depositors (*Rab-ul-Mal*), 66
Depositors risk, 72
Depositors share, 74
Depositor vs. bank, 65
Deposits, 5, 7, 18, 67, 70, 71, 73, 76, 97, 118
Deposits in investment, 7
Deposits in the conventional baking system, 72
Deposits in the equity, 70
Deposits of clients, 6
Deposits product, 8
Deposits side, 104
Derivatives, 44
Desired asset, 10
Development, 31, 54, 63, 64, 67, 73, 98, 138, 178, 185
Development and growth of trade and property, 35
Development Financial Institutions Act 2002 (DFIA), 151
Development financing, 145

Development of agriculture, 35
Development of employment opportunities, 35
Development of Islamic private equity and venture capital markets, 9
Development of Islamic banking system, 65
Development of the constraints framework, 187
Development of the industry, 96
Different modes of financing, 109
Diminishing *Musharakah* agreement, 104
Diminishing *Musharakah* based House Financing Scheme, 111
Diminishing *Musharakah* contract, 105
Diminishing *Musharakah* (DM), 103–106, 108–110, 119, 121, 126, 127, 158, 165, 166, 170, 174
  principle of, 127
  risks in, 132
Direct investment, 72, 97
Disagreement, 11
Disclosure of business secrets, 88, 194
Discounting of securities, 43
Dispute(s), 25, 34, 131, 179
Distribution, 19, 20, 25, 26, 55, 56, 60
Distribution of credit, 69
Distribution of income, 37
Distribution of loss, 24, 25
Distribution of opportunities and wealth, 35
Distribution of profit, 23, 25, 107, 110
Distribution of responsibilities, 9
Distribution of risk, 72
Distribution of wealth and income, 73

Distribution of wealth in the society, 35
Distributive justice, 32, 37, 54–56, 59
Divergent literature, 49
Divine guidelines and prohibitions, 3
Divine injunctions, 35
Divine law, 29
Documentation, 34, 139, 169, 170, 175, 176
Domains of Participatory finance, 108
Domestic agricultural products, 167

E
Economic activity, 38, 42, 76
Economic affair, 33, 38
Economic agents, 3, 59
Economically suppressed class of the society, 37
Economic and business realm, 35
Economic and legal mechanisms, 96
Economic and social wisdom, 50
Economic assessment, 139
Economic behaviour, 65
Economic concerns, 36
Economic development, 50
Economic factors, 72
Economic feasibility of Islamic finance, 49
Economic-financial concerns of human life, 36
Economic games, 91
Economic growth, 33, 54, 68, 69
Economic growth and development, 73
Economic imbalances and exploitations, 40
Economic justice, 54, 55
Economic models, 49
Economic monarchy, 29
Economic motives, 36
Economic progress, 38
Economic realm, 37
Economic sectors, 73
Economics justice, 55
Economic stability, 54, 55, 69
Economic structure, 90
Economic system, 3, 38
Economic system stability, 65, 78
Economic thinking, 70
Economic transactions, 54
Economic units, 71
Economy, 3, 29, 30, 35, 38, 50, 52, 54, 56–59, 72, 73, 98
Economy based on Islamic setting, 98
Educational institutions, 98
Efficiency, 48, 54, 56, 59, 65, 70, 78, 96, 141
Electronic Credit Information Bureau (ECIB) report, 129
Eligibility criteria, 124, 127, 140, 141, 151, 171
Embellishments, 33
Employment, 18, 55, 69, 71
Employment law, 96
Employment opportunities, 71
Enterprise, 16, 69, 123, 145
Entrepreneur's ability, 75
Entrepreneur's actions, 93
Entrepreneur's investment, 75
Entrepreneur employs, 9
Entrepreneur in a participatory system, 72
Entrepreneur risks, 72
Entrepreneur(s), 9, 21, 40, 51, 54, 56, 69, 71, 72, 74, 75, 89, 92–95, 99, 117, 147–150, 154, 174
Entrepreneurs/businesses, 151
Entrepreneurship, 45, 53
Environment, 35, 37, 52, 54, 92, 134, 160, 179, 181
Environmental changes, 181
Environmental demands, 181

Environmental safety, 35
Environment conducive, 34
Epistemological issues, 184
Epistemological source, 50
Equality, 32, 35, 52, 53, 55
Equal opportunities, 3
Equity, 7, 23, 36, 51, 55, 56, 59, 63, 67, 71, 72, 74, 78, 104, 131, 148, 151, 152, 166, 178
　application of, 119, 152
Equity based investments, 74
Equity financing, 72, 165
Equity investment risk, 97
Equity or profit and loss, 70
Equity partnership, 141, 144
Equity premium, 74
Equity premium puzzle, 74
Equity risk premium, 74
Equity shares, 67, 70, 104
Equity theory, 55
Equity window, 67
Eradicating participation in management, 169
Establishing justice, 31
Establishing long term relationships, 75
Ethical behavioral norms, 36
Ethical framework, 56–58, 64
Ethical norms, 47, 57, 58
Ethical objective, 29, 30, 34
Ethical standards, 9, 60
Ethical value, 33, 154
Ethics, 37, 52
Ethics governing, 30
Event of loss, 107
Evil in the society, 34
Evil(s), 38, 58
Evils and injustices of interest, 78
Evils of interest, 86
Evolutionary banking model, 157, 159
Evolutionary framework, 160

Excessive risk, 39, 45
Exchange, 17, 33, 40, 41, 44, 53, 55
Exchange-based modes, 152
Exchange for share in the profits, 68
Exchange of benefits, 76
Exchange of certain commodities, 40
Exchange of money, 39, 42
Exchange of six commodities, 40
Expansion of capitalism, 38
Expenses, 26, 146
Exploitation(s), 37, 39, 45, 52, 54, 56, 64
Export re-finance, 108
Expropriation risk, 96
Extant literature, 88
External financing, 171

F
Failure of Islam, 32
Fairness, 36, 47, 51–53, 55, 57, 59, 64, 91, 92
Fairness and justice, 38
Falah (success), 31
Family law, 31
Family/linage (Nasal), 50
Family needs, 37
Fasad, 51, 52
Fasad in the society, 41
Feasible in practice, 66
Fee, 25, 26, 167
Fees charge, 6
Fiat finance, 69
Finance, 4, 9, 16, 28, 48, 49, 53, 56–59, 63–65, 68–70, 72, 76–78, 87, 89, 91, 94, 95, 104, 105, 108–111, 115–119, 121–124, 126, 127, 129–132, 134, 137–141, 145–147, 149, 151–154, 157, 159–161, 166–178
Finance and conventional commodity operations financing, 167

Finance and real assets, 73
Finance bank, 119
Finance contributes to growth, 37
Finance literature, 50, 64
Finance products, 166, 181
Financial derivatives, 73
Financial environment, 96
Financial history, 173
Financial institution, 4, 43, 47, 49, 64, 68, 70, 95
  participation of, 152
  to earn profit on invested capital, 8
  tolerate loss, 8
Financial intermediation, 71
Financial products, 59
Financial services, 145, 159, 161
Financial system, 5, 48–50, 58, 59, 68, 78, 93, 96
Financial system stability, 78
Financial transactions, 31, 39, 45, 47, 50
Financier, 10, 21, 51, 56, 59, 69, 93, 95, 97, 151, 166–168, 174
Financing agriculture, 145
Financing arrangement, 105, 166
Financing (assets), 141
Financing bank, 134, 172, 177
Financing facilities, 110
Financing, ideal modes of, 121
Financing, *Ijarah* modes of, 127
Financing in Pakistan, 157
Financing limit, 128, 129
Financing mix, 158
Financing Mix of Islamic Banking Industry of Pakistan, 109
Financing mix of Islamic banks, 158
Financing needs, 108, 109, 145, 146, 154, 166, 167
Financing needs of government departments, 167
Financing needs of government for commodity operations, 166
Financing of fixed assets, 167
Financing of Islamic banking industry, 108
Financing only dependable clients and projects, 170
Financing on the prevalent market rate, 168
Financing patterns, 51
Financing period, 116
Financing portfolio, 108
Financing portfolio of the Islamic industry of Pakistan, 109
Financing project, 111
Financing purposes, 3
Financing, risk modes of, 124
Financing scheme, 76
Financing tenure, 111, 128
Financing the ownership, 167
Financing to businesses, 174
Financing to purchase, 111
Fiqh, 29
Fixed/durable assets, 168
Food security, 35
Framework, 29, 35, 37, 58, 59, 89, 98, 99, 157, 160, 164, 181, 184
Framework for an Islamic economic system, 36
Framework of *Maqasid al Shari'ah*, 68
Framework of participatory finance, 157, 161, 180
Framework of Participatory Islamic Finance, 160
Framework of the conventional benchmarks, 65
Framework synthesis, 187
Free loans to the bank, 6
Frm's management, 93
Fundamental needs, 32

G
Gambling, 43–45

Games of chance, 39, 44, 45
GDP growth, 78
General objectives, 31
Gharar, 42–45
Gharar in exchanges, 44
Gharar in the contract, 43
Ghazali's framework, 50
Ghazali's classification, 31
Global economy, 98
Global finance, 4
Goals of Shariah, 76
Gold, 34, 42, 116
Gold banking, 153
"Gold for gold", 40
Goods, 6, 10, 18, 54, 117, 118
Goods and services, 42, 69, 70
Goods financing, 126
Goods financing facility, 110
Goods to the buyer, 10
Govern, 3, 29, 30, 33, 38, 47, 124, 126, 140, 150
Governance system, 4
Governed by the principle of participation, 12
Governed by the principles, 4, 5
Governed by the rules and regulations, 4
Government, 37, 42, 97, 108, 116, 117, 122, 168, 170, 179
Government departments, 116, 167, 171, 172, 176–180
Government financing banks, 180
Government of Pakistan, 160
Governs financial transactions, 3
Grounded theory, 187, 188
Growth, 35, 54, 55, 59, 69, 73, 78
Growth and development *(tanmiyah)*, 35
Growth in the economic activities, 70
Growth of financing activities, 70
Growth of interest, 73
Growth of Islamic banking, 5

Growth of participatory financing, 96
Guarantees, 17, 126, 145, 146, 148
Guidelines for Issuance of *Musharakah* Certificates for *Mudarabah*, 97

H
Hadith, 14, 15, 40, 47
Hajiyyat (complement), 32
Halal, 11, 38
Haram (prohibited) activities, 45
Head Office Credit Committee (HOCC), 148
Higher appraisal and monitoring costs, 88, 194
Higher monthly installment, 113
Higher price, 117
Higher return on investment, 73
Highest share, 108
High financing cost, 99
High inflation, 73
High prices, 37
High risk, 76, 88, 190
High-risk participatory, 138
Hire, 11
History, 55, 123, 153
Hoarding, 37
Holistic constraints framework, 85
Holistic framework, 184
Holistic framework of the constraints, 88
Holistic typology, 89
Holistic view, 58
Holy Prophet (Pbuh), 13, 40
Holy Quran, 11
House and Car Financing, 130
  Assessment and Selection Process for, 133
House financing, 110, 116, 126, 130
House Financing Scheme, 128
House financing scheme of Islamic bank, 111

Human agents, 91
Human life, 3, 35, 36, 38, 47
Human's development, 31

I
Ibada (worship), 33
Ibn Ahsur classification, 31
Ideal, 72
Idealization, 48
Ideal models of financing, 65
Ideal modes, 27
Ideal modes of financing, 85, 103
Ideal modes of Islamic finance, 48
Ideal of Islamic economics, 48
IFIs Major services
 financial services, 4
 Islamic banking, 4
 Islamic funds, 4
 sukuk, 4
 takaful, 4
Ijarah, 9, 14, 65, 104, 109, 127, 158, 168, 169, 175
Immoral, 93
Immoral behavior, 40, 53
Implications of the constraints framework, 98
Import finance, 108
Import financing, 103, 119
Inception, 27, 86, 159
Inception of companies, 43
Income, 38, 42, 54–56, 78, 124, 130, 132, 154, 171–173
Industrial and agriculture sector, 10
Industrial goods, 7
Industry, 41, 160, 161, 181
Industry and commerce, 66
Industry needs, 177
Industry of Pakistan, 180
Industry Size, 5
Inflation, 74
Inflationary pressure, 69

Inflation-driven instability, 69
Informing practice or policy, 188
Inheritance, 33, 34, 41, 53, 131
 rules of, 13
Initial Public Offerings (IPOs), 43
Injustice, 40, 52, 53, 56, 58, 64
Innovations, 145
Insolvency, 72
Insolvency law, 96
Installment(s), 10, 105, 130, 131, 149, 150, 171, 176
Installment sale, 140, 142
Institutions, 52, 59, 96, 98, 153
Institutions invest, 4
Insurance companies, 4, 43
Integrated framework, 29, 31, 35, 57, 60
Integrated Framework of *Maqasid al Shariah* (Higher Ethical Objectives), 30
Integrate model, 31
Intellect(Al'Aql), 33, 50
Intellectual, 30, 35
Interest, 4, 6, 18, 40–43, 45, 51, 53, 56, 58, 63, 65–67, 69, 71, 74, 86, 93, 95, 99, 104, 105, 138, 145, 150, 152, 153, 167
Interest and commitment fee, 167
Interest based and non-participatory, 75
Interest-based banking model, 72
Interest-based banking system, 72
Interest-based borrowing, 65
Interest based debt, 73
Interest-based loans, 42
Interest based system, 48, 70
Interest based system banks, 70
Interest bearing financing, 95
Interest bearing transactions, 42
Interest-free, 45
Interest of bank, 92
Interest of depositors, 93, 97

INDEX

Interest of people, 30
Interest or benefit, 32
Interest or *Riba*, 39
Interest payments, 75
Interest rate, 69, 73
Interest rate risk, 72
Intermediaries, 4, 6
Intermediaries (banks), 71
Intermediation contracts, 3
Interpretative process, 187
Invest, 16, 19, 21–23, 67, 76, 97, 105, 119, 148, 151, 166
Invested by bank, 105
Investigates, 50
Investing, 186
Investing funds, 76, 97
Investing their funds, 91, 95
Investment, 7, 16, 17, 19, 21–23, 25, 33, 35, 42, 54–56, 59, 67, 71, 74, 97, 117, 118, 124, 138, 147, 149–151, 167, 170, 178
Investment Account (IA), 151
Investment Account Platform (IAP), 119, 137, 151, 154
Investment banking, 7, 8
Investment behavior, 87
Investment certificates, 7
Investment deposit, 7
Investment firms, 4
Investment of saving deposits, 70
Investment opportunity, 138
Investments in portfolios, 7
Investments on partnership, 7
Invest money, 66
Invest on partnership, 93
Investor(s), 6, 9, 21, 43, 75, 119, 150–152, 154
Invest their money, 97
Invest this money, 66
Iran, 137–139, 141, 143
Islam, 3, 13, 29, 34, 35, 37–39, 41–45, 47, 50–58, 64, 66, 145

Islam and the Theory of Interest, 66
Islamic Assets, 132
Islamic baking in Pakistan, 157
Islamic baking literature, 64
Islamic banking, 4–8, 16, 28, 39, 43–45, 49, 54, 63–68, 71, 76–78, 85–87, 89–91, 94–99, 103, 104, 108–111, 115–117, 119, 121, 122, 124, 126, 127, 131, 132, 134, 137, 141, 145, 147, 148, 151, 153, 154, 158–161, 163, 165–170, 172, 173, 176–181
  banking assets, 5
  finance, 121
  growth, 5
  inception of, 147
  jurists of, 121
  modes in, 121
  practiced, 8
  share, 5
Islamic Banking and Finance, 4
Islamic Banking Division (IBD), 132
Islamic banking industry, 90, 104, 147, 157
Islamic banking industry of Pakistan, 108, 157–161, 165, 181
Islamic banking industry of Pakistan (Percentage share), 158
Islamic banking in Pakistan, 108, 159
Islamic banking literature, 63
Islamic banking market, 8
Islamic banking models, 63
Islamic banking system, 63
Islamic bank of Pakistan, 105
Islamic banks finance, 179
Islamic banks for participatory financing, 98
Islamic banks on participation basis, 67
Islamic banks practice *Murabahah*, 10
Islamic brotherhood, 64

Islamic capital markets, 54
Islamic commercial banks, 7
Islamic compliant, 7
Islamic countries, 38, 134
Islamic doctrine, 38
Islamic economic principles, 85
Islamic economics and finance, 48
Islamic economic system, 3, 37, 39, 45, 47, 59
Islamic economists, 48, 49, 66, 87
Islamic economy, 38, 64
Islamic faith, 30
Islamic finance, 3, 4, 28, 39, 42–45, 49–51, 53, 54, 56, 58, 59, 63, 76, 86, 95, 96, 98, 138, 152, 174, 175, 185, 186
  axioms of, 48, 50, 51, 57, 60
  different modes of, 9
  Participatory vs. Non-Participatory Modes, 8
Islamic finance assets, 4
Islamic finance context, 42
Islamic finance contract, 152–154
Islamic finance industry, 4, 5
Islamic finance literature, 48
Islamic Finance Market, 5
Islamic finance, modes of, 15, 27
Islamic finance philosophy, 39
Islamic Finance Sector, 5
Islamic finance theory, 49
Islamic Financial Institutions (IFIs), 4, 47–49, 56, 60, 65, 76, 78, 88, 89, 96, 186
Islamic financial instruments, 96, 97
Islamic financial practices, 59
Islamic financial products, 8, 59
Islamic financial service industry, 98
Islamic Financial Services Act 2013 (IFSA), 151
Islamic financial structure, 39
Islamic financial system, 3, 45, 47, 48, 56, 57, 59, 66, 70

Islamic financing
  conventional to, 138
  participatory modes of, 121
Islamic funds, 5, 8
Islamic identity, 76
Islamic industry of Pakistan, 108
Islamic investment banking, 8, 43
Islamic Jurisprudence (*Fiqh*), 11, 16, 29, 30
Islamic Jurists, 11
Islamic law, 4, 30, 37, 38, 86, 97
Islamic legal theory, 32
Islamic lens, 30
Islamic modes, 57, 146
Islamic modes of financing, 146
Islamic Moral Economy (IME), 47
Islamic nations, 5
Islamic participatory financing, 87, 157, 180
Islamic philosophers, 29
Islamic point of view, 37
Islamic principles, 5, 8, 30
  cultural, 30
  economic, 30
  faith, 30
  legal, 30
  political, 30
  social, 30
  worship, 30
Islamic products, 8
Islamic proponents, 29
Islamic public finance, 38
Islamic rules, 30
Islamic rules and laws, 47
Islamic scholars, 8, 30
Islamic *Shari'ah*, 5
Islamic society, 29, 30
Islamic society framework, 29
Islamic subsidiary, 8
Islamic system, 66, 71
Islamic teachings, 38
Islamic trade-finance products, 8

Islamic view, 38, 55
Islamic viewpoint, 42
Islamic window, 8
  commercial banks interested, 8
Islamize, 160
Istisna, 109, 158, 176
  suitable for construction projects, 10
Istisna contract, 10
Istisna (sale agreement), 10

J
Joint businesses, 11
Joint ownership, 11, 12, 116
Joint ownership of a business enterprise, 166
Joint ownership of an asset, 166
Joint stock companies, 43
Judicial system, 93, 96, 97, 99, 134, 179
Judicial system for the resolution of disputes, 179
Jurists, 11, 13, 15, 40, 44
Jurists of Islamic banking and finance, 103
Justice, 3, 30–32, 35, 47, 51–53, 55, 57–59, 64, 65
Justice and economic security of people, 35
Justice and equity in society, 78
Justice in economic and business realm, 35
Justice in wealth, 91

K
Karachi Inter Bank Offered Rate (KIBOR), 168, 174
Key peer-reviewed, 185
KIBOR in Pakistan, 107
Kind of liability, 45
Knowledge, 31, 92, 185

Knowledge in the society, 95
Knowledge supremacy, 38
Kuvat Turk Bank, 153

L
Lack of clarity, 34
Lack of government, 99
Lack of money, 38
Large corporations, 109
Law, 30, 35, 37, 150
Law for Usury (Interest)-Free Banking, 138
Lawful, 38
Lawful or righteous livelihood, 38
Law of Interest-Free Banking, 138
Laws and regulations, 98
Lease asset, 105
Lease (*Ijarah*), 33, 104
Legal aspects, 131
Legal bodies, 98
Legal claim, 34
Legal complexities, 179
Legal disputes, 96
Legal documentation, 179
Legal experts, 131
Legal formalities, 179
Legal framework, 96
Legality of *Shirkah*, 11
Legal mechanisms, 35
Legal opinion, 123
Legal practices, 52
Legal proof, 34
Legal risk, 132
Legal Stamp paper, 133
Legal system, 3, 180
Legal tradition, 96
Lender's part, 40
Lender as premium, 39
Lender(s), 39–42, 51, 53, 56, 71, 73, 75
Lending money to the borrower, 10

Lend money, 39
Letter of Credit (L/C), 118
Level of development, 33
Liabilities and assets, 72
Liabilities side, 6
Liability, 12, 16–18, 67, 71–73, 75, 126
Liability partnership, 9
Liable for loss, 6
Life, 3, 29, 30, 58
Line of business, 9
Liquidation, 20, 26
Liquidity, 8, 153
Literature, 49, 58, 77, 85, 86, 88, 89, 94, 183–187, 196
Literature of Islamic economics, 66
Literature regarding constraints, 98
Literature review, 184, 185
Living standard, 37
Loan, 39, 40, 42, 51, 65–67, 138
Loan applicant, 92
Loans on interest, 6
Local goods, trade of, 117
Local prices, 117
Local trade financing, 103
Logic, 30, 184
Long-term finance, 108
Long-term financing, 166
Long-term investment, 16
Long-term profitability, 71
Long-term viability, 181
Loss, 3, 6, 9, 16, 19, 21–23, 26–28, 39, 40, 45, 51–53, 56, 60, 67, 74, 93, 97, 110, 117, 118, 122, 126, 132, 134, 144, 148, 167, 171, 175
Loss and gain domains, 91
Loss in investment, 5
Loss of connection, 73
Loss of the richness, 184
Loss sharing, 19, 27, 37, 52, 59, 91
Loss sharing ratio

A's share, 24
B's share, 24
ratio of capital contribution, 24
Under *Musharakah* agreement, 24
Lotteries, 44, 45
Low risk non-participatory, 138
Lump sum or in installments, 9

M

Macro-economic reforms, 5
Main modes, 76
Malaysia, 86, 118, 119, 137, 151, 154
Management, 9, 18, 19, 24, 28, 117, 138, 144, 146, 150, 169, 183
Management affair, 169, 173
Management of business, 144
Management of enterprise, 7
Management of Islamic financial institutions, 77, 87
Management of the financing, 176
Management structure, 180
Management structure of *Musharakah*, 169
Manufacturer, 10
Maqasid Al Shari'ah, 29–32, 35, 36, 47, 48, 50, 53, 57–60, 76
framework of, 60
Maqasid Al Shari'ah integrated framework, 36
Marginalization of participatory finance, 76
Market mechanisms, 37
Market needs, 176
Maslahah, 32
Maybank Islamic Berhad, 151
Maysir/Qimar (gambling), 45
Means of investments, 34
Medium enterprises, 171
Meezan bank, 105
Messenger of Allah, 14, 15, 31

INDEX 229

Methodologically, 184
Mit Ghamr Savings Bank, 86
Model banks, 67
Mode of exchange, 119
Mode of financing, 10, 95, 159, 161, 163
Modern industry, 159
Modes, 49, 54
Modes of finance, 3, 48, 95, 110, 169
Modes of financing in practice, 103
Modes of Islamic finance, 8, 10
Modes of non-participatory financing
 Ijarah, 9
 Istisna, 9
 Murabahah, 9
 Salam, 9
Modes of participatory financing
 Mudarabah and Musharakah, 9
Modes of transfer, 34
Modes of worship, 3
Monetary, 17
Monetary/financial transaction, 42
Monetary transaction, 42
Money, 37–39, 41, 53, 56, 97, 126, 133
Money creation, 70
Money creation by banks, 70
Money exchange, 15, 42
Money for their benefit, 42
Money goods, 42
Money market operations, 8
Money markets, 4
Money supply, 69
Money to industry and commerce, 66
Monitoring, 138, 141, 152, 164
Monitoring business/asset, 170
Monitoring cost, 91, 99, 178
Monitoring expenses, 94
Monitoring mechanisms, 97
Monitoring of the projects, 94
Monitoring the business/assets, 173, 178

Monthly installment, 111, 113, 114
Moral, 30, 31, 35, 52
Moral commitments, 154
Moral exploitation, 37
Moral framework, 56–58, 64
Moral hazard, 87, 88, 91–94, 99, 121–124, 126, 134, 139, 141, 144, 164, 177–179, 193
Morality, 68, 78
Moral standards, 92
Moral teachings, 3
Moral uplift, 31
Moral values, 31, 33, 37
Mortgage, 18, 132, 134, 171, 179
Mortgage bank, 133
Mortgage Crisis, 73
Mortgages the assets, 177
Mudarabah, 6, 9, 11, 19, 21, 22, 25–28, 48, 49, 51, 64, 66, 76, 88, 89, 93, 94, 97, 99, 103, 104, 109, 119, 121, 137, 142, 154, 158, 185
Mudarabah, application of, 119
Mudarabah based financing, 103, 119
Mudarabah-based Islamic financial system, 66
Mudarabah basis, 66
Mudarabah Companies in Pakistan, 76
Mudarabah contract, 9, 54, 93
Mudarabah, growth of, 141
Mudarabah laws, 97
Mudarabah modes, 4
Mudarabah modes of finance, 104
Mudarabah Rules 1981, 97
Mudarabahs Ordinance 1980, 97
Mudarabah transactions, 66
Mudarib, 21–27, 66, 119, 152
Multinational corporations (MNCs), 69, 109
Murabahah, 64, 65, 67, 76, 109, 110, 115, 116, 146, 157, 158
 sale contract, 9

Murabahah financing to *Musharakah* financing, 176
Musaqat, partnership in gardening, 13
Musawamah, 109, 110
Musharakah, 6, 11, 13, 16–18, 20, 22, 23, 28, 48, 49, 51, 54, 64, 66, 76, 88, 89, 93, 94, 99, 103–106, 108–110, 116–119, 121, 122, 127, 134, 137, 138, 140–142, 145–149, 154, 157, 158, 161–163, 165–170, 174, 176–178, 185
 origin, 16
Musharakah adaptation, 165, 173
Musharakah agreement, 117
Musharakah and *Mudarabah*, 164
Musharakah, application of, 141
Musharakah contract, 9, 105, 118, 139, 140, 147, 165
Musharakah financing, 134, 139, 140, 147, 159, 160, 162, 176, 181
Musharakah financing, application for, 148
Musharakah, growth of, 141
Musharakah investment, 148
Musharakah mode, 4
Musharakah Mutanaqisah, 104
Musharakah, termination of, 20
Musharakah, viability of, 121, 141
Muslim, 4, 5, 13–17, 38, 51, 52, 54, 59, 86, 93, 96
Muslim countries, 97
Mutual contract, 12
Mutual funds, 4
Muzara, partnership in agriculture, 13, 14

N
Necessities, 32, 130, 171
Necessities for well-being, 32
Necessities guarantees, 32

Needs, 3, 33, 37, 55, 57, 59, 160, 161, 176, 178
Needs loan, 41
Needs of businesses, 69
Needs of consumers, 167
Needs of individuals and society, 33
Needs of SMEs and corporations, 166
Needs of the business, 178
Needs of the customers, 104
Needs of the market, 160
Negligible share, 117
(Neo-) classical economic sense, 91
Net loss, 24
Net Profit, 23
Net share of A and B profit, 24
Nexus, 29, 31, 48, 50, 57, 58, 60
Non-benefiting partner(s), 11
Non-clarity, 42
Non-monetary benefits, 93
Non-Muslim, 5
Non-participation, 57
Non-participatory, 63, 89, 90, 152, 174
Non-participatory agreements, 64
Non-participatory arrangements, 68, 94
Non-participatory financing, 52, 65, 76, 77, 86, 88, 95, 98, 99, 139, 141, 164
Non-participatory modes, 3, 4, 8, 9, 15, 27, 28, 48, 49, 58, 59, 65, 76, 78, 108, 147, 174, 175
Non-participatory modes of financing, 68, 76, 87, 89, 95, 98, 158
Non-perceptual/short-term capital, 166
Non-supportive government, 88, 195
Non-trade operations, 48
'No participation in management affairs feature', 175
Norms, 55

O

Objective and value of *Shari'ah*, 30
Objective of an Islamic state, 38
Objective of Islamic financial system, 47
Objective of *Shari'ah*, 30, 50
Objective of the government, 117
Objective of the study, 183
Objective(s), 4, 21, 26, 33, 50, 56, 59, 65, 184
Objectives of Islamic finance, 50
Objectives of *Shari'ah*, 30, 47, 58
Objectives of the economic system stability, 48
Objectives of the Islamic banking, 76
Ontological issues, 184
Operational needs, 110
Operational needs of a business, 167
Opportunities, 33, 56
Original, 104
Original form, 108
Originality, 85
Originate, 91
Other Islamic Financial Institution (OIFI'S), 5
Outcomes of adaptation, 158, 173
Outright grants, 41
Overview of a body, 187
Overview of Islamic banking, 3
Overview of participation in Islam, 4
Overview of the extant literature, 86
Ownership, 11, 17, 34, 110, 143
Ownership of an asset, 34
Ownership of bank, 178
Ownership of goods and services, 34
Ownership of the asset, 104
Ownership of the car, 116
Ownership of the property, 110
Ownership of wealth, 34
Ownership rights, 34, 35
Ownership risks, 6
Ownership units, 166

P

Pakistan, 86, 97, 105, 109, 111, 116, 122, 127, 128, 131, 137, 147, 154, 158–161, 174, 179
Pakistan Bank's Association (PBA), 132, 172
Pakistan Islamic banks, 108, 116, 181
Parent bank's treasury, 8
Partial objectives, 31
Participation, 11, 13, 14, 27, 48, 49, 52, 57, 59, 63, 64, 70, 73, 95, 147, 152–154, 157, 185
  history of, 13
  in agriculture, 14
  in commercial activities, 14
  in property, 14
  legality of, 15
  origin of, 15
Participation and risk sharing, 73
Participation banking, 141, 153, 154
Participation-based systems, 66
Participation basis, 97
Participation finance, 154
Participation in capital, 16
Participation in management, 169, 177
Participation in services, 16
Participation instead of interest, 65
Participation principle, 71
Participatory, 70, 77, 99, 137, 154
Participatory arrangement, 11, 73, 75
Participatory banking, 67
Participatory banking models, 68
Participatory banking system, 70
Participatory contacts, 77
Participatory contracts, 77
Participatory finance, 6, 28, 29, 31, 47–52, 54, 56–60, 63–66, 68, 69, 73, 76–78, 85–99, 103, 109, 119, 121, 134, 137–141, 144, 147, 151–154, 158, 159,

163–165, 170, 174, 175, 177–181, 183–186
  advantages of, 64
  application of, 137, 154
  axioms of, 57
  idealization of, 63, 64
  risk of, 151
Participatory financing arrangement, 8, 66
Participatory financing contracts, 139
Participatory financing, growth of, 143
Participatory financing in Islamic banking, 91
Participatory financing model, 69
Participatory Financing, Role of, 65
Participatory financing, viability of, 134, 151, 164
Participatory institutions, 153
Participatory Islamic finance, 3
Participatory modes, 3, 4, 8, 15, 27, 28, 48–50, 53, 56–58, 64, 66, 76
Participatory modes of financing, 50, 71, 85, 104, 108, 164
Participatory modes of Islamic financing, 103
Participatory system, 70–74
Participatory system banks, 70
Participatory ventures, 11
Partner, 9, 11–20, 22, 25–27, 52, 60, 63, 71, 75, 93, 104, 106, 122, 123, 134, 138–140, 143, 144, 146, 149, 150, 154, 169, 174, 175
  bear the losses, 12
  gets share in the profit, 12
Partner for depositors, 97
Partner gets share, 168
Partner in the business, 75, 166, 175
Partners, entrepreneurial characteristics of, 138

Partnership, 3, 9, 11, 14, 15, 19, 20, 66, 87, 92, 93, 104, 123, 143, 144, 146, 185
Partnership agreements, 94
Partnership arrangement, 91, 93
Partnership assets, 143
Partnership bias, 7
Partnership capital, 144
Partnership contracts, 48, 65, 76, 78, 144
Partnership paradigm, 90, 92
Partnership, permissibility of, 13
Partnership principle, 98
Partnership share, 143, 144
Partnership (*Shirkat al Inan*), 11
Partnership venture, 144
Partnership with the bank, 104
Partners in development, 5
Partners in loss sharing, 91
Partners in the risks, 71
Partners, moral characteristics of, 138
Partner with business venture, 66
Payment, 9, 10, 17, 18, 25, 28, 39, 43, 71, 75, 111, 131, 146, 148, 171
Payment behavior, 132, 171
Payment for purchase, 116
Payment of loan, 39
Payment plan, 111
Payments for the purchase of bank's share, 105
Payments to the lenders, 75
Peaceful life, 32
Period, service or industry, 9
Permissibility, 13, 16, 57
Permissibility of the profit, 39
Personal, 30
Pertinent literature, 76
Philosophers, 52
Philosophy, 4, 47, 51, 59, 63
Philosophy of Islamic banking and finance, 68

INDEX

Philosophy of *Maqasid Al Shari'ah* and participatory finance, 50
Philosophy of *Shari'ah*, 29, 50
Philosophy of the *Maqasid Al Shari'ah*, 50
Physical assets, 42
Place of business, 9
Pledge, 15
Point of contract, 10
Policy, 57, 59, 147, 148
Policy guidelines, 59
Policy implications, 98, 196
Policy practice, 59
Political structures, 96
Political system, 3
Poor, 34, 37, 41, 56
Poor management, 72
Poor people, 38
Poor systems, 93
Post-contract monitoring, 94
Potential losses, 91
Practice, 13, 25, 30, 76, 109, 121, 134, 153
Practice Islamic banks, 85, 109
Practice of Islamic financial institutions, 76
Practice of participatory finance, 104, 108
Practice of the participatory financing in Islamic banking, 103, 108
Practices of IFIs, 77
Practices of the Prophet Muhammad, 47
Practitioners, 49
Pre-agreed ratio, 9, 21, 117–119, 168
Pre-contract project, 94
Premium, 42
Price, 4, 10, 20, 45, 104, 116, 117, 126, 130, 131, 146, 150
Price in *Salam*, 10
Price mechanism, 37
Price of *Istisna*, 10
Price or subject matter, 42
Price over installments, 10
Price payment, 40
Prices increase, 73
Prices of agriculture commodities through commodities, 117
Prices of domestic agricultural products, 116
Pricing of goods, 40
Primary interest, 70
Principle, 11, 21, 45, 51, 52, 55, 59
Principle-agent problem, 87
Principle of diminishing *Musharakah*, 110, 116
Principle of *Ijarah*, 115
Principle of participation, 67, 71
Principle of *Shirkah*, 11
Principle of *Shirkat ul Aqad*, 105
Principle of *Shirkat ul Milk*, 104
Principles for wealth, 38
Principles of economic and distributive justice, 35
Private and public sector corporations, 45
Private property, 37
Private property and enterprise, 37
Prize bonds, 44
Process, 72, 91, 124, 125, 138, 139, 157, 160, 185, 186, 188
Process of adaptation, 165, 181
Process of altering, 160
Process of diminishing *Musharakah*, 105
Productivity, 53
Productivity and profitability, 71
Product repositioning, 165, 178, 180
Products and services, 98
Professor of Economics, 72
Profit, 3, 5, 6, 9–12, 16, 18, 19, 21–23, 25–28, 37, 39, 40, 44, 51–53, 56, 57, 59, 63, 67, 71, 93, 95, 106, 107, 110, 117–119,

122, 124, 126, 144, 146, 148, 149, 167–169, 173–175
Profitability, 75, 94, 138, 153
Profitable business, 95, 122
Profitable trade and work, 35
Profit above KIBOR, 168
Profit and losses of the business, 167
Profit and losses of the venture, 71
Profit and loss of the business, 110
Profit and loss sharing agreement, 7
Profit-and-loss sharing banks, 86
Profit and loss sharing basis, 110
Profit and loss sharing from inception, 158
Profit and loss sharing in banks, 86
Profit and loss sharing (PLS), 8, 9, 11, 19, 53, 65, 67, 70, 71, 168, 174, 185
Profit and risk sharing, 97
Profit ceiling, 106
Profit distribution, 148, 174
Profit distribution system, 116
Profit earning, 11
Profiteering, 34
Profit for management, 146
Profit from a risky project, 93
Profit of the business, 168, 174
Profit or losses, 169
Profit Rate (Rent), 112, 114
Profits and losses of venture, 97
Profit sharing, 27, 86, 93, 110, 168
Profit-Sharing Investment Account (PSIA), 119
Profit sharing ratio, 19, 22, 25, 26, 93, 107, 118
  A's share, 23
  A's share as *Rab-ul-Mal*, 23
  B's share, 23
  B's share as *Mudarib*, 23
  per capital contribution ratio, 23
  Under *Mudarabah* agreement, 23
  Under *Musharakah* agreement, 23

Profit to the lender, 40
Profit to the seller, 9
Progressive life, 32
Prohibition of interest, 39, 45, 68, 78
Prohibition of *Riba*, 45
Prohibitions, 39
Project/commodities, 171
Project financing, 108
Project's life, 113
Proliferation of *Murabahah* financing, 68, 87
Property, 11, 12, 15, 20, 34, 37, 41, 51–53, 110, 111, 131–134, 148, 166, 169, 172, 179
Property assessment, 132
Property/asset, 127
Property law, 96
Property, partnership in, 13
Property rests, 9
Property rights, 41, 45, 53, 96, 97, 99, 131, 134, 179
Property rights framework, 41, 53
Property rights of lender to the borrower, 41
Property, share of, 127
Prophet Muhammad (peace and blessings of Allah be upon him), 13–15, 27, 30, 39, 47, 52
Propositions, 58
Prosperity of society, 5
Protection of depositors' interest, 88, 190
Protection of family/linage (*Nasal*), 32
Protection of life (*Al-hayah*), 32
Protection of mind (*Al'Aql*), 32
Protection of religion (*Al-Din*), 32
Protection of wealth, 33–35, 53, 54
Protection of wealth (*Al mal*), 32
Prudential regulations, 96, 97, 99, 148, 160
Public finance, 38

Public interest, 30, 32, 33
Public Interest (*al-Maslahah*), 31
Public sector corporations, 116
Public well-being, 30, 32
Purchase, 11, 24, 111, 113, 116, 133, 141, 150, 166, 169, 186
Purchase bank's share, 116
Purchaser, 10
Purchase the asset, 9
Purchasing of goods, 39
Purchasing price, 167
Pure *Musharakah*, 175, 176
Pure *Musharakah*, origin, 166
Purview of *tanmiyah*, 35

Q

Qur'an, 13, 15, 27, 30, 31, 38, 39, 41, 44, 47, 49, 51–53

R

Rab-ul-Mal, 21–27, 66
Rate of inflation, 73
Rate of interest, 5, 66, 73
Rate of return, 40, 56, 71, 73, 74
Rationale, 30
Real assets, 73
Real economy, 37
Reality-oriented school, 48, 49
Realm of justice, 32
Real sector's growth, 73
Reasonable profit, 4
Receivables, 18, 123
Reduced constraints to SMEs financing, 68
Reduced Regulatory Constraints, 179
Reduced Uncertainty, 177
Regime of law, 34
Regulations, 96
Regulatory constraints, 96, 99, 173, 179, 180, 188

inefficient auditing and accounting system, 165
lack of government support, 165
lack of liquid and deep secondary markets, 165
non-supportive regulatory framework, 165
restrictive prudential regulations, 165
weak judicial systems, 165
weak property rights, 165
Regulatory framework, 89, 96–99, 134, 160, 179
Relationship, 26, 51, 138, 146
Relationship between central bank and commercial banks, 66
Relationship between entrepreneurs, 75
Relationships, 188
Reliability, 124, 126, 171
Reliability and trustworthiness, 92, 99, 164
Reliability and trustworthiness in the market, 91
Reliability of a business/asset, 178
Reliable businesses, 170
Religion, 3, 13, 29
Religion (Al-Din), 50
Religious, 52, 54, 86, 98, 153
Religious authorities, 47
Religious legislations, 31
Religious norms, 145
Religious obligation, 67
Religious rituals, 3
Reluctance to share profit, 88
Repayment, 176
Repayment ability, 70
Repayment behavior, 130
Replacement of interest, 86
Resolution of disputes, 180
Responsibility of government, 49
Restriction, 9, 21, 25, 176

Restructuring *Musharakah*, 165
Revenue, 11, 72, 126, 149
Review, 184
Reviewer, 184
Review paper, 186
Revised management structure, 165, 169
Revised Risk Management Structure, 165, 170
Revolutionary framework, 159, 160
Riba, 39, 40, 42, 45, 51–53, 56, 64
Riba al Fadl, 40
Riba (Interest), 39, 45
Rich, 41, 56
Rich archival record, 152
Rich historical relevance, 152
Rich people, 41
Right, 17, 18, 20, 24, 45, 52, 53
Right for assets, 34
Right of free enterprise, 37
Right of liquidating, 179
Rights and liabilities, 11
Right to charge, 40
Right to have food for survival, 32
Right to interfere, 93
Right to live, 32
Right to participate, 169
Right to religion, 32
Right to the property, 41
Right to the property of borrower, 41
Risk, 6, 44, 54, 56, 59, 60, 69, 72–74, 93, 121–124, 126, 127, 131, 133, 134, 137, 147, 148, 151, 153, 154, 171, 175, 177
Risk and reward, 12
Risk assessment, 127
Risk averse, 91, 95, 98
Risk averse attitude, 65
Risk-averse depositors, 67, 88, 99, 164, 191
Risk free rate, 74
Risk (hazard), 93

Risking his capital, 41
Risk in participatory financing, 97
Risk is shared, 72
Risk management, 123, 127, 177
Risk Management Department (RMD), 132
Risk management practices, 170
Risk management properties, 75
Risk management structure, 170, 177, 180
Risk of default, 93
Risk of earning profits, 5
Risk of loss, 6
Risk premium, 74
Risk sharing, 45, 49, 51, 63–65, 67, 72, 78, 151, 174, 177, 185
Risk-sharing features, 50
Risks of venture, 69
Risk transfer, 73
Risky assets, 180
Risky avenues, 97
Risky modes of financing, 178
Risky product, 170
Risky projects, 91, 95
Root of all evil, 38
Rub-ul-Mal, 21
Rules, 97
Rules and principles, 39
Rules for *Riba* in sales, 40
Running finance, 105, 176
Running *Musharakah* agreement, 107
Running *Musharakah* (RM), 103–107, 109, 110, 116, 119, 121, 122, 124, 126, 147, 165–167, 170, 172–174, 176
Rural agriculture sector, 145, 154
Rural development, 49, 145

S

Sadaqah (charity), 33
Sadaqat (voluntary charity), 34

Salam, 10, 33, 109, 158
Salary, 26, 129
Salary of the people, 173
Sale, 11, 20, 24, 104, 118, 126, 149, 150
Sale contract, 10
Sale of foreign goods, 118
Sales, 173
Sales-based modes, 27
Sales values, 132
Sapital, 19
Saving, 35, 54, 130, 131, 138, 141
Saving units of the economy, 4
Sectors of the economy
  agriculture, 6
  business, 6
  industry, 6
Securities law, 96
Security, 123, 144
Selection of projects/assets, 171
Self-interest, 37, 91
Selling price, 116, 167, 168
Service fee, 19, 21
Services, 4, 18, 25, 26, 54, 124, 132, 145, 146, 149, 154, 161, 170, 172, 178
Services of a manufacturer, 10
Services of legal experts, 179
Services of registered property, 172
Services to consumers, 108
Set of rules, 3
Share, 13, 14, 16–23, 25, 26, 33, 56, 67, 69, 95, 108, 118, 122, 126, 141, 143, 144, 146, 150, 151, 153, 168, 172, 174, 176, 180
Shared among all partners, 110
Shared by the government departments, 180
Shared equitably, 44
Share gain share, 185
Shareholders, 5
Share in ownership, 11
Share in the Global Islamic Finance Assets, 5
Share in the profit, 75, 168
Share losses, 91, 175
Share of A
  Share of A as a Co-owner, 24
Share of B
  Share of B as a Co-owner, 24
  Share of B as a *Mudarib*, 24
Share of *Murabahah* financing, 158
Share of *Musharakah*, 108
Share of *Musharakah* and *Murabahah*, 159
Share of *Musharakah* financing, 158
Share of participatory financing, 108
Share of partners
  A's contribution, 23, 24
  A's share, 23, 24
  B's contribution, 23, 24
  B's share, 23, 24
  capital, 23, 24
  loss, 24
  profit, 23
Share of risk, 40
Share of running *Musharakah*, 108
Share of the asset, 11
Share of various Islamic services, 5
Share profit, 193
Shares of joint stock companies, 49
Share the bank's profit, 66
Share the borrower's profit, 66
Share their net profits, 7
Share the loss, 11, 110
Share the profit, 66
Share the resulting profit, 11
Shari'ah, 3, 4, 9, 27, 29–33, 36, 39, 40, 44, 45, 47, 50–52, 56–60, 64, 67, 76, 85, 87, 160
  rules of, 59
Shari'ah compliance, 48, 59, 60, 76, 160

238 INDEX

Shari'ah compliant, 4, 8, 45, 48, 108–110, 126, 167
Shari'ah compliant debt-based contracts, 54
Shari'ah compliant financing, 108
Shari'ah compliant modes of finance, 8
Shari'ah law, 96
Shari'ah prescribed conditions, 65
Shari'ah principles, 7
Shari'ah rules, 43
Shari'ah supervisory boards, 65
Shari'ah's objectives, 32
Shariah, 11, 15–17, 33–35, 59, 63, 105, 138, 147, 153
Shariah Board, 148
Shariah compliant, 76
Shariah rules and guidelines, 17
Shariah supervision, 105
Sharing profit and loss, 66
Shirkah, 11–14, 16
Shirkah, partnership
   in trade, 13
Shirkah, permissibility of, 15
Shirkah, practice of, 13
Shirkat, 16
Shirkat-al-Milk, 166
Shirkat-Ul-'Aqd, 12, 21
   referred to as *Shirkat al 'Inan* or General Partnership, 12
Shirkat-Ul-'Aqd (Participation by Contract), 12
Shirkat-ul-'Aqd, types of
   Shirkat-ul-A'amal (Participation in services), 12
   Shirkat-ul-Amwal (Participation in capital), 12
   Shirkat-ul-Mufawada (Universal or Unlimited participation), 12
   Shirkat-ul-Wujooh (Participation in credit worthiness or goodwill), 12

Shirkat-ul-A'amal (Participation in services)
   called *Shirkat Al-Abdan*, *Shirkat Al-Sana'i'* or *Shirkat-Ut-Taqabbul*, 12
parterns
   join hands to offer services to their customers, 12
partners
   fee or wages shared in a pre-agreed ratio, 12
Shirkat-ul-Amwal (Participation in capital)
   contribute capital, 12
   contribution of partners needs, 12
   co-ownership in a business enterprise, 12
partners
   control over the assets, 12
   profit shared in a pre-agreed ratio, 12
   shared in the ratio of capital contribution, 12
partners jointly, 12
Shirkat ul Aqad, 166
Shirkat ul Milk, 11, 12, 127, 166
Shirkat ul Milk (Participation in Ownership), 11
Shirkat-ul-Mufawada (Universal or Unlimited participation)
partners
   acts an agent, guarantor, and trustee on the behalf of other partners, 13
   conditions difficult to satisfy because determination, 13
   participation does not factually exist, 13
   share an equal basis capital, profit, risk, and management, 13

Shirkat-ul-Mufawada (Universal or Unlimited participation) partners wealth and privileges to justify unlimited liability and equal rights, 13
Shirkat-ul-Wujooh (Participation in credit worthiness or goodwill) partner
    do not invest capital, 12
    profit is shared in a pre-agreed ratio, 12
    purchase commodities on a deferred price, 12
Short-run loss, 75
Short-selling, 43
Short-term, 75
Short-term activity, 140
Short-term capital, 165
Short-term investment, 16
Sleeping partner, 7, 18, 19, 22, 169, 173
Small and Medium Entrepreneurs (SMEs), 8, 68, 69, 108, 109, 122, 126, 170, 177, 180
Small enterprises, 171
Small enterprises and startups, 69
SME, application in, 122
SME financing, 121, 165
Social, 35, 50, 52, 54, 55, 57, 58, 64, 98
Social behaviors, 30
Social connotation, 50
Social dimensions in Islamic economics, 50
Social environment, 92
Social evils, 32
Social growth, 33
Social harms, 37
Social impact, 47
Socialism, 38
Social justice, 36, 50, 52–54, 56, 57
Social level, 29, 35

Social life, 41, 52
Social role of participatory finance, 49
Social setting, 89, 164
Social system, 3
Social uplift, 31
Social values, 9, 60
Social welfare, 37, 47–50, 54, 60, 67, 86
Social welfare system, 37
Social well-being, 32, 33, 35, 50, 51, 57–60
Society, 30–33, 35, 37, 40, 44, 45, 51–58, 60, 64, 68, 92, 99, 127, 164
Society's technological base and knowledge, 31
Socio-economic, 37
Socio-economic justice, 32, 48, 50, 56, 65, 78
Socio-economic objectives, 27, 54, 58, 60, 68
Soft commodities, 116
Special Assets Management (SAM), 132
Specific objectives, 31
Speculative behavior, 45
Spheres of life, 3, 35
Spirit, 4, 5, 51, 52, 56–58, 63
Spirit of Islam, 68, 78
Spirit of Islamic banking and finance, 85
Spirit of Islamic finance, 76
Spirit of *Shari'ah*, 48
Spirit of the Islamic financial system, 78
Spiritual values, 31
Spread of risk, 73
Stability, 34, 53, 56, 59, 69, 78, 153, 181
Stability of the banking system, 71
Stable exchange, 34
Stakeholders, 160

Stakeholders of the Bank, 65
Standard, 17
Standardized participatory financing contracts, 97
Standard *Musharakah*, 159, 161
Standards, 97, 130, 180
Starting Month Payment, 112
State Bank of Pakistan (SBP), 108, 129, 147, 148, 160, 172
State Bank of Pakistan's prudential regulations, 97
Step-Up Monthly Installment option, 114
Step-Up Monthly Installment Plan, 111, 113, 114
Stream of literature, 87
Struggle, 29, 35, 37
Substance, 51, 59, 60
Substance-in-economy, 59
Sudan, 86, 108, 117, 137, 144, 145, 154
Sudanese Islamic Bank (SIB), 137, 145, 154
Sukuk, 5
Sunnah, 11, 13, 15, 27, 30, 47
Supply of money, 69, 70
Systematic Literature Review approach, 183
Systematic review, 85, 89, 183–185
System conducive, 96

T

Tahsiniyyat (embellishments), 32, 33
Takaful, 5, 134, 148, 177
Takaful Contribution, 112, 114
Takaful (Islamic insurance), 171
Tangible assets, 17, 22
Tanmiyah (growth and development), 33, 35
Taxation, 37, 95, 99, 122, 164, 179
Taxation policies, 96

Tax law, 96
Tax shield benefits, 88, 195
Teachings of Islam, 38
Teachings of *Qur'an*, 39
Technological base and knowledge, 31
Tentative payment, 112, 114
Tentative Payment Schedule (Unequal Monthly Installment Plan), 113
Termination, 20, 27, 28, 144, 178
Termination of *Mudarabah*, 26
Termination of *Musharakah*, 20
Terms and conditions, 4
Theory, 55, 63, 66, 153
Theory and practice of Islamic finance, 48
Theory and practice of the Islamic banks, 87
Theory of Islamic banking, 86
Theory of preferring participation, 49
Theory of two-tier Mudarabah, 66
Three contracts
  lease, 104
  partnership, 104
  sale, 104
Thubat (stability and proof), 33, 34
Tijarah, 109
Total investment, 23, 24
Total payment, 116
Total Price of House, 111
Total share, 108
Trade, 6, 7, 21, 25, 39, 41, 44, 95
Trade-based financing modes, 65
Trade finance needs, 108
Trade financing, 108, 117, 119
  Muslim, 65
Trade in stocks, 43
Trading/*Murabahah*, 7
Traditional banks, 71
Transactional contract, 3
Transaction costs, 96
Transaction Cost Theory, 91
Transaction of sale, 40

Transaction period, 106
Transaction(s), 6, 18, 25, 34, 39, 42, 43, 51, 65, 76, 91, 92, 117, 118, 139–141, 148, 151
Transactions of credit, 40
Transactions of the contemporary, 43
Transparency, 34, 37, 53, 148
True Islamic state, 98
Trustworthiness, 98, 139, 177
Turkish Banks, 153
Two-tier Mudarabah, 66
Type of partnership
  investor(s) (*Rab-ul-Mal*) and entrepreneur(s) (*Mudarib*), 9
Types of risks, 40
Typology, 31, 157, 158
Typology of adaptation, 158, 165, 181
Typology of constraints, 77, 85, 89, 188
Typology of constraints participatory financing, 77
Typology of the constraints, 89, 98

U

Uncertainty, 22, 25, 42–45, 89, 90, 94, 99, 151, 173, 177, 178, 180, 188
Uncertainty conditions, 87
Uncertainty, contemporary business, 164
Uncertainty in participatory financing, 90
Uncertainty in participatory financing arrangements, 91
Uncertainty in the viability of participatory financing, 164
Undertaking to purchase, 110
Undisputed assets, 179
Unequal Monthly Installment option, 112
Unequal Monthly Installment Plan, 111–113
Unfair loan, 69
Unfairness, 91
Unfair treatment in taxation, 95
Unit Sale Price, 112, 114
Untrustworthiness, 88, 189
Using services of external agencies in the assessment process, 172
Usury-Free Banking Law, 144
Utility, 32

V

Value of deposits, 72
Values, 30, 51
Value system, 50, 51, 57, 64
Value system of Islam, 4, 5
Variants of Participatory financing, 104
Venture being financed, 97
Venture capital, 68
Venture financing, 54
Venture(s), 18–20, 27, 51, 56, 63, 68, 75, 78, 89, 117, 119, 122, 144, 151, 152
Viability, 71, 137, 144, 154, 179
Viability of Islamic finance, 98
Viability of *Musharakah* and *Mudarabah*, 77
Viability of participatory financing, 98, 99
Viability of the venture, 69
View economic progress, 38
View needs of the society, 33
Views the economic activities, 38
View the legal frameworks of Islamic countries, 97

W

Wages, 11
Wakalah, 6, 19

Weak properly rights, 88, 194
Weak regulatory and legal framework, 88, 195
Wealth, 5, 33–35, 37, 38, 53–56
Wealth (Al mal), 50
Wealth creation, 70
Wealth (mal), 33
Wealthy, 33
Wealthy class of the society, 69
Welfare, 30, 32, 51, 52, 58
Welfare of individuals and society, 3
Welfare of people in the society, 47
Welfare of society, 4
Well-being, 3, 32, 33, 45, 50, 56–59, 64
Whole bank, 8
Wisdom of participatory finance, 50
Wisdoms of the Qur'anic prohibition of *Riba*, 41
Working capital finance, 108
Working capital financing (WCF), 103, 109, 157, 162
Worldview of Islam, 31
Worldwide, 5
Worldwide assets, 5
Worldwide Islamic finance assets, 4, 5
Wuduh (clarity), 33, 34

Z

Zakat, 14, 15, 37
 law of, 15
Zakat (obligatory alms), 34

Printed in the United States
by Baker & Taylor Publisher Services